Kafka
Literature as
Corrective Punishment

Franz Kafka

Literature as
Corrective Punishment

Franz Kuna

INDIANA UNIVERSITY PRESS

BLOOMINGTON AND LONDON

Library of Congress Cataloging in Publication Data
Kuna, Franz, 1933–
    Franz Kafka : literature as corrective punishment
    "Chronology of Kafka's works" : p. 189
    Bibliography : p. 190
    1. Kafka, Franz, 1883–1924
PT2621.A26Z7666 1974   833'.9'12   74–4813
ISBN : 0-253-33168-4

Printed in Great Britain

Contents

Acknowledgments 7

Author's Note 8

Introduction 9

1 Kafka's World 13
  The Literary Scene in Prague
  Literature as Exorcism
  Ethical 'Stirnerism'
  Crisis of Consciousness

2 Literature as Corrective Punishment 33

3 *Metamorphosis* 49

4 *America* 64
  The Stoker
  Uncle Jacob
  The Hotel Occidental
  A Refuge?
  The Nature Theatre of Oklahoma

5 *The Trial* 99
  Tribunal in the Hotel
  Ascensio by Writing
  The Arrest
  Joseph K.'s Response
  The Two Levels of Consciousness
  Seekers and Sex
  First Interrogation
  Three Possibilities of Acquittal
  'Before the Law'
  The End

6 *The Castle*   136
      Landscape of Death
      K. and Klamm
      K. and Frieda
      The Promise of Mystical Experience
      A Divine Comedy
      The Parody of Self-Importance
      Amalia and Olga
      Conclusion

Notes   183

Chronology of Kafka's Works   189

Select Bibliography   190

Index   194

Acknowledgments

I wish first of all to express my special gratitude to Cedric Williams for revising my English and for generously providing valuable advice.

I am indebted to the editors of the *Journal of European Studies*, of the Penguin volume *Modernism*, and the editor of the *Publications of the English Goethe Society* for permission to make use of material which has previously appeared in their publications. In the first chapter I have repeated some of the things I said in my contribution to *Modernism* and incorporated the concluding paragraphs of my essay on Hofmannsthal's 'Chandos Letter' in *PEGS*. The second chapter is an extended and slightly revised version of my article 'Kafka and Sacher-Masoch' in the *Journal of European Studies*. My debts to recent Kafka criticism will become only too apparent in the text itself.

Passages from Kafka's works in translation are quoted from the following definitive editions (see also Select Bibliography).

By permission of Schocken Books Inc., New York, and Martin Secker and Warburg Limited, London: *Amerika* (Schocken edition)/*America* (Secker and Warburg edition), tr. Willa and Edwin Muir (copyright © 1927, 1946, 1954 by Schocken Books Inc.); *The Metamorphosis* from *The Penal Colony* (Schocken edition)/*In the Penal Settlement* (Secker and Warburg edition), tr. W. and E. Muir (copyright © 1948 by Schocken Books Inc.); *The Diaries of Franz Kafka 1910–1913*, ed. Max Brod, tr. Joseph Kresh (copyright © 1948 by Schocken Books Inc.); *The Diaries of Franz Kafka 1914–1923*, ed. Max Brod, tr. Martin Greenberg with the co-operation of Hannah Arendt (copyright © 1949 by Schocken Books Inc.); *Letters to Felice*, ed. Erich Heller and Jürgen Born, tr. James Stern and Elisabeth Duckworth (copyright © 1967, 1973, Schocken Books Inc.).

By permission of Schocken Books Inc. from *Briefe* (copyright © 1958 by Schocken Books Inc.) in the author's own translation.

By permission of Martin Secker and Warburg Ltd and Alfred A. Knopf, Inc., New York, from *The Trial*, tr. W. and E. Muir, with additional material tr. E. M. Butler (copyright 1925, 1935, 1946 by Schocken Books Inc.; copyright renewed 1952, 1963, 1974 by Schocken Books Inc.—copyright 1937, © 1956 by Alfred A. Knopf, Inc.; copyright renewed 1964 by Alfred A. Knopf, Inc.); and *The Castle*, tr. W. and E. Muir, with additional material tr. Eithne Wilkins and Ernst Kaiser (copyright 1926, 1946 by Schocken Books Inc.; copyright renewed 1953, 1974 by Schocken Books Inc. —copyright 1930, 1941, 1954 by Alfred A. Knopf, Inc.; copyright © renewed 1958 by Alfred A. Knopf, Inc.—copyright 1930 by Martin Secker and Warburg Ltd).

Author's Note

Full details of the texts, both original and in translation, to which I have referred are given in the Select Bibliography. Translations for which no source is given are my own. Page references are taken from the following editions identified in my text by the appropriate capital letter :

Metamorphosis and Other Stories, tr. W. and E. Muir, Penguin, 1961 (M).
America, tr. W. and E. Muir, Penguin, 1967 (A).
The Trial, tr. W. and E. Muir, Penguin, 1953 (T).
The Castle, tr. W. and E. Muir, Penguin, 1957 (C).
The Diaries of Franz Kafka 1910–1913, tr. Joseph Kresh, Schocken Books, New York, 1948 (D1).
The Diaries of Franz Kafka 1914–1923, tr. Martin Greenberg with the co-operation of Hannah Arendt, Schocken Books, New York, 1949 (D2).

Introduction

Boris Kuznetsov, in his recent book, *Einstein and Dostoevsky*, makes the following interesting comment on the relationship between the idea of macroscopic harmony and individual existence :

There had to appear (and survive) in nineteenth-century culture the *image* of the lonely, insulted, defeated human being, ignored by the macroscopic scheme of existence. It had to be an image, not a concept, for only an image can convey the inimitable, individual qualities of people, and this is the concern of poetics, not of logic, confronting the mind with the specific picture of an individual.

This image has survived, most urgently and intensively, in Kafka's work. More so than Dostoyevsky, Kafka felt the need to protest against a modern concept of statistical harmony which no longer took account of the happiness of *every* individual. This was brought home to him as a fact by his own experience, when in the Workers' Insurance Office for Bohemia, 'the dark nest of bureaucrats', he had to look after the welfare of insured workers. Once he remarked about them to Max Brod : 'How undemanding these people are. They come to petition us. Instead of attacking the building and smashing everything into matchwood, they come to petition us.' The rationalised superstructures embodied in our social institutions are based on principles which are anathema to the modern conscience. They rule over statistically averaged processes in which justice may be done to the greatest possible number but in which the fate of a single individual may very well be immaterial. Kafka never grew tired of pointing out the consequences of the modern mania for rationalised systems and bureaucratic utopias. In *The Castle* he demonstrated both the possibility of fatal injustice—when K.'s file is destroyed—and the need for individual protest—when Amalia tears up Sortini's letter. But this does not mean that Kafka fought on one front only, against the menacing manifestations of a mundane and utilitarian world. As is well known he conducted an equally fierce war against the 'evil intentions' of the individual, particularly when this individual was himself. This led Kafka frequently to a contradictory assessment of reality. Whilst he never had any doubts as to the real nature of the observable world, he came to develop a highly ambiguous attitude towards that reality. Kafka's 'revolt against the real' (Erich Heller) was not as consistent as is commonly assumed. Sometimes he viewed reality as the wicked creation of the demiurge, from which the real God was excluded. It was then up to the individual to take matters into his own hands and work out a programme for salvation. Sometimes however he viewed the created world as a reality *sui generis*, as something that did not rest on arbitrariness and was therefore capable of providing an authentic transcendental backcloth to individual existence. 'The world is in order', as Kafka put it to his young friend Gustav Janouch. 'Only we are transfixed like the wooden figure in the church.'

In the following pages I have attempted to analyse in more detail some of the assumptions on which Kafka's writings are based. It was Kafka's conviction that existence was divided into an objective and a subjective sphere and that despite man's (and God's) inability to establish a connection between the two a constant attempt had to be made to yoke them together. This modification of a time-honoured philosophical axiom allowed Kafka on the one hand to provide a penetrating critique of the idea of 'objective' existence, and the many contemporary versions of it, and on the other hand to explore thoroughly the predicament of the individual, which he diagnosed as a 'paralysis of conscience'. What first impresses itself on the reader of Kafka's work is a vision of an incomprehensible world, a mood of total impotence in the face of the unintelligible power of circumstances, as a consequence of which 'the inner world of the subject is transformed into a sinister, inexplicable flux' (Georg Lukács) requiring exorcism by the harshest punitive measures. Yet it is equally true that beneath the nightmare a more positive assessment of reality can be detected. Though for most of the time it was impossible for Kafka to make such an assessment an integral part of his poetics, he could on occasion intimate that, as he explained to Janouch, reality is also 'the strongest force shaping the world and human beings. . . . Dreams are only a way round, at the end of which one always returns to the world of most immediate reality.' The final chapter of *The Castle*, for example, describes such a return. One must also understand the therapeutic and utopian quality of Kafka's nihilism. If he could not bring himself unambiguously to celebrate the positive aspects of human existence, then he at least indirectly pointed the way, by pushing the nihilistic view of it to its limits.

Though the present study is in the first instance designed for a more general readership I have at the same time attempted to dwell on problems which hitherto have received less attention than they deserve. Some of the things I have suggested above are examples of such problems. The second chapter is a revaluation of a perennial problem in Kafka criticism : the intimate relationship between Kafka's life and his work. Professor E. M. Wilkinson's recent and excellent paper, 'Tragedy in the Diachronic Mode' (*Publications of the English Goethe Society*, 52, 1972), unfortunately appeared too late to be included in the discussion. I should otherwise have liked to argue more forcefully, and with more confidence, that Kafka's works are literature in a decisively 'diachronic mode', with the proviso that the heterogeneous material out of which they are made is not so much of a historical as of a biographical and contemporary nature. If, in this context, I have refrained from reopening the discussion on Kafka's relationship to his father then I did so for the simple reason that I could have added little of substance to Professor Politzer's important essay, 'The Letter to His Father' (in *Franz Kafka Today*, ed. A. Flores and H. Swander), in which he argues the 'fictional' aspects of what was otherwise a real enough, if less disastrous than is commonly assumed, conflict between father and son. In my approach to the works, which I have selected for fuller discussion, I have tried to be as varied as possible, paying particular attention to the sociological (*Metamorphosis*), biographical (*The Trial*) and metaphysical implications (*The Castle*) of Kafka's oeuvre. The chapter on *America* will, I hope, demonstrate an interesting departure from what was to become Kafka's chief mode of writing. In my close readings of the works I have been guided by the conviction that in the case of Kafka we are dealing with literature written to be read, as J. A. Mazzeo once said about Joyce, with exegetical methods rather than with methods inspired by organicist theories. As far as I have been able to arrive at any general conclusions I have incorporated them in the text, and have not attempted to write a Conclusion with a capital C.

I
Kafka's World

Austrian and German literature in the nineteenth century share a predicament which was not known to other literatures at the time. The view that in England, France and Russia literature, and intellectual life in general, enjoyed a healthy communion with the socio-political conditions from which they organically grew (frequently expressed, amongst others, by Georg Lukács) may be too simple to carry absolute weight, but it is a perfectly valid judgment if we compare the situation in these countries with that in nineteenth-century Austria and Germany. When Thomas Mann was asked the question (and this is a question which Germans ask themselves about once every decade) whether Schiller was still a living force, he began his answer by saying that no Frenchman would dream of asking whether Racine and Corneille were still living forces in his day. At the same time he pointed to the lack of continuity in German literature and, as he does in many of his other responses to the 'German problem', to the extraordinary ardour on the part of German writers to celebrate their inwardness and isolated position. Much work has recently been done, by historians and critics alike, towards explaining this strange gap between literary and political developments. It is now generally accepted that the radical separation of literature from its socio-political context, its both despairingly and arrogantly sustained apolitical posture, has something to do with the way the Germans went about building their nation in the nineteenth century. What we find in Austria is merely the other side of the same coin.

For centuries the Empire formed a unified whole, sacred and untouchable to the many different nations it comprised, a kind of political arcadia (sustained by benevolent absolutism) which miraculously escaped serious disruption throughout the nineteenth century but which was split wide open by the events during and following the First World War. Intellectually speaking, Austrians were so unprepared for the final catastrophe that the former aspirations for unity and wholeness not only lingered on within the narrow confines of the drastically reduced nation but became the desperate concern of cultural politics. Hofmannsthal's idea of the new Austria as a model for the new Europe to come is a perfect example of this. Austrian literature after 1918 is very largely a record of the traumatic experience created by the sudden disappearance of the old Monarchy. This it became because the inhabitants of the vast 'Commonwealth of Nations' were educated in the belief that an indestructible *Spiritus Austriacus*, rather than anything more concrete, sustained every aspect of their existence. That is to say, long before the Empire ceased to exist as a political reality Austrians were encouraged to embrace an elaborate historical and geographical myth, with strong aetiological, theological and pseudo-existential overtones. As Claudio Magris[1] has argued, this 'Habsburg myth' began to appear long before 1900, as soon as the first cracks in the political and social fabric of the Empire became visible. It was given currency by Metternich's vast and subtle propaganda machine, but literature became its chief vehicle. In a situation in which the relationship between practical politics and ideological aspirations becomes strained an awkward choice presents itself to the writer. He can choose either to put his art in the service of what are considered to be the predominant spiritual concerns of the age or to set himself up as a critic of these concerns. On the whole Austrian writers opted for the former, showing only little awareness of the ambiguous situation in which they found themselves. That is to say, Austrian literature in the nineteenth century was 'majestic', the mouthpiece of accepted opinions and emotions, not only supporting but in itself being a kind of operant myth. The critique was conducted very much on the borderline between literature and day-to-day polemical writing, reaching its highest possible pitch in the work of Karl Kraus.

By the end of the century Austrian writers and intellectuals had become fully aware of the impossibility of their position. The more stagnant and static life in their patriarchal society became (was this one of the reasons why Kafka so frequently toys with the idea of a matriarchal society?) the less possible it was for these writers 'to ally themselves with any kind of broader social or political activity'.[2] In other words writers were doomed more than ever to cling to the myth they had inherited, adapting, elaborating and spiritualising it. Yet the political vacuum, combined with what was after all more than visible, the bureaucratic machinery of the multi-national state, created an indefinable but acute state of anxiety, even of paranoia. Like Kafka's Castle the power which held the crumbling yet still splendid and alluring edifice together was both there and not there. It is not by accident that the sense of impending doom, mortal pessimism and self-doubt were most poignantly expressed not by the Viennese but by the German writers in Prague. Their isolation and sense of frustration were almost total. They could not identify with the newly-stirring forces around them (in their case Czech nationalism) or cling on very much longer to the larger, anachronistic whole to which they belonged in an indeterminate sort of way. Nor could they clearly envisage what the forms of the new society, and their own role in it, might prove to be. Intellectual life in Prague, more than anywhere else, mirrors the contradictions and psychological malaise which came to the fore, immediately before and during the war, in all corners of the Dual Empire. The following pages are devoted to further examination of this intellectual climate, and how it affected Kafka and his work.

The literary scene in Prague

By the turn of the century the German-speaking community in Prague was no more than an isolated outpost in the midst of a predominantly Czech population. Despite the decline in sheer numbers there took place a remarkable resurgence of literature and of intellectual life in general. At one point the term 'a Prague German' was almost a synonym for 'writer'. But the sudden efflorescence of cultural activities does not disguise the fact that on the whole they remained a provincial and parochial affair. The German literature of Prague never had a modernist movement of any significance. Writers like Hugo Salus (1866–1929), Friedrich Adler (1857–1938), Camill Hoffmann (1878–1944) and even Paul Leppin (1878–1945) were either thoroughly traditional or only mildly infected, as if by a spring fever, by 'the modern spirit' as it flourished in most other European cities. When the first 'modern' writers began to make their voices known, from about 1906 onwards, they were doomed to become imitators not only of the tradition they inherited but of the Modernism which had been flourishing for some time almost everywhere else. Too much (or too little) was asked of these writers : to catch up with developments which were already twenty or thirty years out of date. The problem was by no means a new one for Prague writers. At a time when Schiller, Goethe and the early Romantics were leaving their imprint on the rest of Europe, Prague was still producing unwieldy theatrical productions reminiscent of the seventeenth-century Jesuit pageants, and a whole flood of historical and gothic novels of the most provincial kind.

Nor did the social background of the city provide much encouragement to the budding writer, particularly when he happened to be German, or Jewish, or both—as most of the writers who concern us here were. Johannes Urzidil, himself an early emigrant from the 'Dublin of the East', says this about the social situation in Prague :

The German-speaking poets and authors of Prague had simultaneous access to at least four ethnic sources : the Germanic tradition to which they belonged culturally and linguistically; the Czech tradition, which everywhere surrounded them as an element of life; the Jewish tradition, even when they were themselves not Jewish, since it formed one of the main historical and ubiquitously evident factors in the city; and the Austrian tradition, into which they were all born and within which they all grew up. . . .[3]

This account leaves out the frictions, the almost unbearable fragmentation of all creative and intellectual efforts in the comparatively small city. Nor does it indicate the distribution of the various groups. In 1900 Prague had a population of over 400,000 (over 90 per cent) Czechs, about 10,000 non-Jewish Germans, and 25,000 Jews, of whom 14,000 spoke Czech and 11,000 German. There was hardly anything which the minority groups had in common, nor did they, in turn, have much in common with the dynamic and nationalist interests of the vast majority of Czechs. Despite idealistic attempts at collaboration in intellectual circles the situation in Prague remained one of fragmentation, projecting a peculiar hothouse atmosphere in which all kinds of creeds, such as Socialism, Zionism, German nationalism, Bohemianism, Humanism and an artificial type of Cosmopolitanism clashed vehemently. These clashes had of course the usual side-effects : cliquishness, intrigues, in-fighting, snobbery. The worst about it all, however, was that the whole thing was a peculiarly local affair, without any 'higher' meaning whatsoever. Whatever apologists like Max Brod may have said fifty years later, Prague in the early decades of this century provided a classical situation for the development of hysteria, claustrophobia and alienation among intellectuals. At least three major waves of emigré German writers left Prague for no other reason than the drab atomisation of life in their city. Rilke left as early as 1896. By 1906 Victor Hadwiger had gone. In 1912 Franz Werfel left; to be followed, within the next eight years, by Egon Erwin Kisch, the 'roaming reporter', Willy Haas, one of the editors of the *Herder-Blätter*, Paul Kornfeld, and others. In 1915 Kafka made the following interesting remark in his diaries : 'Always this one principal anguish : If I had gone away in 1912, in full possession of all my forces, with a clear head, not eaten by the strain of keeping down living forces !'[4] It is true that many of those who had left kept returning on brief visits, and that interest in their work was revived by those who had stayed behind, but by about 1912 Modernism in Prague had ceased to exist as a significant force. What was left was on the one hand a small group of writers of highly different outlooks, of whom Max Brod (1884–1968) was still a kind of spiritual leader, and on the other one of the greatest German writers—Franz Kafka.

One of the attempts to create a centre for modernist activity in Prague was the foundation of 'Young Prague', a group of writers who gathered mostly around Oskar Wiener in 1905–06 and who were represented in the *Moderne Flugblätter*. Their contributions were later collected under the title *Frühling*. Another such attempt was the plan for forming a 'Freie deutsche Künstlervereinigung', a 'free German association of artists', to be directed against the literary popery of the older generation. A third was Leppin's magazine *Wir* which stopped publication, however, after its second number in 1906. But in the same year Max Brod, the spiritual leader of a group which included Oskar Baum, Felix Weltsch and Kafka, published his first collection of short stories, which bore the provocative title *Tod den Toten* (1906; 'Death to the Dead'). The book was meant as an attack against the excessive preoccupation with the past which some of the modernists shared with the older generation. Brod's first novel, *Schloss Nornepygge* (1908), had a startling effect on the young generation of writers in Berlin, who had gathered around Kurt Hiller. It portrays a young hero who is haunted by hopelessness, nihilism, and by what Brod called 'Indifferentismus'. In 1910 Hiller invited Brod, 'the indifferent', to read from his own works at Hiller's literary club, Der Neue Club, in Berlin. For a while exciting contacts between Prague and Berlin seemed to establish themselves. Brod contributed to the periodical *Der Sturm*, as he did later to *Die Aktion*; Hiller and his friends wrote for the Bohemian *Herder-Blätter* (1911–12). In 1912 Franz Werfel (1890–1945), whose first collection of poems, *Der Weltfreund* (1911), was hailed with enthusiasm, went to Berlin—and stayed. But Brod and his friends soon realised that the spontaneous links between Berlin and Prague rested on a kind of misunderstanding. The mood in Prague changed rapidly, from 'indifferentism' to commitment. The foundation of the 'Johann Gottfried Herder-Vereinigung zur Förderung ideeller Interessen' in 1910 and of the *Herder-Blätter*, its official organ, was a direct expression of this change. From now on social, religio-cultural and political activities were going to be more important than literature. The aim of the Herder-Vereinigung was to act as a bridge linking the more radical doctrines current at the time and to spread the gospel of a liberal humanism. Herder became the powerful symbol for all these endeavours. It is not surprising that in this large-scale search for new meaning enthusiasm for the past was aroused once more. Despite Brod's earlier views, the dead came alive again. *Epigonentum*, crude and unsophisticated, flourished. The choice of models was predictable and eclectic : the Bible, Homer, Plato, Schiller, Goethe, Flaubert. One of the leading periodicals was called *Witiko*, after Adalbert Stifter's novel bearing the same name. Max Brod devoted much of his time after 1912 to historical novels, confidently reviving some of the more old-fashioned nineteenth-century narrative techniques in the process, and Louis Fürnberg, a 'Rilkean' poet who later became a communist, wrote a 'Mozart-novelle' in imitation of Eduard Mörike's *Mozart auf der Reise nach Prag*. After 1918 socialism and communism were for many, like Kisch, F. C. Weiskopf and Fürnberg, the natural ways out of an artificial and ideologically highly strung situation. Others simply cultivated memories of the old Prague as an imagined fairy-land, in exile. Max Brod was one of the last to leave (in 1939), and to revive interest in the 'Venice on the

Moldau' and its intellectual life by the many passionate and polemical accounts which flowed from his pen during the Fifties and Sixties.[5]

Kafka was the only writer in Prague who did not allow himself to submit to any of the short-lived ideologies of the day. His main works did not reach the public until after his death. If he had to survey the scene it was through a glass darkly. Considering himself as 'the most typical Western Jew'—but he meant very much the same thing when he called himself a 'bachelor'—he thoroughly mistrusted the noisy political activities of his contemporaries and, on a more general level, felt threatened by the typical manifestations of Central European politics and Habsburg myth-making. The only creed Kafka did not reject out of hand was socialism. Though he never was a professed socialist, as some of his friends and many of his contemporaries were, he felt attracted to the moral and intellectual aspects of socialist thinking. Michael Mareš, a Czech socialist leader, whose acquaintance Kafka made in October 1909, writes this about Kafka's political engagement: 'As far as I know, Kafka was not a member of any of the . . . anarchist clubs, but it can be said he sympathised with them as a man of deep social conscience. He had a very great interest in such meetings (as his presence at them showed), but he never participated in the discussions.'[6] Though Kafka was familiar with the dialectical methods of socialist theory—as his stories *The Great Wall of China* and *Metamorphosis* clearly reveal—his own brand of socialism was more a form of humanist revolt, a desired condition of both the world and the soul, than active political commitment. It was a necessary counterdoctrine to the capitalist degradation of life, the rapid economisation of human existence. What Kafka told Gustav Janouch is also frequently echoed in his literary work: 'The factories are merely organisations for increasing financial profit. In such a matter, we all have a merely subordinate function. Man is today only an old-fashioned instrument of economic growth, a hangover from history, whose economically inadequate skills will soon be displaced by frictionless thinking machines.'[7] Threats of this kind are not to be answered by 'a fierce anarchist whom they endure as a curiosity in the *Prager Tagblatt*'[8] but rather by such an all-embracing metaphysical socialism as that outlined by Dostoyevsky in *The Brothers Karamazov*:

Socialism is not just a worker's question or that of the so-called fourth estate, it is rather in an eminent sense an atheistic demand : the question of the contemporary realisation of atheism, the question of the Babylonian Tower that was built without God, not in order to reach heaven from earth but to pull heaven down to earht.[9]

In *The Great Wall of China* Kafka develops the idea further, but it is in *The Trial* and *The Castle* that he sets the stage for the grand battle between man and heaven.

Literature as exorcism

Kafka was uniquely qualified for the kind of literature which broke away decisively from literary traditions and conventions, and which developed original patterns of its own. Kafka's mistrust of literature as an institution was complete. His idea of paradise was a place where there are no books. But he had a compulsive interest in fictional works of a strongly autobiographical kind (Goethe, Dostoyevsky, Strindberg, Grillparzer, Kleist, Kierkegaard) and in works which use language analytically (biblical exegesis and works of a scientific, psychological and philosophical nature). His remark on Schopenhauer is typical in this respect : 'Schopenhauer is an artist in language. That is the source of his thinking. For the language alone, one must not fail to read him.'[10] The idea of language as pure exorcism fascinated Kafka. There is a sense in which Austrian literature right down to Peter Handke can very largely be seen as a rhetorical ritual of exorcism. In the works of Schnitzler, Musil, Broch, and most contemporary Viennese writers, the spiritual muddledom and what is frequently referred to as 'the sickness of the Austrian mind' (in the widest geographical and teleological meaning of this term) have been consistently on trial, the trial normally ending with the hero condemned to silence. Kafka is the climax of this tradition. But whilst the writers mentioned above had a habit of selecting a collective malaise Kafka put the spotlight on a single individual, most rigorously in *The Trial*. Whilst Kafka's contemporaries in Prague, in their synthetic mood, were searching for new laws and values, he himself undertook a radical examination of how the individual can emancipate himself from the old laws and values in the first place. Where literature during the first decades of this century offered either utopian solutions or a gay apocalypse Kafka tormented himself with penal fantasies. But it must not be assumed that the early stories Kafka intended to collect under the title *Punishments* (a plan which was never realised) are nothing but the products of a hidden desire for self-torment. They are uncompromising experiments motivated by a need for truth and new ways of apprehending reality analytically. Moreover, Kafka's radical view of art as inquisition should not blind us to the possibility that beneath the dark surface of his work there glimmers something more positive, the hope that salvation might lie in the very act of pushing the dialectic to its extremes. It is here that Kafka's public image appears to be in need of some correction.

Kafka is perhaps the most significant of 'post-Nietzschean' writers, if by 'post-Nietzschean' we mean the twentieth-century response to Nietzsche's 'Artisten-Metaphysik' (aesthetic metaphysics) as outlined in *The Birth of Tragedy*. Musil and others 'discussed' Nietzsche or 'adapted' certain Nietzschean habits of thought for their own purposes. But Kafka's very art is grounded, on the one hand, in the kind of nineteenth-century radical pessimism we know from Schopenhauer and, on the other, in Nietzsche's vision of life and art (which resulted from a commitment to this pessimism). 'Profound pessimism', as Nietzsche explained in his 'extravagant' book of 1871, is the precondition for the eventual ability whole-heartedly to embrace existence. The nightmarish aspects of Kafka's work have been fully analysed, perhaps too fully; but it also needs pointing out that much is comic, and ironic, in Kafka. When he switches to the horrors of existence it is not in order to 'prove' the tragedy of it all but in order to create a desire and curiosity for existence redeemed. In their own way Kafka's works are, despite their ambiguity, a subdued celebration of life. This is particularly true of the novels *America*, the 'brightest' of Kafka's works, *The Castle*, his most ambitious attempt to explore man's existential dilemma, and such stories as *Metamorphosis* and *A Hunger-Artist*. Long after Kafka's death, and well outside the walls of Prague, a body of literature sprang up which is frequently referred to as the Kafka Tradition. But the 'tradition' can easily be distinguished from its radical initiator. The difference between, say, Camus and Kafka appears to lie in the fact that the former allows his characters to find solace in a spiritual (admittedly absurd) position whilst the latter questions the validity of the human urge to embark on a spiritual quest as such. In Kafka the religious hero, with his temptation to impose an alien order on reality, and the artist, with his temptation to assert the timelessness and impersonality of his art, are the first to be put on trial. This can only be done if reality is seen not only as the evil environment such as is frequently depicted by Kafka but also as the redeeming influence through which man can achieve reconciliation with the controlling powers of his existence.

Ethical 'Stirnerism'

'What am I?' asked Tolstoy, prophet and father-figure of the young generation that grew up in European cities around 1900, in 1882, when he made a unique attempt to solve the spiritual crisis of his life by writing down what soon was to become one of his most admired works, *A Confession*. Towards the end of the nineteenth century this became 'the overwhelming question' of the day; not only for the Prufrocks or the self-conscious and self-styled 'moderns' but for anybody who was remotely concerned with the problems of life, truth, and personal identity. The question 'What am I?' resounded through at least one and a half decades in a chorus made up of the sombre voices of committed writers and philosophers, the light gossip of columnists, the harsh voices of angry young men writing political pamphlets and literary manifestos, and the incessant chatter and patter around the tables of Viennese and Prague coffee-houses. But science too joined in. Ernst Mach and Sigmund Freud posed what, to them and to many other scientists, had become one of the most vexing moral and scientific problems, the identity of the self, each of them giving their far-reaching answers in the light of their respective systems. The question 'What am I?', clearly, had become a public one. Tolstoy himself had already asked it not only with a view to himself but with a view to the whole age. His *Confession* combines both fictional and autobiographical elements, as most famous confessions do, and is an earnest attempt to persuade his contemporaries of the need to pause and consider their life. Together with the writings of other Moderns, such as Dostoyevsky, Ibsen, Barrès, and Maeterlinck, it exerted a deep influence on the generation of the Nineties, turning their quest for 'truth' almost into a fashion. Hofmannsthal gratefully acknowledged the debt he owed to the 'author of *Anna Karenina*', and pointed out in an early review of three of Barrès' novels that Tolstoy, by asking an apparently loaded question, did not intend to make the world Christian again but to point to the unity of all living things.

Tolstoy had answered his question 'What am I?' with breathtaking simplicity : 'A part of the infinite.'[11] It was an answer that was like oil on wounds to all disappointed aesthetes, melancholic moralists, and worn-out seekers of self—for a while at least. In the long run the answer engendered a confusing display of anything from subtle scepticism to crude dogmatising about the nature of the Infinite. Hofmannsthal, who committed himself to the Tolstoyan ethic, without Tolstoy's peculiar powers of belief, suffered, and mirrored in his writings, the whole chameleon-like metamorphosis of the 'infinite'. For a while the 'infinite' was a synonym for 'life', one of the Nietzschean key-words of the Nineties, and conservative catch-word *par excellence* as Thomas Mann noticed. But after about 1905 it became anything from 'Geist' to 'das Soziale', 'das Österreichische' and 'das Europäische'. Hofmannsthal is the supreme example of a writer whose suggestive and non-ideological vocabulary of the Nineties later changed into a complex but nevertheless dull system of metaphysical and socio-political rhetoric.

Tolstoy's answer, however, was only one of many possible answers in a universal attempt to solve the problem of human identity. Earlier on in the nineteenth century the German philosopher Max Stirner (1806–56) came up with a totally different version of asking, and answering, the question of the age. Stirner looked at the problem from a generic point of view. 'In the times of spirits' (i.e. when he was a child), he writes,

thoughts grew till they overtopped my head, whose offspring they yet were; they hovered about me and convulsed me like fever-phantasies—an awful power. The thoughts had become *corporeal* on their own account, were ghosts, such as God, Emperor, Pope, Fatherland, etc. If I destroy their corporeity, then I take them back into mine, and say : 'I alone am corporeal.' And now I take the world as what it is to me, as *mine*, as my property : I refer all to myself.[12]

Or, putting it more abstractly :

I on my part start from a presupposition in presupposing *myself*; but my presupposition does not struggle for its perfection like 'Man struggling for his perfection', but only serves me to enjoy it and consume it. I consume my presupposition, and nothing else, and exist only in consuming it. But that presupposition is therefore not a presupposition at all : for, as I am the Unique, I know nothing of the duality of a presupposing and a presupposed ego (an 'incomplete' and a 'complete' ego or man); but this, that I consume myself, means only that I am. I do not presuppose myself, because I am every moment just positing or creating myself, and am I only by being not presupposed but posited, and, again, posited only in the moment when I posit myself; i.e. I am creator and creature in one.

If the presuppositions that have hitherto been current are to melt away in a full dissolution, they must not be dissolved into a higher presupposition again—i.e. a thought, or thinking itself, criticism. For that dissolution is to be for *my* good; otherwise it would belong only in the series of the innumerable dissolutions which, in favour of others (e.g. this very Man, God, the State, pure morality, etc.), declared old truths to be untruths and did away with long-fostered presuppositions.[13]

These two passages are worth quoting at length, not because of their stylistic virtues, but because they give expression to the philosophy of egoism, which flourished at the turn of the century as a by-product of the aestheticism and moral protest of the day, with rare force and eccentricity. The great liberators of the nineteenth century, Schopenhauer, Nietzsche, the early Wagner, did not achieve what Stirner achieved : the immunisation of the concrete individual self, the man of flesh and blood, against all abstractions and the worship of impersonal forces. Stirner's answer to the question 'What am I ?' was : 'I am I'. The I proceeds out of and returns to the 'creative nothing', and while the I exists its concern is with itself alone. 'Stirnerism' was a unique protest against the nineteenth-century worship of such abstractions as 'absolute spirit', 'universal essence', 'tradition', 'history', etc., and served as an important model for a similar need, between 1890 and 1914, to emphasise the concrete reality of the individual. Stirner's influence can be detected even after 1914, in a sentence like the following from *The Man Without Qualities*, in which

Musil attacks the abstractions that were so popular in the nineteenth century:

It [the nineteenth century] had been clever in technical and commercial matters and in research, but outside these focal points of its energy it had been quiet and treacherous as a swamp. It had painted like the Old Masters, written like Goethe and Schiller, and built its houses in the Gothic or Renaissance style. Insistence on the Ideal dominated all manifestations of life, like the headquarters of a police-force.[14]

But the important fact about Stirner's philosophy is its affinity with existentialism. Like existentialism it defended the unique free individual, though this defence was carried out in a provocative way. Stirner's radical philosophy of egoism contained nothing that would have prevented it from being read as a primer of narcissism, the most fascinating evil the nineteenth century knew—and only reluctantly condemned. Kierkegaard's writings clearly reveal the moral ambiguity of early existentialism. The question for individual truth was experienced as a moral triumph, the narcissistic aspects of the quest as guilt. It was Gogol, however, who mercilessly explored the moral implications of egoism, something which Stirner had omitted to do. His 'dead souls' are grim versions of egoists who fail to achieve the primary purpose of all quests (including the quest for the self), identity, and they are the direct forerunners of Kafka's condemned heroes. It is known that Kierkegaard and Gogol were two important influences in Kafka's life and work. Whether Kafka was acquainted with Stirner's philosophy in detail is debatable.[15] But that is not the problem here. The problem is the nature of Kafka's own philosophy of egoism. If lying can be shown to be 'a universal principle', as Joseph K. shows it to be, then there is every reason to believe that salvation lies with one's own soul alone. This is exactly what Joseph K. believes, at least to begin with. The first chapter of *The Trial* is a literary version of undiluted Stirnerism. But Kafka never forgives his heroes for what he himself frequently considered as natural a means as any of protecting the self, and combating the lies of the world: healthy egoism. He condemns them all, and the penalty is frequently death. Like Gogol, Kafka leaves us in no doubt about the necessity of such rough justice. The K.s are not merely egoists, they are narcissus-figures. Their quest for unity fails, because they cannot see what is outside themselves. They end up with a glimpse of some terrible reality existing monolithically in their own breasts: their own soul. So, like Narcissus, they must die. Reasoning of this kind may be no more than the familiar logic of traditional ethics, yet the pattern has proved uniquely fruitful in the development of truly 'modern' literature, literature that has sought 'to restore art to its pure essence'[16] and to avoid confusion with extrinsic elements, such as morality, religion, or psychology.

Art has its own peculiar laws. Stirnerism, we might say, is on the side of 'modern' literature, in the same way as nineteenth-century 'pessimism'—the Nietzschean variety—is and nineteenth-century 'optimism' is not. Things become interesting when there is a clash between the 'modern' and the 'traditional', as there is in Tolstoy's question and answer. Whilst the problem of identity—the question 'What am I?'—is in the interest and within the scope of modern literature, the exploration of the 'infinite' is not, as Musil's *Törless* proves. But this is precisely what Hofmannsthal attempted to do in his famous *Chandos Letter*: to link the problem of identity with a mystical belief in the unity of all life, Hofmannsthal's version of the 'infinite'. The result was an intriguing experiment in terms of literary autobiography, an over-refined statement of the mysticism current at the turn of the century, and a total failure in terms of 'modern' literature. Since Hofmannsthal's *Chandos Letter* provides an interesting contrast to Kafka's own thinking on the matter, it is worth briefly dwelling on its essential message.

Crisis of consciousness

Hofmannsthal's imaginary letter, which purports to have been written on August 22, 1603 by Philip, Lord Chandos, younger son of the Earl of Bath, to Francis Bacon, was originally published in the Berlin daily *Der Tag* under the title *Ein Brief* (1902; *The Letter of Lord Chandos*). In this letter the writer expresses, and gives a detailed explanation of, his intention to renounce all future literary activity. He begins by giving an account of what he wrote, or planned to write, as a young man, when the whole of human existence and of the world appeared to him as one great unity. The *Letter* then proceeds to analyse the various stages of what Chandos diagnoses as 'a disease of my mind', the inability to speak or think of anything coherently, to conceive the whole of existence as one great unit, to attach meaning to such abstract concepts as 'spirit', 'soul', or 'body', and to form an opinion of any kind. Ultimately he despairs of language itself. This is how Chandos puts it :

the abstract terms of which the tongue must avail itself as a matter of course in order to voice a judgment . . . crumbled in my mouth like mouldy fungi.

For me everything disintegrated into parts, those parts again into parts; no longer would anything let itself be encompassed by one idea. Single words floated round me; they congealed into eyes which stared at me and into which I was forced to stare back—whirlpools which gave me vertigo and, reeling incessantly, led into the void.[17]

All that is left to Chandos are his 'good moments', as he calls them, moments in which 'a pitcher, a harrow abandoned in a field, a dog in the sun, a neglected cemetery, a cripple, a peasant's hut . . . can become the vessel of my revelation'. He compares these moments, 'epiphanies' as Proust and Joyce would have called them, to 'whirlpools, but of a sort that do not seem to lead, as the whirlpools of language, into the abyss, but into myself and into the deepest womb of peace'. They persuade him to renounce all languages known to human beings, even Latin, and hopefully to rely on a 'language none of whose words is known to me, a language in which inanimate things speak to me and wherein I may one day have to justify myself before an unknown judge'.

This brief summary does not do justice to the wealth of literary allusions which Hofmannsthal, in a manner not dissimilar to Eliot's, incorporated into his highly self-conscious and literary account of 'Sprachskepsis', nor can it give an impression of the extent to which every detail in the *Letter* is intended to carry weight and to assimilate the author's own experience to archetypal models in the tradition of communicating a crisis of consciousness. Above all the *Letter* imitates a time-honoured religious, and rhetorical, pattern, the movement from words to silence. But it does this in a peculiar way. All the models which refer to the problem of communication, or a crisis of consciousness—such as were abundantly used and given currency by, say, the Romantics

—tend to reveal a sense of intellectual rebirth, frequently incorporating a positive decision in their dialectical scheme. They all express the hope of imaginative change, intensification of the moral life, and new creativity. Chandos appears to be the only man in a crisis who is neither able nor willing to find a way out of it. Why? The answer cannot be given in a single sentence.

Poets have felt uncomfortable, in the face of language that 'prattles on its *pebbled* way, instead of its bed or channel',[18] since at least the Romantic period. Coleridge, after exposing the 'trashy style' of Drayton, writes this to his friend William Sotheby: 'In my opinion, every phrase, every metaphor, every personification, should have its justifying cause in some *passion*, either of the poet's mind or of the characters described by the poet' (ibid.).[19] By the end of the century Coleridge's demand for the truthfulness of metaphoric statements had become a common concern for writers of all kinds. A climax was reached when writers, mostly under the pressure of a personal crisis (real or fictional), began to discover for themselves an identity between language and experience. In a state of utter despair and amidst thoughts of suicide Tolstoy remembered the oriental fable of the traveller who is surprised in the desert by a wild beast. Tolstoy applied it to his own situation as follows:

Thus I hang upon the boughs of life, knowing that the inevitable dragon of death is waiting ready to tear me, and I cannot comprehend why I am thus made a martyr. I try to suck the honey which formerly consoled me; but the honey pleases me no longer, and day and night the white mouse and the black mouse gnaw the branch to which I cling. I can see but one thing: the inevitable dragon and the mice—I cannot turn my gaze from them.

This is no fable, but the literal incontestable truth which every one may understand. What will be the outcome of what I do to-day? Of what I shall do to-morrow? What will be the outcome of all my life? Why should I live? Why should I do anything? Is there in life any purpose which the inevitable death which awaits me does not undo and destroy?[20]

'This is no fable,' Tolstoy says, 'but the literal incontestable truth.' And this is what Chandos feels about the rats in the cellar and Carthage burning. Of Chandos's sense-impressions one can say that he does not offer them as a proof of God but as a proof of authentic experience and of authentic metaphoric speech. But the same applies to Chandos's memories : when Chandos remembers the dying rats in the cellar, or Carthage burning, then the memory is not of the past but is synonymous with his present suffering. When Hofmannsthal reviewed Alfred Biese's *Philosophie des Metaphorischen* he was slightly disappointed with the book, because he had not expected merely 'a collection of the choicest metaphors' but a 'Philosophie der subjektiven Metaphorik'.[21] In the *Letter* Hofmannsthal presents such a philosophy. The examples he gives are metaphors, not for a reality which transcends them, but for the most private experience of the individual. In this sense they are 'literal' metaphors or 'incontestable truths'. They are like Trakl's 'Chiffren', or like Kafka's 'perfect' sentences. 'When I arbitrarily write a single sentence,' Kafka writes in his *Diaries*, 'for instance, "He looked out of the window", it already has perfection.' (D1,* 45.) They are the results of a moral revolution within the individual, as Hofmannsthal explained frequently before 1900, and of a new 'Gerechtigkeit' (justice) in matters of the intellect as Kasimir Edschmid put it much later, strangely echoing Hofmannsthal's vocabulary throughout his *Frühe Manifeste*. Miss Mary Gilbert has provided us with the insight that Hofmannsthal's essays between 1900 and 1908 'are veiled manifestations of a creative energy which could not, for a while, find an outlet in the directions of an overt lyric form; the reason for this lies in a deep-seated need for greater reality, and this need provides, in the essays, the steady undercurrent of preoccupation'.[22] Critics like Walter Jens, Fritz Martini and Walter Höllerer have felt, rightly to my mind, that this 'need for greater reality' also provided us with a more or less consistent, and one of the first, expressionist documents in the *Chandos Letter*. But at the same time it turns out to be a very Janus-faced document. The more reasons we have for believing that the *Letter* is an outstanding achievement, in terms of 'modern' poetry, that Chandos, the integrating consciousness of the *Letter*, reveals himself to us as a tough and typically modern poet rather than a shipwrecked artist of yesterday, the more we find ourselves concluding that Chandos's negative decision at the end is not a 'No' to yesterday's art but a 'No' to tomorrow's. Like all literature of excessive sincerity the *Chandos Letter* ends up denying

* See Author's Note, p. 8, for a key to abbreviated references to works by Kafka.

29

what it started out to say. What Michael Hamburger reports about the lack of books on modern literature in Hofmannsthal's library is symptomatic of Hofmannsthal's instinctive aversion from what turned out to be the only influential version of Modernism: 'Despite his acquaintance with Werfel none of Kafka's works can be found in Hofmannsthal's library. Amongst the younger poets there is no trace of Trakl.'[23]

One respects Hofmannsthal's demand, implicitly stated in the *Chandos Letter*, that the writing of poetry could no longer be a matter of perpetuating and imitating the polished achievement of the past, that it had to submit itself to an act of radical analysis and to a confrontation with the brute elements. But the decision to give it all up, like Eliot's farewell to poetry in *Little Gidding*, cannot be taken seriously. The demand for the separation of the man who suffers from the mind which creates merely suggests that the poet has divided loyalties. It is a demand, moreover, which the spirit of the *Letter* is a supreme testimony against. An even more impressive testimony against it is the artistic achievement, and the personal suffering, of a Trakl and a Kafka who were despairingly committed to seeing in the Chandos experience the potentiality of form, and could not merely be interested in its vocabulary. If Hofmannsthal's decision as stated towards the end of the *Letter* makes any sense at all, then apart from its symbolic function it does so only insofar as it reflects Hofmannsthal's personal refusal to enter upon 'a ruinous and exhausting undertaking'—'the writing of major poetry' in our age.[24]

As Max Brod frequently pointed out, Kafka was deeply impressed by Hofmannsthal's *Letter,* and echoes of it are present in his early writings. The closest parallels can be found in the fragment *Description of a Struggle*. The characters in this story experience an even more radical feeling of universal disintegration than Chandos. Not only words and concepts crumble in their mouths, but the very world around them. Instead of standing still the spire of the Town Hall moves in little circles. The window-panes rattle, the lamp-posts bend like bamboo sticks, and 'the Virgin Mary's cloak is coiling round her pillar and the wind is tugging at it'.[25] The people who should be walking on the pavement are in a state of floating motion. 'Now I realise, by God, that I guessed from the very beginning the state you are in', says the narrator to his companion, the 'supplicant'.

Isn't it something like a fever, a seasickness on land, a kind of leprosy? Don't you feel it's this very feverishness which is preventing you from being properly satisfied with the real names of things, and that now, in your frantic haste, you're just pelting them with any old names? You can't do it fast enough. But hardly have you run away from them when you've forgotten the names you gave them. The poplar in the fields, which you've called the 'Tower of Babel' because you didn't want to know it was a poplar, sways again without a name, so you have to call it 'Noah in his cups'.[26]

The supplicant has joined a complete stranger, the narrator, on his walk in the hope of learning from him 'how things really are, why it is that around me things sink away like fallen snow, whereas for other people even a little liqueur glass stands on the table steady as a statue'. As an example of other people's confidence in the familiar world he recalls the following incident:

When as a child I opened my eyes after a brief afternoon nap, still not quite sure I was alive, I heard my mother up on the balcony asking in a natural tone of voice: 'What are you doing, my dear? Goodness, isn't it hot?' From the garden a woman answered: 'Me, I'm having my tea on the lawn.' They spoke casually and not very distinctly, as though this woman had expected the question, my mother the answer.[27]

Chandos himself might have given this archetypal situation as an example of his 'good moments', moments of experience which he can thoroughly trust and rely upon. Beneath the surface of this casual and conventional conversation the supplicant senses a solidity and significance he himself cannot experience. To him the little scene, being wholly itself, is laden with universal meaning. Characteristically enough his companion protests against such an interpretation of a simple occurrence as if it were the explanation of everything:

That story you told me . . . I really don't find so remarkable. Not only have I heard and experienced many stories of this kind, I have even taken part in some. The whole thing is perfectly natural. Do you really mean to suggest that had I been on that balcony in the summer, I could not have asked the same question and given the same answer from the garden? Quite an ordinary occurrence![28]

In a wider sense this sober assessment is Kafka's polemical answer against Hofmannsthal's attempt, and similar ones by other modernists, to postulate the Leibnizian 'harmony' between the inner and outer worlds as a *fact* of individual experience. Kafka too read Leibniz, as everybody else did at the time, but only in order to proceed to a radical critique of man's craving for harmony. *The Trial* and *The Castle* are monuments to Kafka's dedication to his self-imposed task of dismantling the key assumptions underlying the idea of a harmonious order. What Einstein, very much at the same time, did in physics Kafka did in the field of ethics and aesthetics.[29]

Whilst Hofmannsthal stuck to his formula of the mystical unity of the world and experience, manipulating literature for the purpose rather than purifying the medium itself, Kafka began to prepare himself for the more difficult task of attacking the view that the inner and outer world form an objective dialectical unity, that they are inseparably married in spite of their apparent opposition. To Kafka Leibniz's system was a fantastic construct of the human mind, Hegel's interpretation of it no more than an elaborate hocus-pocus. He ultimately followed Kierkegaard according to whom the individual exists within an opaque, impenetrable 'incognito'.[30] Stirner's gay and arrogant philosophy of egoism had to be transformed into a serious ethical position vis-à-vis the external world. As far as Kafka's writing was concerned this implied the 'ruinous and exhausting undertaking' of substituting his own angst-ridden vision of the world for objective reality.

2
Literature as Corrective Punishment

'I sometimes amuse myself with the idea that men may soon grow tired of books and their authors, and the savant tomorrow come to leave directions in his will that his body be burned in the midst of his books, including, of course, his own writings.' Half a century later one writer almost fulfilled Nietzsche's daydream, toying with the idea of spiritual suicide and, at the end of his life, expressing the will that his writings be burnt. Nothing reminds us more urgently than this radical decision—which was never acted upon—of the intimate relationship between Kafka's life and his work.

As in the case of Kafka's incestuous fantasies not much is known about the physiological consequences of his masochistic disposition. But the extent to which he invited torment and humiliation from his fiancée Felice Bauer (see chapter on *The Trial*), and other people he loved, reveals how serious a role it must have played in his life. The consistently masochistic philosophy of life (Politzer goes as far as calling Kafka 'a mystic of masochism') which permeates his work (most obviously *The Judgment, Metamorphosis* and *In the Penal Settlement*) suggests that masochism was something he had to come to terms with. Despite the obvious difficulties of the task, an attempt will be made in this chapter to show in what sense Kafka's fictional work can at all be said to be an account of his most private experience. Let us begin by examining a telling reference to another highly autobiographical writer, Sacher-Masoch, which Kafka, with surprising effect, incorporated in one of his stories.

No direct references to Leopold von Sacher-Masoch are to be found in Kafka's writing, despite the fact that, as critics have not failed to point out, many situations and relationships presented in Kafka's works are of a typically 'masochistic' kind, or have at least a masochistic flavour about them. But in one of his stories, *Metamorphosis*, Kafka appears to have embodied an unmistakable reference to Sacher-Masoch's most notorious and popular work,

Venus in Furs (1870). This book forms part of an uncompleted cycle of novels, modelled on Balzac's *Comédie Humaine*, which Masoch planned to publish under the general title of *Das Vermächtnis Kains*. The work was to consist of six parts : Love, Property, Money, the State, War and Death. Only *Das Eigentum* and *Die Liebe*, which contains *Venus im Pelz*, were completed. The title of the latter soon became a household name with the intelligentsia throughout Europe. Despite the taboos relating to themes involving masochism, sadism, incest, etc., sexual pathology was freely discussed in the proliferating underground literature of the day, and oblique references to it made their appearance in serious fiction.

In his book *Kafkas Dichtungen*[1] Kurt Weinberg comments on the 'picture of the lady muffled in so much fur' (M, 40)— which is only casually mentioned at the beginning of *Metamorphosis* but which later in the story becomes for Gregor Samsa the dearest object left to him—and its 'possible' relationship with Sacher-Masoch's *Venus in Furs*. Walter H. Sokel's comments on the same subject are even more tentative than Weinberg's[2] but he points more confidently to the similarity between 'De Sade's orgies, Sacher-Masoch and Stekel's sado-masochistic case-histories'[3] and certain situations in Kafka's *The Trial* and *America*. It is now generally recognised that Kafka had a passionate interest in literature involving the discussion of autobiographical detail of a problematical kind, but critical comment on Kafka's knowledge of the psychological and pathological writing proliferating around him remains scarce and cautious. This is partly due to the generally purist attitude of recent Kafka criticism (a healthy state of affairs, but now and then leading to naïveté), and partly to Kafka's extraordinary gift for disguising his sources.

One of Gregor Samsa's few possessions is the picture of a lady in furs which he has recently cut out of 'an illustrated magazine', and which now hangs on one of the walls of his room, in 'a pretty gilt frame'. When in the second section mother and sister begin their clearing-up operation it is none other than this picture which Gregor tries to salvage and, if necessary, to defend at all costs. ('He clung to his picture and would not give it up. He would rather fly in Grete's face.') In a situation in which all things are being taken away from Gregor he is prepared to defend at least his own identity : 'his masochistic-loving self-sacrifice' (Weinberg), of which the picture of the lady, in her threatening posture, is a symbol. At the end of the story Grete's newly-developed, positive womanhood ('als am Ziele ihrer Fahrt die Tochter *als erste sich erhob* [my emphasis] und ihren jungen Körper dehnte') is being contrasted with the negative gesture and demonic nature of the lady in furs ('die, mit einem Pelzhut und einer Pelzboa versehen, aufrecht dasass und einen schweren Pelzmuff, in dem ihr ganzer Unterarm verschwunden war, *dem Beschauer entgegenhob*' [my emphasis]).[4] Whilst both Weinberg and Sokel comment fully on the masochistic implications of the picture, they both emphasise, however, the accidental nature of the reference to Sacher-Masoch. A broader interpretation of Kafka's story is given in the next chapter; it will be suggested in this one that it is not only the object, the picture, that reminds us of Masoch and his *Venus in Furs* but the situation as a whole, as described at the beginning of *Metamorphosis*, and, not unexpectedly, Gregor Samsa's very name.

Sacher-Masoch's novel begins with the narrator's dream about a beautiful woman wrapped in gigantic furs who engages the dreamer in a philosophical discussion on the eternal hostility existing between men and women, a hostility which 'Northern' man in particular has failed to transform into a meaningful relationship between the sexes. 'You can only exorcise and curse me' (i.e. adopt a self-consciously Christian attitude), the woman says, 'or sacrifice yourselves in bacchic frenzy at my altar'[5] (i.e. fall into a pagan-masochistic behaviour-pattern). It turns out that the dream was suggested by an oil-painting which the dreamer discovers the same evening in the living-room of his friend Severin. The painting shows a nude in dark furs whose right hand plays with a lash, while her bare foot rests carelessly on a man, lying before her like a slave or a dog. The features of this man, Severin's, reveal profound sadness and passionate devotion; 'he looks up to her with the ecstatic, burning eyes of a martyr'.[6] (One is reminded of Gregor's desperate attempt to cling to 'the picture of the lady muffled in so much fur', the object of his fatal but satisfying devotion, as he 'pressed himself to the glass, which was a good surface to hold on to and comforted his hot belly'.) When the narrator tells his friend that he has seen the very woman portrayed in the picture, Severin confesses : 'I, too, only I dreamed

35

my dream with open eyes.'[7] And this is precisely Gregor Samsa's position, when he wakes up from his troubled dreams into a 'dream with open eyes', the horror *and* the beatitude of his strange predicament. There has been much critical comment on Gregor Samsa's thoughts when he light-heartedly contemplates his new situation : 'Wie wäre es, wenn ich noch ein wenig weiterschliefe und *alle Narrheiten vergässe*' [my emphasis]. ('What about sleeping a little longer and forgetting all this *nonsense*?') (M, 9.) This cryptic sentence becomes at least partly comprehensible if it is related to Severin's 'foolish' adventures, to the 'silly story'[8] of his affliction and ultimate cure. In order to give full expression to his desire to subordinate himself completely—'a genuinely modern point of view'[9]—Severin signs a contract, by which he becomes the unrestricted property, 'the slave', of Wanda. In return Wanda will play the role of torturer, of 'Venus in Furs' with the whip in her hand. What began as a fantasy, as a vague intuition of the supreme power of woman over man, turns into the brutal reality of a totally submissive life, from which Severin will only emerge after the utmost degradation.

Both Kafka's and Sacher-Masoch's heroes suffer the same predicament. They have both chosen the role of 'anvil' (a Goethean metaphor developed at length by Masoch), Severin's Wanda and Gregor's world around him each acting as 'hammer'. The slave-motive, too, if only in disguise, is retained by Kafka. Gregor lives in bondage to his parents, whose debt to his superior he has taken it on himself to repay. The thought that he will be able to settle the matter, in five or six years, and thereby regain his freedom is of course nothing more than wishful thinking. The ties which bind him to his parents are merely a reflection of the larger ties which bind him to society as a whole,[10] the nature of this bond being clearly defined by Gregor's attachment to his picture (of the lady in furs). Metaphoric hints at Gregor's insignificance and at the absolute superiority of the world around him —symbolised, amongst other things, by his boss's manner of speaking to his employees 'von der Höhe herab' ('from above') and by his father's immense feet—are also reminiscent of Sacher-Masoch's emphasis on Wanda's absolute power, particularly his picturesque-heroic description of Wanda with her whip towering like a magnificent demon over her *tied-up* victim.

It is difficult not to relate Kafka's Gregor to the Gregor *alias*

Severin of Masoch's novel. When Severin agrees to become Wanda's slave, he must also give up his name and exchange it for one appropriate to his inferior position : 'From now on your name is no longer Severin but *Gregor*'[11] (italics by Sacher-Masoch), says Wanda. As it happens there is a parallel incident, fully recorded in James Cleugh's biography of Sacher-Masoch, *The First Masochist*, in Sacher-Masoch's own life. In 1869 Masoch met one Fanny Pistor, who appears to have shown an immediate understanding of his sexual tastes. They agreed at once 'to embark upon a liaison, to be marked materially by a prodigality in which furs and foreign travel were to be conspicuous, and spiritually by the utter subordination of the male to the female partner. This compact was not merely oral. It was written down, signed, sealed and delivered with the greatest formality and precision.'[12] Fanny also suggested that Leopold's name be changed to Gregor, a typical name for a manservant in imperial Austria. If all the evidence points to Kafka's Gregor being a symbolic name, in the manner indicated, then the temptation is great to read Gregor's surname, SAMSA, as an anagrammatic abbreviation of the first masochist's name : *SA*CHER-*MAS*OCH. That the last two letters had to be turned round is of course due to Kafka's well-known practice of making the names of some of his heroes rhythmically consonant with his own name. It will be noted that the elaborate allusion is not so much a 'literary' one as an allusion to an actual life-situation : to the unenviable predicament of a fellow human being who happened to describe it in a pseudo-literary work. We shall return to this point later.

Kafka commented in his diary on August 15, 1913 on his acute sense of alienation from the world around him, an alienation which in its 'innern Bestimmtheit und Überzeugtheit' ('inner decisiveness and conviction') has become so total and pronounced that he anticipates new possibilities for his future life, including the one 'in einer Ehe trotz allem bestehen zu können, ja sie sogar zu einer für meine Bestimmung vorteilhaften Entwicklung zu führen'. ('To pass the test of marriage in spite of everything, and even to steer it in a direction favourable to my development.') His intention is 'mich bis zur Besinnungslosigkeit von allen absperren. Mit allen mich verfeinden, mit niemandem reden.' ('Shut myself off from everyone to the point of insensibility. Make an enemy of everyone, speak to no one.') This intention coupled with another one, to accept a partner in marriage, would then be a perfect expression of his 'Bestimmung', to let all displays of human activity bear witness to his own sense of total isolation. A confession of love to his wife would take the form of an exquisite self-torment; it would be conducted in the sight of a partner whose chief attraction would lie in her combination of utter confidence in practical life and inability to comprehend the inner isolation of the other. Kafka actually imagines such a situation in the form of a dialogue between one Leopold S. and Felice, which by way of example follows on from his more general reflections:

LEOPOLD S. (*a tall, strong man, clumsy, jerky movements, loosely hanging, wrinkled, checked clothes, enters hurriedly through the door on the right into the large room, claps his hands and shouts*): Felice! Felice! (*Without pausing an instant for a reply to his shout he hurries to the middle door which he opens, again shouting*): Felice!
FELICE S. (*enters through the door at the left, stops at the door, a forty-year-old woman in a kitchen apron*): Here I am, Leo. How nervous you have become recently! What is it you want?
LEOPOLD (*turns with a jerk, then stops and bites his lips*): Well, then, come over here! (*He walks over to the sofa.*)
FELICE (*does not move*): Quick! What do you want? I really have to go back to the kitchen.
LEOPOLD (*from the sofa*): Forget the kitchen! Come here! I want to tell you something important. It will make up for it. All right, come on!
FELICE (*walks toward him slowly, raising the shoulder straps of her apron*): Well, what is it that's so important? If you're making a fool of me I'll be angry, seriously. (*Stops in front of him.*)
LEOPOLD: Well, sit down, then.
FELICE: And suppose I don't want to?
LEOPOLD: Then I can't tell it to you. I must have you close to me.
FELICE: All right, now I am sitting.[13]

This is masochism in its most sublimated form, and again, the abbreviation Leopold S. (read Leopold von Sacher-Masoch) may be no other than Kafka's shorthand for a human predicament that would otherwise go without a name.

The fact that obvious references to Sacher-Masoch in Kafka's work are less frequent than one might justly expect has led critics to assume that Kafka was unfamiliar with Sacher-Masoch's work. It is safer to assume the opposite. As a writer and journalist Masoch enjoyed a wide reputation and a considerable following. Among his admirers were Victor Hugo, Zola, Ibsen, and Ludwig II of Bavaria. In his later years he was fêted in Paris by the French newspapers *Le Figaro*, the *Revue des Deux Mondes*, and made a Chevalier of the Légion d'Honneur. By the turn of the century few can have been ignorant of Sacher-Masoch or failed to browse through one or other of his best-selling novels. Bearing in mind Kafka's intense interest in literature relating to psychology and pathology it is more than likely that Masoch's work too came his way in one form or another. The sparseness of actual references should not surprise us, this fact being due not only to the taboo still in force up to the Thirties preventing overt reference to sexual pathology in fiction, but also to Kafka's almost legendary shyness and reticence in personal matters. Hints and guesses, the oblique speech of strained metaphors and anagrams, are all we can expect when entering Kafka's fiction and fictionalisations.

A vexing question though remains: why does Kafka deliberately leave the reader in the dark as to the precise origin of his references, when he could have elegantly dropped, in the manner of Thomas Mann, the necessary hints? This is a question of the mode of existence of allusions in Kafka's fiction, a question which can best be answered by adopting a comparative approach. Structured and modified as the allusion to Masoch's Venus in Furs appears in *Metamorphosis*, the reference as such remains, in the first place, private to Kafka. But Kafka is not the only modern European writer who developed a habit of incorporating obscure detail into the texture of his work. Musil's practice of mounting a complex narrative structure on material whose full contextual relevance (in the light of Musil's biography and particularly his early MS. versions) becomes apparent only after diligent research has been analysed by a number of critics, particularly by Wilhelm Bausinger.[14] Musil's difficulty in demonstrating, to himself and his readers, the ontological nature of his writings frequently brought him to the brink of despair. 'Eine solche Aufgabe [to combine ontology with aesthetics] wird ja wohl lohnend sein,' he writes in a letter (to Wotruba, April 3, 1940), 'aber solange sie nicht gelöst ist, müsste man rein immer erzählen, dass man ein armer Narr ist.' ('A task of this kind will certainly be rewarding, but until it is accomplished one would simply have to go on narrating—poor devil that one is!') Musil partly solved his problem by piling up integrated narrative sequences whose full structural, i.e. ontological, significance could only be established by the often accidental discovery of their multiple contextual relevance (as determined by the author's letters, diaries, early MS. versions, *and* the most recent place of occurrence). Thus it was no longer necessary to provide the 'full' narration. The onus passed on to the reader. This state of affairs is clearly reminiscent of Joyce's desire for a life-long reader of his fiction, a desire which must not be confused with, say, Thomas Mann's recommendation to read his *Magic Mountain* more than once. As he explains in his 'Preface to *The Magic Mountain*', the musical structure and the formal intricacies of the book cannot be grasped after one reading only. Though Mann too emphasises the fragmentary nature of his individual works, he does not tantalise his readers by buried meanings and deliberate obscurities of an external kind, nor is there anything in his work that is meant to undermine our instinctive belief in the power of words to express and sustain, in the final analysis, existence. Whilst writers like Kafka, Joyce, and Musil hint at the possibility of an unmediated unity of 'life' and 'art', Mann firmly postulates the mediated unity of the literary work of art and its power to transcend time and to make reality appear contingent. It is true that Kafka, Joyce and Musil too make every effort to eliminate time and circumstantiality in their fiction but, strangely enough, they also retain a vigorous impurity which makes the clocks tick again and the debris of circumstantial evidence fracture the neat arrangement of the surface. Richard Ellmann reports the story[15] that when Joyce was dictating some of *Finnegans Wake* to Samuel Beckett, someone knocked at the door, Joyce said 'Come in', and Beckett wrote it down in the manuscript. He offered to erase the phrase, but Joyce preferred to let it stand; it can still be found in the published version. Robert Martin Adams has argued convincingly that 'something like it' must have taken place in *Ulysses*. 'Certainly an event of this sort would account very happily for the occurrence in Bloom's thoughts of Stephen's phrase about Shakespeare walking in Gerard's rosery of Fetter Lane, greyedauburn (p. 276). The theory of Joyce's surpassing readiness to accept accidents is tidier than any notions which present themselves of Stephen's thoughts passing into Bloom's mind or of Bloom identifying with Stephen.'[16]

It can easily be seen that textual and structural incongruities like Musil's notorious hypothetical characters (in *The Man Without Qualities*) whose aesthetic and supra-aesthetic function can only be determined in the light of extrinsic knowledge,[17] Kafka's cryptic sentence about Gregor Samsa's 'Narrheiten' ('nonsense') in *Metamorphosis*, and the examples drawn from Joyce, are equally relevant manifestations of one and the same modernist intention : to evoke a range of obscure and initially private detail in order not to emphasise formal patterns but to retain the accident of creation. Though established critical opinion inhibits our temptation to identify authors with their fictional heroes, works like *Ulysses, The Man Without Qualities, Metamorphosis*, and all Kafka's later works, demand from us that, to elaborate on one of Professor Adams's insights, the personae of Joyce, Musil and Kafka outside their work carry almost as much 'dramatic weight' as the personae of Bloom, Ulrich, Samsa and the K.s within it; 'and the complex interrogatories, exchanged across the frame of fiction, contribute richly to its anxious, self-exploratory, and "modern" character'.[18] Modernist writers are committed to no less a task than achieving an identity of aesthetic experience and direct vision. In the words of Adams, the modernist work of art, with its harsh cacophonies, broken textures, and deliberate incongruities, becomes an object 'which might be categorised as either "life" or "art"'.[19] This fits Kafka's case admirably, as his letters, diaries, and the work itself amply prove. As already indicated, Musil's method of suggesting how life and art might become one depends on a complex system of cross-references between his fiction and the private record of his physical and intellectual life. Kafka's method of relating his life to his writing is even more radical than Musil's. When we are quite literally 'finding out' about the pitiful predicament on which Kafka mounted Gregor Samsa's we are confronted by a dramatic discovery, by Kafka's 'Gregor, c'est moi !'. Kafka does not, like Musil, merely lead us into the secret conspiracy between art and life; he shocks us straight into it.

Kafka's way of accepting 'accidents' and of incorporating them in his fiction is at once more spontaneous and more affirmative of predicaments external to the work, i.e. less 'literary', than is

41

normally the case in modernist writing. A good 'Joycean' example in Kafka's work is provided by the last, indented, sentence of *The Judgment* : 'In diesem Augenblick ging über die Brücke ein geradezu unendicher Verkehr.' ('At that moment there passed over the bridge an almost limitless stream of traffic.') In the *Diaries* we find the following comment on the genesis of this story : 'The fearful strain and joy, how the story developed before me. . . . How everything can be said, how for everything, for the strangest fancies, there waits a great fire in which they perish and rise up again. How it turned blue outside the window. A wagon rolled by. Two men walked across the bridge' [the bridge across the Moldau, which Kafka could see from his window]. And he adds : 'Only *in this way* can writing be done, only with such coherence, with such a complete opening out of the body and the soul.'[20] In his creative mood the writer is not only open to the 'strangest fancies' generated within his mind, or to the work of others consciously or unconsciously supporting the drift of his thoughts (Kafka acknowledges 'thoughts about' Freud, Wassermann and Werfel, when writing *The Judgment*), but above all to the impersonal events and circumstances around him. There is still a sense in which Joyce's decision to let the accidental 'come in' stand is the deliberate and almost arrogant permission, on the part of the author, to allow humdrum reality a brief appearance in the outer realms of the literary universe—only to be swallowed up by it, like the image in Rilke's poem 'Der Panther' that enters through the eye but ceases to exist in the heart of the animal. The image thus annihilated is just as indicative of the absolute powers of the creative self (of which the panther is a symbol) as Joyce's 'come in' is indicative of the inner strength and coherence of the work of art. What Kafka sees through the window of his room enters the work as a piece of final and concrete evidence for the justness of his literary fantasy. The story ends where it began : conspicuously in the confines of an autobiographical situation.

Literature since Flaubert, it has been said, mediates between the world of reality and the world of dreams, achieving 'a glad reunion between reality and richness, a dialectical synthesis of the naturalistic tradition and the symbolistic reaction'.[21] If this is true, then Kafka is the odd man out. His collaboration is not with the richness found in the literary tradition, nor is it with what naturalism defined as reality, but with the tortured immediacies of his naked self. There is no cosmopolitan iconoclasm, not even an *alter ego*, in Kafka's work. He is the Dubliner permanently chained to his native soil, his work 'the uncreated conscience'[22] of a self-condemned man. Maturin, the great nineteenth-century analyst of guilt, writes in *Melmoth* : 'It is certain, that when we are conscious of guilt, we always suspect that a greater degree of it will be ascribed to us by others. Their consciences avenge the palliations of our own, by the most horrible exaggerations.'[23] Kafka's work takes cognisance of this fact, not metaphorically but literally. The ending of *The Judgment* is more than a metaphor of confirmation : it is the author's total submission to the world hurriedly and in a frenzy endorsing the judgment. The result is not so much literature as 'corrective punishment'.[24]

For Kafka literature and life are at once fatally linked and divided. Out of the awareness of the ultimate division between the two arises the need to yoke them together, violently if necessary. Kafka achieves this by putting himself behind the veil of an apparently neat literary surface, as if planting a mine in a field. The autobiographical material in Kafka's work has a centrifugal function rather than a centripetal one. The jackdaws encircling the castle are not so much literary signs, traditional symbols of death, as synonyms for an actual threat in Kafka's life. The Czech for jackdaw is *kavka*, which at the same time was the emblem Kafka's father had chosen for his business. As so often in Kafka literariness gives way to literalness. To the critic extrinsic knowledge no longer renders merely an explanation of causes, but of effects. Many similar instances are readily available in Kafka's work, diaries and letters. The allusion to Sacher-Masoch in *Metamorphosis* is perhaps the most uncanny of them all. Under the disguise of a conventional reference unobtrusively supporting the symbolic design of the story it is the most horrific psychological pointer to an appalling predicament. As such it is a symptom of the dissolution of the fictive sense, a dissolution which can be witnessed in Kafka's work long before it became the programme of the present *avant-garde*.

This is not the place to re-open the discussion on Kafka's ambiguous request of his friend Max Brod to destroy all his unpublished diaries, manuscripts and letters, 'restlos und ungelesen' ('completely and unread'), in the event of his death. The works which had already appeared in print were not pardoned either. 'Nur hindere ich, da sie schon einmal da sind, niemanden daran, sie zu erhalten, wenn er dazu Lust hat.' ('Of course, since they are already in print, I won't prevent anybody from keeping them, if he feels inclined to.') 'Feel inclined' for what? In the light of Kafka's reflections, ranging from the dead-earnest to the cynical, on the intricate mesh of his life and writing, this ironic phrase can only refer to the doubtful inclination, on the part of the curious reader—'hypocrite lecteur!—mon semblable—mon frère!'—to preserve the supreme documents of a most tragic message. Kafka's art is both, an experiment in self-portrayal *and* an affirmation, however precarious, of the self-protective quality of art.

As an experiment in self-portrayal, of the Kafkan variety, art becomes a source of shock, destroying what Walter Benjamin called the 'aura' of the unique work of art as art. There is a sense in which 'the stuff of life' stands in the very way of the divine machinations of art, just as the brute facts of the modern world stand in the way of the 'sacral essences' (Kermode's phrase) of great criticism, of criticism with an 'aura'. As a critic Benjamin believed both in portraying the barrage of contemporary discontinuities and in sustaining the 'sacred' task of the truly great critic. 'His major essays take cognisance of the shock as well as of the aura. He believed both that the material of great criticism was being destroyed, and that it ought to be destroyed. In wanting to be a great literary critic he discovered that he could only be the last great literary critic.'[25] The parallel to Kafka is obvious. His radical decision to draw the hell-inspired (as Kafka himself indicated) equation between life and literature—'Ich habe kein literarisches Interesse, sondern bestehe aus Literatur, ich bin nichts anderes und kann nichts anderes sein' ('I have no literary interests, but consist of literature, I am nothing else and cannot be anything else'), he wrote to Felice on August 14, 1913—could not fail to bring up an awkward question : what kind of 'I' was it that so briskly asserted the identity of self and the transcending power of art? The answer, a truly devastating one, we find in the letters to Felice and in the harsh judgment of *The Trial*. Everything Kafka wrote after about 1914 was to be inspired by the success he felt whenever he had his hero-victims, and himself, wriggling on a pin, whenever he wrote something that epitomised the threat of void and the lack of hope he sensed. Those who have accepted the premises of Kafka's art have learned to admire its sky-tearing hypostasis, but to Kafka himself this must have appeared a doubtful achievement. To quote from *Melmoth* again : 'When art assumes the omnipotence of reality, when we feel we suffer as much from an illusion as from truth, our sufferings lose all dignity and all consolation. We turn demons against ourselves, and laugh at what we are writhing under.'[26]

Kafka's well-known habit of self-indictment did not stop at the personal level. In *The Trial* and *The Castle* he proceeded to project the war against himself on to the cosmos, imagining unknown powers who would not only take pleasure in magnifying his personal sense of guilt out of all proportion but ultimately in revenging themselves on their rebellious victim. In order to understand the nature of this curious undertaking we must now turn to an odd but fashionable creed to which many Prague intellectuals subscribed and which went by the name of Marcionism. In 1916 Albert Einstein wrote to Hedwig Born, thanking her for a book by Max Brod which she had lent him : 'I believe that I met him in Prague. I think he belongs to a small circle there of philosophical and Zionist enthusiasts, which was loosely grouped around the university philosophers, a medieval-like band of unworldly people whom you got to know by reading the book'.[27] This sarcastic reference to the Brod circle, of which Kafka of course was a member, was not wholly without justification. It was not only that the mental habits of these writers and intellectuals had a scholastic flavour about them but that despite their modernist poses they had a peculiar taste for the obscurer aspects of ancient religion and philosophy. In 1916 the philosopher Christian Ehrenfels published his *Kosmogonie*, in which he presented a kind of Marcionist cosmology, ideas in fact he had developed in lectures and private discussions much earlier on. He was the centre of what is now known as Prague Marcionism, a wholly local phenomenon which did not spread far beyond the group of people who had a common interest in it. Marcion, a heretic of the second century, came to reject the Old Testament on the grounds that the Demiurge or Creator-god of the Jewish religion of Law was utterly incompatible with the God of Love revealed in Christ. Study of the Old Testament indicated that this Jewish God constantly involved himself in contradictory courses of action, that he was fickle, capricious, ignorant, despotic and cruel. Marcion and his community shared with gnostic teaching the distinction between an evil Creator-god and a supreme, remote and unknowable Divine Being. The function of Christ was to come as the emissary of the supreme God, bring 'gnosis' and redemption from the evil environment in which man was placed by the demiurge. Ehrenfels, who elaborated these ideas, emphasised the need of the human intellect to form a partnership with God in the unavoidable cosmic duel, and practically viewed man as co-creator with God. Though the gnosis that flourished in Prague between 1890 and 1930 appealed to different writers for different reasons, it was above all inspired by the claustrophobic situation they all found themselves in. As German Jews they comprised a minority within a minority, which was insulted and under attack from all sides. Whereas in most other places the Jews still enjoyed a relatively comfortable existence, in Prague they found themselves struggling against mounting odds to preserve their culture. 'Theirs was a siege mentality : Marcionism expressed the desperation of a beleaguered minority that yearned to silence its tormentor.'[28]

Kafka had a double reason for embracing Marcionism. There was not only the social and cultural dilemma he suffered in common with others but also his personal sense of being trapped. In his 'struggle against the world' he frequently sided with the enemy, turning with suicidal vehemence against his own self. No struggle can be endured for very long if it cannot be projected on to a higher, more impersonal plane. Marcionism not only provided this plane but became the fictional blueprint for Kafka's last two novels. But whereas Marcion promised redemption after death from the despotism of the capricious creator-god Kafka did not hold out any such hope. Man's belief in salvation was yet another delusion inspired by the demiurge. However, the most important point about Kafka's Marcionism is that he was not so much interested in its cosmology as in its symbolical relevance to the human condition as he understood it. Others, like Alfred Kubin in *Die andere Seite* (1909) and, to a lesser extent, Gustav Meyrink in his *Golem* (1915), produced crude literary accounts of Marcionism, without going much further. Kafka exploited its potentiality as a critical weapon with which to fight hopes as they were aroused, in too easy a fashion, by Leibniz's belief in harmony, Hegel's idea of the 'Absolute' and even Kierkegaard's 'leap' into the dark. What modern man needed was not encouragement of his futile longing for synthesis but a thorough critique of his ethical and metaphysical concepts. In his major works Kafka has provided this critique. His literary method is reminiscent less of Gnosticism than of something much more contemporary, logical positivism. If harmony between man and the universe cannot be verified by experience, then it is not worth keeping as a philosophical idea, and moral obligations associated with it must be banned from ethics. Kafka must be credited with having initiated something like a Copernican revolution in literature. Kant has said that since man has failed in his attempt to obtain *a priori* knowledge of objects by making knowledge conform to objects, he should then be proceeding precisely on the lines of Copernicus' primary hypothesis :

In the light of the failure to explain satisfactorily the movement of the heavenly bodies on the basis of the supposition that they all revolved round the spectator, he tried to see whether he might not have better success if he made the spectator revolve and the stars remain at rest. A similar experiment can be tried in metaphysics, as regards the *intuition* of objects. If intuition must conform to the constitution of the objects, I do not see how we could know anything of the latter *a priori*; but if the object (as object of the senses) must conform to the constitution of our faculty of intuition, I have no difficulty in conceiving such a possibility.[29]

Similarly, if the desired cooperation with God cannot be achieved by assuming that the created world is the best of all possible worlds then we must assume the opposite and not hesitate to make suggestions towards its improvement. This is precisely how the K.s proceed. Their 'Besserungsvorschläge' are attempts to correct possible errors in the created world. Kafka did not share the common belief amongst contemporary sociologists 'that a human institution cannot rest upon an error and a lie'.[30] Nor did he believe that 'Society is a reality *sui generis*', that 'it has its own peculiar characteristics, which are not found elsewhere and which are not met again in the same form in all the rest of the universe. The representations which express it have a wholly different content from purely individual ones and we may rest assured in advance that the first add something to the second.'[31] It is the bitter experience of the K.s that not only is the present world weighed down by bureaucracy but that a heavenly bureaucracy stands in the way of all hopes for salvation. They also discover that both are founded on arbitrariness and a system of lies (*The Trial*) rather than on anything more reliable. The last point in Durkheim's dictum, that society adds something to the individual, is merely granting to society what is denied to the individual. If anything, the two must constantly correct each other. With regard to the invisible world Kafka could hardly be expected to come up with much more than a caricature of heavenly justice. With regard to the visible world, however, the revised Marcionist model allowed for a subtle dialectical exposition of man's existential problem.

3
Metamorphosis

Without advocating specific spiritual values of their own, early twentieth-century writers were generally but passionately preoccupied with defending the 'spirit' against what they considered the evils of the day : naturalism, determinism, positivism and the like. In the wake of rapid urban developments another 'enemy of the spirit' was quickly identified : materialism—though many preferred to call it capitalism. The nineteenth-century city novel had already dealt, in breadth rather than in depth, with the degrading influence of wide-scale mechanisation on man. Now a more analytical, also more professional, approach was adopted, or sometimes simply added to the earlier method of contrasting the wicked modern conditions with the 'good societies' of the past. The object of analysis, and universal scorn, was not so much the new social situation itself as the product of this situation, what sociologists later called 'economic man'. One of the most memorable comments on this new-style 'hero' of the capitalist society can be found in Thomas Mann's *Death in Venice* :

Gustav Aschenbach was the poet-spokesman of all those who labour at the edge of exhaustion; of the overburdened, of those who are already worn out but still hold themselves upright; of all our modern moralisers of accomplishment, with stunted growth and scanty resources, who yet contrive by skilful husbanding and prodigious spasms of will to produce, at least for a while, the effect of greatness—There are many such, they are the heroes of the age.[1]

This new type of heroism, collective and self-negating in kind, that is being practised in the new forms of social organisation, what Dostoyevsky called the anthill, the chicken coop and the crystal palace, is a 'heroism of weakness' (Mann) based on illusions of strength and greatness, a devitalised affair, a sell-out to impersonal forces. Reality is thus no longer a man-made thing, the product of the unique activity of concrete human individuals, but a supra-individual entity confronting the individual person like some sacrifice-demanding monster.

Mann's ironic sketch of economic man, a masochistic creature who seeks salvation by putting his will at the service of a highly impersonal system, finds a more fully developed, and in its implications more terrifying parallel in Kafka's story *Metamorphosis*. Since critics have paid little attention to the social implications of Kafka's work I shall select this particular story for the purpose of commenting on Kafka's devastating critique of modern social and economic systems.

Kafka was not the first to use the insect metaphor in order to portray an existence hopelessly alienated from the 'normal'. Dostoyevsky has his underground man say: 'Now I want to tell you, gentlemen, whether you care to hear it or not, why I could not even become an insect. I tell you solemnly that I wanted to become an insect many times. But I was not even worthy of that.'[2] The reasons he gives for failing to become 'even . . . an insect' are hyperconsciousness and pride, two evils which the nineteenth century frequently branded as dangerous aberrations of the mind. Ultimately it is these very qualities which cause him to sink more deeply into his own mire and are responsible for his destructive ability to sink into it completely. 'The main thing was that all this did not seem to occur in me accidentally, but as though it had to be so. As though it were my normal condition, and not in the least disease or depravity, so that finally I even lost the desire to struggle against this depravity.'[3]

Gregor Samsa too will eventually resign himself to the conditions of his insect-life. But to begin with he puts up a struggle, not so much for the reasons provided by the underground man but for reasons which lie outside him. From his meditations in bed—symbol of a dangerous isolation from the external world—we learn that he is a commercial traveller frantically trying to overcome what he considers to be a temporary indisposition, so that he can catch his train and once more follow the well-established routine of his job. He reveals a mentality which is thoroughly conditioned by the norms and requirements of his work, by the need to be punctual and, above all, by his acute anxiety about living up to the expectations of his superiors. But parallel to the mental agonies of his terror-stricken conscience runs another, calmer train of thought, leading to a more sober review and assessment of his present situation. The degrading and inhuman aspects of his job are clearly defined by Gregor: 'O God, he thought, what an exhausting job I've picked on! Travelling about day in, day out. It's much more irritating work than doing the actual business in the warehouse, and on top of that there's the trouble of constant travelling, of worrying about train connections, the bad and irregular meals, casual acquaintances that are always new and never become intimate friends. The devil take it all!' (M, 9f.)

Gregor's boss is an insensitive monster sitting on high, like a god, at a desk and talking down to employees. There is no escape from him or the impersonal system he represents, not even through illness. The doctor merely regards 'all mankind as perfectly healthy malingerers'. Moreover, the smallest omission at once gives rise to the gravest suspicion, as if all employees were nothing but scoundrels, as if there were among them not one single loyal devoted man, 'who, though he might have wasted an hour or so of the firm's time in a morning, was so tormented by conscience as to be driven out of his mind and actually incapable of leaving his bed'. (M, 15.) The firm Gregor works for shows a unique inability to view its employees as human beings. The chief clerk who appears in order to inquire into the circumstances of their hitherto faithful servant's failure to report for work responds to Gregor's pleading by categorically stating his and the firm's point of view. Gregor's failure to turn up for work is seen as a case of obstinacy, of acting against his better self, that of 'a quiet, dependable person', of neglecting his business 'in an incredible fashion', 'barricading' himself in his room and 'making a disgraceful exhibition' of himself. Moreover, Gregor's work has not been up to standard recently, and there may even be truth in the firm's suspicion that Gregor has fiddled the cash payments entrusted to him.

The main aspects of economic man debased to a functional role, as they were amply analysed by early twentieth-century philosophers and sociologists, emerge in Kafka's story in paradigmatic fashion. The exclusive demands of the economic system ('we business men', as the chief clerk puts it) for dependability, loyalty, efficiency and productivity create in its victims a sense of total alienation from the essentials in life, such as our need for experiencing the vitality of existence (what Kafka calls getting regular meals and enough sleep) and for meaningful human contact. Life becomes a devitalised affair, symbolised in *Meta-*

morphosis by the insect metaphor, and reality a menacing structure that no longer corresponds to anything actual. The worst aspect of Gregor's predicament is perhaps that he bears the responsibility for allowing himself in the first place to be forced into this subordinate and self-annihilating role.

Dostoyevsky's underground man explains about himself: 'I am a certain low-ranked civil servant. I was in the service in order to have something to eat (but only for that reason), and when last year a distant relation left me six thousand roubles in his will I immediately retired from the service and settled down in my corner.'[4] And he adds ironically: 'I used to live in this corner before, but now I have settled down in it.' Gregor Samsa has a similar attitude towards his job. He works in order to keep himself, and his sister and parents, alive. Moreover, there are debts to be paid back, which his parents owe to his boss. Gregor does not expect to inherit a fortune, but he looks forward to the time when he will have saved enough money to settle the debts and to cut himself 'completely loose' from his tyrannical employer. On the face of it there does not seem to be much wrong with the generous intention of helping one's parents to pay their way. But both the son and the parents, who have accepted the proposition, overlook a crucial fact. The generous gesture has on the one hand resulted in the son's complete subordination to a devilish system, and on the other in the parents' renunciation of their will for survival. Gregor's decency has created a situation in which he, like the underground man, is doomed to behave like 'a coward and a slave', a situation which is amply demonstrated by his, and his parents' self-abasement before the intruding chief clerk. The parents have been reduced to a condition which they share with all other poor and enslaved people. As it is put later on in the story:

They fulfilled to the uttermost all that the world demands of poor people, the father fetched breakfast for the small clerks in the bank, the mother devoted her energy to making underwear for strangers, the sister trotted to and fro behind the counter at the behest of customers, but more than that they had not the strength to do. (M, 47.)

Is *Metamorphosis* then, in the first instance, a story about economic enslavement followed by a loss of will? Not really. As we shall see later, Gregor's struggle is seen from both a negative and a positive point of view. In the case of his family a significant transformation takes place as soon as it becomes obvious to them that Gregor can no longer be expected to recover from his 'illness'. Gregor's initial intention to secure the financial welfare of his family prematurely reduced his father, and the rest of the family, to almost invalid status, both mentally and physically. Having 'got used to' and 'gratefully accepted', but without any 'special uprush of warm feeling', the money the son brought in, Herr Samsa is a man

who used to lie wearily sunk in bed whenever Gregor set out on a business journey; who welcomed him back of an evening lying in a long chair in a dressing-gown; who could not really rise to his feet but only lifted his arms in greeting, and on the rare occasions when he did go out with his family, on one or two Sundays a year and on high holidays, walked between Gregor and his mother, who were slow walkers anyhow, even more slowly than they did, muffled in his old great-coat, shuffling laboriously forward with the help of his crook-handled stick which he set down most cautiously at every step and, whenever he wanted to say anything, nearly always came to a full stop and gathered his escort around him. (M, 42f.)

What is left is a mere fossil of former power and energy, somebody who has handed over the status of *paterfamilias* to his son and who has become docile in his dealings with the outside world and a cringing figure in the face of the authorities. But a significant change takes place in him after Gregor's catastrophic failure to continue supporting the family. And Gregor is the first to become aware of this change and to suffer its consequences. Encountering his father for the first time after his own metamorphosis he is amazed at his father's new appearance:

Could that be his father? . . . Now he was standing there in fine shape; dressed in a smart blue uniform with gold buttons, such as bank messengers wear; his strong double chin bulged over the stiff collar of his jacket; from under his bushy eyebrows his black eyes darted fresh and penetrating glances; his one-time tangled white hair had been combed flat on either side of a shining and carefully exact parting. (M, 43.)

The parallel to the metamorphosis of the father in *The Judgment* is obvious. Here the transformation is presented in a perhaps less stylised but no less dramatic a fashion. The restoration of the father's powers is depicted not in terms of references to some primitive god but of an allusion to the familiar appearance of the old Emperor Franz Josef. From now on the father is no longer the bedridden old man he used to be but somebody who is reluctant to leave his seat of power, the chair he now normally sleeps in with his uniform on. There is even a resurgence of his sexual energies, portrayed by Kafka with his usual delicacy and economy. At the end of the apple-throwing episode Gregor has just enough presence of mind left to see 'his mother rushing towards his father, leaving one after another behind on the floor her loosened petticoats, stumbling over her petticoats straight to his father and embracing him in complete union with him.' (M, 44.) When finally Gregor watches his father once more taking control over the family's financial affairs—'now and then he rose from the table to get some voucher or memorandum out of the small safe he had rescued from the collapse of his business five years earlier' (a handsome sum has in fact been preserved, and each member of the family, excepting Gregor, is now working again)—he is in no doubt as to the genuineness of his father's complete 'recovery'. And there is a new firmness and sense of determination in Herr Samsa's dealings with the outside world. When he feels that the family deserves a rest from it all he does not mind writing letters to his own, his wife's and his daughter's employers to ask for a day off. When there is a slight disagreement with the three lodgers the family had taken in earlier on, he simply chases them out of the house, thereby getting rid of the last traces of an alien and freedom-robbing system. Miraculously enough, even his attitude towards Gregor, whom he had almost tried to kill, changes. There is a new tolerance towards his son's indisposition; the door between Gregor's bedroom and the family's sitting-room is left ajar, 'by general consent as it were', so that lying in the darkness of his room, he can see them all at the lamp-lit table and listen to their talk. This reflects an interesting attitude towards whatever Gregor's unfortunate metamorphosis stands for, a characteristic attempt and ability to assimilate an apparently insuperable catastrophe into their own lives. But before we can go more fully into this we must first look at yet another significant metamorphosis in the story, that of Gregor's sister.

When Gregor's transformation into a gigantic insect is first discovered it is his sister Grete who responds with sympathy and an extraordinary sense of insight into her brother's predicament. It is she who, in complete self-forgetfulness and as if nothing in particular had happened, takes on the duty of looking after the incapacitated Gregor. 'In the goodness of her heart', and 'with fine tact', she attends to the business of feeding the insect, always sensing immediately its secret wishes and desires. Gregor enjoys the full benefits of 'the enthusiastic temperament of an adolescent girl' who has faithfully devoted herself to an abhorrent task. In time Grete becomes the acknowledged 'expert in Gregor's affairs as against her parents'. But before long things change. Gregor reaches the climax of his suffering when his sister eventually grows out of her 'adolescent' devotion to her brother, gets more and more irritated and repulsed by the creature's presence and turns into a mature and practically-minded woman who is ultimately responsible for Gregor's death. Since the story hinges on this significant change of attitude on the part of Grete we must consider it in more detail. It may best be considered in relation to the catastrophic climax of the story.

One evening Grete plays her violin. Since the lodgers have just finished their supper and appear to be interested, the recital takes place in their room. But it is soon obvious that the lodgers, like the chief clerk the symbols of an external, non-spiritual order, are not only bored by the violin-playing, but profoundly disturbed and irritated by it.

And yet Gregor's sister was playing so beautifully. Her face leaned side-ways, intently and sadly her eyes followed the notes of music. Gregor crawled a little farther forward and lowered his head to the ground so that it might be possible for his eyes to meet hers. Was he an animal, when music had such an effect upon him? He felt as if the way were opening before him to the unknown nourishment he craved. He was determined to push forward till he reached his sister, to pull at her skirt and so let her know that she was to come into his room with her violin, for no one here appreciated her playing as he would appreciate it. He would never let her out of his room, at least, not so long as he lived; his frightful appearance would become, for the first time, useful to him; he would watch all the doors of his room at once and spit at intruders; but his sister should need no constraint, she should stay with him of her own free will; she should sit beside him on the sofa, bend down her ear to him and hear him confide that he had had the firm intention of sending her to the Conservatorium, and that, but for his mishap, last Christmas—surely Christmas was long past?—he would have announced it to everybody without allowing a single objection. After this confession his sister would be so touched that she would burst into tears, and Gregor would then raise himself to her shoulder and kiss her on the neck, which, now that she went to business, she kept free of any ribbon or collar. (M, 53f.)

Readers versed in the literature of German Romanticism and Poetic Realism will not be surprised to find that music (the sound of a violin in particular) is offered here as the symbol of a spiritual quest. Gregor's main concern has been to find the right kind of food to sustain his insect existence. He does not like milk (always a symbol of life and healthiness, cf. the German 'Lebensmilch', milk of life), preferring instead foul and rotting things. But even these do not satisfy him in the long run—they merely create an unquenchable appetite for food he cannot name. His raids on the pantry each time end in frustration. Gregor has reached a situation in which earthly things no longer satisfy him. To his surprise he finds that music, which he never liked before his transformation (milk being his favourite drink then), may be the pointer to the unknown nourishment, i.e. to the immaterial values he is craving for. Strangely enough, he has to become an insect, a creature uncontaminated by the predominantly material instincts of the human world, for an understanding of music and matters of the spirit to be achieved.[5] Of the Samsa family only Grete possesses this understanding, but in her case it is unconscious and merely a phase. However it is enough to create a strong and intimate bond between her and her brother.

Kafka discreetly hints at the sister's openness to the spiritual: 'searchingly and sadly her eyes followed the notes of music'. When Grete plays her violin she is not so much playing as 'examining' the music, as if it were leading her to something she subconsciously longs for. But the business saddens her, because she knows her longing will remain unfulfilled. The experience goes deep enough to absorb her completely, as if her music-making was incompatible with the normal world around her. When Gregor is too daring and tries to work himself forwards towards his sister, to the alarm of the horrified lodgers, the violin-playing suddenly comes to an end and a critical stage in her life, a crisis of consciousness, a temporal oscillation between the immanent and the transcendental worlds, resolves itself once and for all :

Meanwhile Gregor's sister, who stood there as if lost when her playing was so abruptly broken off, came to life again, pulled herself together all at once after standing for a while holding violin and bow in nervelessly hanging hands and staring at her music, pushed the violin into the lap of her mother, who was still sitting in her chair fighting asthmatically for breath, and ran into the lodgers' room to which they were now being shepherded by her father rather more quickly than before. The pillows and blankets on the beds could be seen flying under her accustomed fingers and being laid in order. Before the lodgers had actually reached their room she had finished making the beds and slipped out (M, 55).

Grete has found her way back again from her musical escapades into the unknown, and will no longer be distracted by them in her active commitments to the requirements of this world. She has been saved by the physical objects surrounding her, as Marlow, in Conrad's *Heart of Darkness*, is saved by the 'rivets' he has to attend to. All that is left of the music is 'the noise made by the violin as it fell off his mother's lap from under her trembling fingers and gave out a resonant note'. As soon as she passes out of her adolescent phase the unknown no longer has a grip on Grete's existence. She is free now, as if an unpleasant spell has been removed from her. Under her 'accustomed fingers', her magic touch, the world (like the pillows and the blankets on the beds) will fall into place, as it were, of its own accord. In terms of her own and her parents' life Grete's decision to get rid of the insect, but to honour the memory of the brother she once knew, makes sense. After Gregor's death a natural order returns to the Samsa household. The lodgers are driven out of the house and a butcher's boy is seen proudly climbing the stairs 'with a tray on his head', signifying the return of more vital spirits than have hitherto visited the stricken family. The Samsas have liberated themselves, by an act of will, both from the distractions and degradations of this world (our impersonal economic system) and of the world beyond (our insatiate but world-denying quest for the unknown). The story ends on a note of spring and general rebirth.

We must now once more return to Gregor's predicament in order to understand the full thematic implications of *Metamor-*

phosis. We have already suggested that Gregor's struggle has both a negative and a positive side to it. The more he moves towards the fulfilment of his destiny—an unequivocal commitment to the unknown—the more he becomes alienated from the normality of life around him. To begin with he is concerned with not forgetting his 'human past', with keeping some form of contact with the human world. That is to say, he is eager to reconcile the demands of his insect-existence with the demands of normal human life. But he does not succeed, for these differing demands seem mutually exclusive. Soon the typical behaviour-pattern of a being possessed by the need to reorientate the course of his life, i.e. to transcend the materialistic basis of his existence, powerfully asserts itself. Fast losing his interest in the food his sister provides him with, and in the strenuous business generally of retaining a sense of normality, he unashamedly follows his animal instincts. In particular he finds a new way of passing his time, by crawling criss-cross over the walls and ceiling. 'He especially enjoyed hanging suspended from the ceiling; one's body swung and rocked lightly and in the almost blissful absorption induced by this suspension it could happen to his own surprise that he let go and fell plump on the floor' (M, 36). These are the acrobatics of spiritual man. Yet we are left in no doubt as to the value of these exercises. They remain on the level of entertainment and have no consequences. Even the most desperate attempts at clinging to the ceiling will not conquer the heavens. On one occasion, when particularly harassed by self-reproach and worry, 'he began . . . to crawl to and fro over everything, walls, furniture and ceiling, and finally in his despair, when the whole room seemed to be reeling round him, fell down on to the middle of the big table' (M, 41). The religious overtones of the sentence are obvious. Instead of the spiritual desperado finding his tabernacle and permanent rest somewhere, a still-born messiah lies flat on the table. The pious intentions of sending his sister to a conservatorium ('last Christmas') are also part of the messianic ambitions of the insect.

The passage quoted on page 55 reveals Gregor's dilemma to the full. Kurt Weinberg has drawn attention to the parallels between this passage and Hartmann von Aue's *Gregorius*, a Middle High German epic about religious matters, but has to my mind grossly exaggerated, as he does throughout his otherwise useful book, the mere rhetorical significance of the allusion. *Gregorius* is a narrative poem of sin and punishment, involving an incestuous relationship. Kafka's point is that man absorbed in spiritual matters knows of no dignified ways and means of expressing these matters. Instead of finding a more appropriate objective correlative for his spiritual concerns, he can only express these concerns in the form of such things as an incestuous fantasy or the kind of sentimental desires we find in the Beauty and the Beast story. At the height of his a-worldly ambitions Gregor is thrown back on his all too human resources. He suffers the final degradation of his life. Hitherto only the outward style of his living was affected, now his whole mental life gets perverted in the total pursuit of the absolute. An intensely felt desire of a transcendental kind, a yearning for union with the spiritual and isolation from a contaminated world, translates itself into an intensely felt human emotion (as only perversity can create), that of incestuous union with his sister. And this is Gregor's tragedy: the inability to demonstrate with dignity his other-worldly desires and ambitions in the world he has to live in. In a very real sense his only way out is death, an insight he cannot spare himself for too long. Ultimately, his death is of his own doing:

The decision that he must disappear was one that he held to even more strongly than his sister—if that were possible. In this state of vacant and peaceful meditation he remained until the tower clock struck three in the morning. The first broadening of light in the world outside the window entered his consciousness once more. Then his head sank to the floor of its own accord and from his nostrils came the last faint flicker of his breath (M, 58).

Kafka provides us with a more vivid and shocking version of what modern writers since Schopenhauer, Nietzsche and Mann reiterate: that our more idealist goals can only be achieved through disease and death. As Thomas Mann puts it in an address on his *Magic Mountain*: 'There are two ways to life: the one is the ordinary, direct and worthy way. The other is bad, it leads over death, and that is the way of genius.' Critics who attribute to Gregor beastliness and wanton regression to an infantile existence, brutishness and authoritarianism to the father, or harshness and cruelty to the sister, completely obscure the two different choices Kafka explores in *Metamorphosis*. Paradoxically enough,

59

both Gregor and his family are after one and the same thing, what V. S. Naipaul has recently called, with perhaps less emphasis on the existential implications than Kafka provides, living 'in a free state'. The goal is the same, only the methods differ. The Samsas have chosen the common, the bourgeois way, Gregor the way of the genius, the one that takes him through his own death. The two choices are equally valid, they merely reflect two different instincts in the human lot, the one our commitment to the vitality of life (symbolised by the butcher's boy or Grete's newly gained sexual maturity), the other our equally powerful need to transcend it (symbolised by Gregor's withdrawal from life). There is only one absurdity : to resign our will to the total pursuit of material benefits, in the false hope of buying our freedom thereby. Kafka does not offer this point by way of a pious moral but, as a close reading of *Metamorphosis* will bear out, in the course of a penetrating analysis of human existence.

Throughout the story there is a dialectical relationship between the natural and the supernatural world. This raises the question of the mode and status of the one kind of existence in relation to the other. Before we attempt to resolve this question, let us first dispose of another matter—something that is the enemy both of the natural and supernatural order, our modern utilitarian economic structures. Kafka's indictment is made crystal clear in *Metamorphosis*. When the chief clerk suffers the encounter with the insect he utters a loud 'Oh!'—'it sounded like a gust of wind' —'clapping one hand before his open mouth and slowly backing away as if driven by some invisible steady pressure' (M, 21). Kurt Weinberg, who appears to believe that Kafka's Red Indians are frequently symbols of Christianity, sees in the chief clerk 'an Indian on the war-path' and interprets the scene as a reference to 'the future dominance of the Roman *Ecclesia militans* as the vanguard of the new Covenant'.[6] This unlikely interpretation seems to reflect a serious failure to distinguish between the substance and the rhetoric of symbolism. The chief clerk continues to retreat. 'He was already at the hall, and the suddenness with which he took his last step out of the living-room would have made one believe he had burned the sole of his foot. Once in the hall he stretched his right arm before him towards the staircase, as if some supernatural power were waiting there to deliver him' (M, 23). The chief clerk appears to be somebody in flight from a mysterious power he cannot possibly face for too long, and from which he must seek deliverance. He is standing on holy ground which is in danger of burning his feet, and desperate to reach 'the stairs going down' (M, 21). The symbolism is obvious enough to make us think of the popular image of the devil who is in danger of being marked by the sign of the cross if he does not quickly retreat and go back to hell. It is casual enough to communicate Kafka's primary intention, not to establish an overtly religious point but to indicate the extraordinary powers we possess when called upon to defend ourselves against influences alien to our life. Later on it will be the father's turn to exorcise the pseudo-forces to which he has temporarily subscribed. The retreat of the three lodgers is portrayed in similarly comic and grotesque terms, with the emphasis on the hurried departure and the symbolic connotations of the staircase image (cf. M, 61f.).

What is the relationship then between the two opposing forces as symbolised by Gregor's and his father's modes of existence? Herr Samsa's hatred of his son appears to indicate that this relationship is no less than one of deadly combat. But to see it simply as that is to overlook the important change of attitude the father undergoes. To begin with, the father fights Gregor at every point, almost killing him in the process. This is plausible, because he has to rediscover his own strength of will and independence, in order to reinstate the only sensible foundations of his and his family's existence. It is also plausible that this process of finding his own self should take the form of a fight against forces alien to it, in other words Gregor's search for the unknown, his failure to contribute any longer to the welfare of the others. The father has, literally, to clear up the mess in his own house before he can proceed further. Once the battle is won, the fight can be relaxed, and the *modus vivendi* can be worked out which includes Gregor in some form. Now 'towards evening the living-room door, which he used to watch intently for an hour or two beforehand, was always thrown open, so that lying in the darkness of his room, invisible to the family, he could see them all at the lamp-lit table and listen to their talk, by general consent as it were, very very different from his earlier eavesdropping' (M, 45). The family has now found a way of incorporating the thing otherwise transcending their most immediate needs. Characteristically enough, this particular form of tolerating the transcendental—only at relaxed moments, in the evening, at candlelight, and never face to face—reveals itself as a perfect analogue to real life. This is roughly the role religion plays in the busy world. And that is perfectly in order, Kafka seems to say, reminding us of Brecht's dictum : 'Erst kommt das Fressen, dann kommt die Moral' ('First comes grub, then comes morality'). Gregor's demands on this world, his possessiveness and total commitment to the unknown, are monstrous and incompatible with the life we know and have to live. In a later story, *A Hunger-Artist*, Kafka looks at the matter more objectively and abstractly, emphasising the need for a balance between the two antagonistic forces operative in our lives. In *Metamorphosis* too the mood is one of objective analysis of the problem, but at the end of it all the benefit of the doubt is given to the real world (as opposed to the unknown). Gregor is ultimately judged according to the way the family, the world, sees him—by being turned into something loathsome, by being made redundant, by his spiritual acrobatics being exposed as something absurd and even perverse. His transcendental yearning is never affirmed as something noble, it is always measured in terms of what he thereby *loses*. The stress is on nostalgia for normality, with the story towards the end turning quietly into a subdued but warm celebration of life. There is a sense in which Kafka's idealism can be seen, as so often in his work, to lack the courage of its own conviction. It is never really validated in its own terms. At the point where the craving for 'unknown nourishment' is acknowledged, it is, as we have seen, perverted and debased.

Gregor's case is one of acute alienation from life. That much is obvious. But we must not believe that Kafka revels in 'alienation' for its own sake, as does so much of existentialist literature. True, in Kafka's work too we find the spiritual melancholy of, say, Max Weber's reflections on alienation, or Durkheim's deep conviction of endemic social disorganisation in Europe, but above all we find Georg Simmel's cool and analytic temper. 'Alienation is, for him [Simmel, the most literary of German sociologists], almost solely methodological; it is a means of fresh analysis of human personality and its relation to the world rather than the basis of any kind of spiritual or ethical evaluation.'[7] This is also true of Kafka, particularly of *Metamorphosis* and *The Castle*. Alienation is something to be overcome, and not to be cherished.

It is a symptom of the inhumanity of modern society that can be turned into an analytical tool for the discovery of genuine choices. Gregor does not remain in an unresolved state of alienation, he pushes himself towards a commitment that cannot be symbolised adequately except by his death. Gregor's father regains his former strength only by reacting vigorously to his son's alienation, until he becomes 'the masterpiece of existence' (to use a Durkheimian phrase) we encounter at the end of the story. The images of rebirth point to his and his family's successful vitalisation of that sense of society which alone can maintain individuality. The father's metamorphosis is based on the proposition that, as R. A. Nisbet says of the Western sociological tradition, 'what is fundamental and decisive in man proceeds from what is *within* man—from instinct, sensation, the inner drives of self-interest or altruism—rather than from the social structure and from conventional morality'.[8]

It is clear that, as in the case of Mann, Proust, Hesse and Pirandello,[9] Kafka's thinking on these matters overlaps to a considerable extent with that tradition in sociology which found its most eloquent spokesmen during the early part of the twentieth century. In agreement with this tradition Kafka suggests that there are not two but three orders of being—the transcendental (Gregor), the 'natural' (the Samsas at the end of the story) and the 'unnatural' enslavement to an economic system, from which Gregor and his family emerge in different ways. The irony, of course, is that the family would seem to have joined that system by the end. They are not doing anything different from what Gregor used to do. The point however is that their attitude to work has changed to one of whole-hearted commitment. It is not the nature of the job that matters so much as whether one does it reluctantly, half-heartedly, resentfully—or gladly and gratefully. Why did Gregor's metamorphosis take place in the first place? It is none other than a token of Gregor's dissatisfaction with (and therefore unsuitability for) a 'normal' existence. He is a parasite mentally long before he becomes one physically. As in *The Trial*, the retribution is a projection of the hero's own doubts and suspicions on to a conscious plane.

4
America

Written mostly during the period from which *The Judgment* and *Metamorphosis* date, Kafka's first novel shows the two major directions in which his early narrative mode could develop. In a diary entry of February 9, 1915 Kafka noted : 'If the two elements —most pronounced in "The Stoker" [the first chapter of *America*] and "In the Penal Settlement"—do not combine, I am finished. But is there any prospect of their combining?' Malcolm Pasley has defined these two elements as Kafka's use of the 'dream-symbol' on the one hand, and the 'intentional symbol' on the other. 'Where the *Stoker* element predominates, we have the controlled flow of evocative pictures—pictures which have imposed themselves upon Kafka's inner eye, and whose full import may not be clear even to the author himself. Charged with emotional life, such symbols are "over-determined" in Freud's sense : they have multiple reference, and resist all efforts to exhaust them by a translation into conceptual terms. Where the *Penal Settlement* element predominates, we have instead a technique of deliberate allusion, a carefully organised structure of suggestive hints. It is as if the "dream-material" had been X-rayed from without and made translucent.'[1] Or to use Graham Hough's straightforward definition : 'If the concept comes first and is then translated into a visible equivalent, this is allegory. If the visible object comes first and an immaterial reality is seen behind it or through it, this is symbolism. . . . Or if we employ Coleridgean terms, allegory is a product of the mechanical fancy, symbolism of the intuitive imagination.'[2]

In practice no easy distinction can be made between the two. Kafka's narrative structures have a Janus-faced quality about them, as have the changing shapes and images of picture-puzzles. We now tend to take much in *The Trial* to be typical products of the 'intuitive imagination', but Kafka himself said that after repeated disappointments he returned to the novel with hopes which were obviously founded on nothing except mechanical fancy ('auf eine mechanische Phantasie') (D2, 91). In reply to an inquiry as to whether the figures in *The Stoker* had been drawn after existing models he flatly denied the idea, emphasising the autonomy of the images and their dream-like movement. On the other hand the story has since been successfully interpreted as an allegory of 'Innerlichkeit'.[3] But the most impressive differences between, say, *The Stoker* and *In the Penal Settlement* do not lie in their respective modes of *expression* (whether they belong to a theme-dominated or image-dominated type of literature) but in their respective *narrative* modes. Whilst *In the Penal Settlement* firmly belongs to the dream-narrative form, despite its 'intentional' symbolism, *The Stoker* reflects an uneasy mixture of the dream-narrative and the mode of realism. The latter Kafka considered as belonging to 'the shameful lowlands of writing' (D1, 276), and he expresses his distaste for the 'many shallow passages followed by unfathomable depths' in realist writing (D1, 287). Kafka is even more explicit in his diary entry of October 8, 1917, where we read :

Dickens' *Copperfield*. 'The Stoker' a sheer imitation of Dickens, the projected novel even more so. The story of the trunk, the boy who delights and charms everyone, the menial labour, his sweetheart in the country house, the dirty houses, *et al.*, but above all the method. It was my intention, as I now see, to write a Dickens novel, but enhanced by the sharper lights I should have taken from the times and the duller ones I should have got from myself. Dickens' opulence and great, careless prodigality, but in consequence passages of awful insipidity in which he wearily works over effects he has already achieved. . . . There is a heartlessness behind his sentimentally overflowing style. These rude characterisations which are artificially stamped on everyone and without which Dickens would not be able to get on with his story even for a moment (D2, 188).

Mark Spilka has given us a full account of Dickens' influence on Kafka's writing.[4] What we need to notice here is that Kafka, who in his mature works developed, with a single-minded dedication, a narrative mode of his own, falls back, if only once, on what is essentially a nineteenth-century narrative form, complete with its repertoire of well-established tricks and effects. It would be a mistake to believe that nineteenth-century realism had nothing whatsoever to do with Kafka's dream-narrative. Writers like Dickens and Keller, the German *Novelle* and the tradition of the grotesque, which was very largely carried along on the wave of realism, prove the opposite. And Martin Greenberg has grossly overstated his case by more or less dismissing *America* out of hand for its 'realism'. Even in this novel Kafka's narrative mode is no less ambiguous than is the structure and quality of his imagery. What most clearly sets *America* apart from everything else Kafka wrote is a phenomenon which was observed by F. D. Luke in his essay on *Metamorphosis*. Comparing Thomas Mann's *Death in Venice* to Kafka's story he writes : 'Mann is more firmly related than Kafka to convention, to the external object, the world of reality and civilised society. . . . The nightmare described in *Death in Venice*, Aschenbach's last "dream" of pagan eroticism and barbaric frenzy, is an elaborately written artificial literary vision, and when Mann introduces Aschenbach's last monologue by calling it "dream-logic", this description is quite inappropriate : he is merely apologising in advance for a highly sophisticated train of thought reasoned at a conscious level on Mann's familiar lines.'[5] Whilst Mann's writing is of a characteristically 'literary' nature, i.e. supported by common cultural legends and literary fiction, Kafka 'creates wholly original narrative patterns of his own', as if there was nothing else to fall back on. But not so in *America*. For once he produces literature with cross-references to other literature. Kafka himself has grudgingly acknowledged his debt to Dickens. The novel is also readily recognisable as having been written in the spirit of the 'Bildungsroman', of the more picaresque type. As such it does not succeed in avoiding imitation of a familiar reality, however much Kafka might have tried to suppress the aspect of mimesis even in his first novel. Moreover, his narrative is, contrary to his usual method, clearly supported by typically literary motifs and leading ideas. As Malcolm Pasley has pointed out, the story is 'a version of the constantly frustrated quest for a lost Paradise, and belongs to the category of *Märchen* or myth. The discovery of the rich uncle, for instance (who subsequently rejects him, like Cinderella, for failing to return by midnight), is a pure fairy-tale motif.'[6] Brunelda's flat is some kind of 'Venusberg' turned upside down. The Nature Theatre of Oklahoma, 'the biggest theatre in the world', is a revival of the Baroque concept of the world as a huge stage, and expresses more particularly 'the Whitmanesque idea of an all-embracing, all-accepting American immensity'.[7]

The chapter is clearly inspired by the sense of utopian endings, which Austrian writers, down to Robert Musil, have always been proud of. The whole idea of the book is of course mounted on a famous myth rather than on direct experience, the myth of the New World, as Kafka abstracted it mostly from Benjamin Franklin's autobiography and other books about America.[8]

Kafka's worried question whether there is any prospect of the two elements (of convention and innovation) combining must be answered in the negative in the case of his first novel. We know that all of Kafka's major works remained unfinished, but for different reasons. *The Trial* and *The Castle* remained unfinished because there was no way of finishing them. Their circular movement turns all apparent endings into new beginnings. The conclusion of *The Trial* is a forced conclusion, the conclusion of *The Castle* a kind of petering out of the main theme. *America* remained unfinished because Kafka could not bring himself to complete it along the lines dictated by the conventional scheme he had chosen. Kafka's imagination merely turned the conventional material that had infiltrated his narrative upside down, but he did not succeed in annihilating it, as is required by his mature method.

Very generally speaking, this method is based on a principle of reduction on the one hand and on perspectivism on the other. 'Reduction' was not only a key-concept in Husserl's phenomenology but a fundamental idea operative in most turn-of-the-century psychology and philosophy. Literature was quick to absorb the phenomenological thinking of the time, and in one way and another writers like Hofmannsthal, Rilke and Musil were all concerned with reducing the diverse and complex to the uniform and simple, frequently employing a more old-fashioned and corresponding metaphysics of essences and entities. As usual, Kafka was the most radical in applying reductionist principles, Franz Brentano's in particular, to creative writing.

The consequences of reductionism in literature are manifold. As far as narrative technique is concerned the method requires that there be no distinction between narrator and what is narrated, between observation and what is observed; and that plot, character and theme are identical. Since the emphasis is on the essential and elementary the chief intention is to abstract the subjective from experience and the accidental from our perceptions of the phenomenal world. Kafka himself knew that total reductions to essences and phenomena is not possible, but only approximations. He liked to view his writing as 'stehender Sturmlauf' (assault by standing still) or 'stehendes Marschieren' (marching on the spot), phrases which recall words which Lewis Carroll put into Alice's mouth : 'Keep running until you reach the point of standing still.' As far as whole narrative units are concerned reductionism leads to compression of the narrative material, with the effect that the plots of single stories resemble myths rather than mimetic structures. When Isaac Bashevis Singer lets one of his characters say that Kafka's *Castle* is 'too long for a dream, allegories should be short',[9] then he is communicating the general feeling that in his novels too Kafka's impulses lead him in the direction of the allegorical, mythical and parabolic. It is in fact possible to say that the novels are either elaborated and embellished single stories (or myths) or that they are collages of single stories (or myths). From about *The Trial* onwards Kafka adds perspectivism (the art of hypothetical thinking as he, like most writers at the time, encountered it in the later works of Nietzsche) to his reductionist method. His last but one story, *The Burrow*, is a brilliant example of 'hypothetical' narrating, a radically perspectivist review of the protagonist's existential problems.

Superficial readers of Kafka frequently come away with an impression of sameness which they feel to be characteristic of his writing as a whole. But despite the close family resemblance that exists between the individual works there is a clear development from Kafka's early, imagistic and pointillist, prose to his later writing in which he repeatedly attempts to crystallise in language the basic postulates of his unformulated philosophy. Kafka's mature method is designed to pierce what Benjamin Lee Whorf called 'the inscrutable blank of invisible and bodiless thought'.[10] From the point of view of both form and content *America* is a transitional work. But it is nevertheless an important and fascinating milestone in Kafka's career, a unique attempt to write against the grain of conventional literature.

'The Stoker'

Published independently under this title in Kurt Wolff's series

'Der jüngste Tag' (1913), this story also forms the first chapter of *Der Verschollene* (*The Man Who Disappeared*, Kafka's working title for the novel, which Max Brod changed to *America* when he published it in 1927). Whilst plot-wise it is only loosely connected with what follows, it nevertheless effectively embodies the aesthetic idea of the whole. The story is both a symbol and allegory of dislocation. From a structural point of view it presents itself as a series of symbolic, indeed dream-like, situations replete with significance. From a textural point of view it presents itself as an allegory from which a single, if complex, theme can easily be abstracted. Karl Rossmann, an innocent boy of sixteen packed off to America by his parents (his *physical* dislocation from Europe) because a servant girl has seduced him, arrives in New York on a Hamburg liner, where a sequence of extraordinary events leads to the *spiritual* estrangement from his origins. The apparent freedom he is heading for is a menacing one, symbolised by the Statue of Liberty which Rossmann sees 'in a new light', with the sword rising up 'as if newly stretched aloft'. About to leave the ship he discovers that he has forgotten his umbrella down below. So instead of disembarking he hurries back, to where he has come from. The delay in the action signifies Karl's inner condition. He is not yet prepared to set foot on the new continent. The umbilical cord tying him to the old world has to be cut first, and by himself. Running down endlessly recurring stairs and corridors with countless turnings he finally stops before a little door, hammering unthinkingly on it. His action betrays an acute anxiety, an attempt to find, like a chased animal, a hole to hide in. Instinctively, Karl had found his way to the centre of the ship, to the stoker's room. What follows is a masterly design in intentional, and yet unfathomable, symbolism. The stoker turns out to be a huge and abrupt but essentially good-natured man, the archetype of a Central European father-figure. Walter Sokel has interpreted the 'stoker-element' of the story as a portrayal of 'Innerlichkeit' (inwardness or inner nature), and it is difficult to see why so many critics have found it necessary to disagree. True, Kafka's portrayal of inwardness is not the uninhibited celebration of the inner nature of man, as was commonly offered in early twentieth-century German literature (Hofmannsthal, Rilke, Hesse), but, like Musil's, a critique of it. As we shall see, despite his spontaneous intimacy with the stoker Karl Rossmann will ultimately have to break free from him. What kind of man then is the stoker?

To find out we must look at the story's plot, of which the stoker's character is an integral part. Karl has stumbled into the man's room when he was about to pack his things and leave the ship. The Chief Engineer, a Rumanian with the name of Schubal, has expressed dissatisfaction with the stoker, 'a German on a German ship', and the way he goes about his job. There have been no specific complaints, rather a continuous clash of temperaments. Whilst the stoker takes an intuitive approach to his work, Schubal likes everything to be done according to rule. The Chief Engineer, an alien upstart, has declared war on German intuition and 'inwardness'. Despite the rather indeterminate nature of this conflict Karl encourages the stoker to put his case to the Captain. Predictably enough the stoker, in his inner frustration, is unable to formulate his complaint rationally and coherently. 'Certainly he was talking himself into a sweat . . . from all points of the compass complaints about Schubal streamed into his head, each of which, it seemed to him, should have been sufficient to dispose of Schubal for good; but all he could produce for the Captain was a wretched farago in which everything was lumped together' (A, 26). When Karl tries to intervene, advising his new friend to put things more simply, to take his 'grievances in order' and to tell the most important ones first and the lesser ones afterwards, the stoker's speech disintegrates completely. He is quickly 'past all bounds', loses his temper, and directs a torrent of inarticulate words against Karl. The stoker's identity, based on his sense of 'inner truth', is shattered like the nucleus of an atom. Language has no objective or meaningful correlatives for the stoker's indefinable state of mind. The truth of his existence can only be measured by the strength of his desperation when challenged by rational ways and procedures. When Karl takes comfort in the thought that in case of need the stoker could simply overwhelm the others present in the room, then we can see how Kafka embodies in a minor incident the kind of answer most of his contemporaries gave when faced with the problem of reconciling their vision with an apparently unyielding reality: apocalyptic violence.

The stoker's unfortunate plea for justice finds a significant contrast in Schubal's clear and methodical statement:

'I have come here because I believe this stoker is accusing me of dishonesty or something. A maid in the kitchen told me she saw him making in this direction. Captain, and all you other gentlemen, I am prepared to show papers to disprove any such accusation, and, if you like, to adduce the evidence of unprejudiced and incorruptible witnesses, who are waiting outside the door' (A, 30f.).

This is a fine speech, but does it necessarily demonstrate that Schubal is in the right? Why, for instance, did he immediately deduce from what the maid in the kitchen told him that the stoker was going to complain about him? Was it his guilty conscience that had sharpened his apprehension rather than anything more objective? Or, are the witnesses he managed to collect in such a hurry really as 'unprejudiced and incorruptible' as he makes them out to be? And does Schubal not distort the truth from the start when he uses the word 'dishonesty' where 'national prejudice' might have been a more appropriate one? After closer analysis it becomes clear that Schubal's 'model speech' is full of holes. It is not so much a statement of truth as the cunning rhetorical strategy of a man who is well versed in legal and administrative matters.

Schubal's speech is not the only example in the story of how public patterns of language distort the real truth. One of the gentlemen present in the room is Senator Jacob, Karl's uncle, who has come to meet his nephew on the ship. In an attempt to identify himself to Karl the Senator unwittingly reveals to everybody present what Karl has hitherto regarded as his most private secret:

'He [Karl] was seduced by a maidservant, Johanna Brummer, a person of round about thirty-five. It is far from my wishes to offend my nephew by using the word "seduced", but it is difficult to find another and equally suitable word. . . . Now this Brummer . . . had a child by my nephew, a healthy boy, who was given the baptismal name of Jacob, evidently in memory of my unworthy self. . . . To avoid the scandal . . . and the payment of alimony, they [Karl's parents] packed off their son . . . to America . . . and the poor lad, but for the signs and wonders which still happen in America if nowhere else, would have come to a wretched end in New York . . . if this servant girl hadn't written a letter to me . . . giving me the whole story, along with a description of my nephew and, very wisely, the name of the ship as well' (A, 34f.).

Karl is astonished at his uncle's ability 'to make a great song' out of it all, a structured narrative of what to him is no more than an indeterminate event of the past. Here is how Karl's experience with the girl appears once more before his inner eye:

Hemmed in by a vanishing past, she sat in her kitchen beside the kitchen dresser, resting her elbows on top of it. She looked at him whenever he came to the kitchen to fetch a glass of water for his father or do some errand for his mother. . . . And once . . . she led him into her room, sighing and grimacing, and locked the door. Then she flung her arms round his neck, almost choking him, and while urging him to take off her clothes, she really took off his and laid him on her bed, as if she would never give him up to anyone and would tend and cherish him to the end of time . . . it was as if her eyes were devouring him, while his eyes saw nothing at all. . . . Then she lay down by him and . . . pressed her naked belly against his body, felt with her hand between his legs, so disgustingly that his head and neck started up from the pillows, then thrust her body several times against him—it was as if she were part of himself, and for that reason, perhaps, he was seized with a terrible feeling of yearning. With tears running down his cheeks he reached his own bed at last. . . . That was all that had happened (A, 35f.).

In comparison with his uncle's 'factual' account Karl's own memories of the incident read like the fragments of an unfinished narrative. Whilst the uncle's report demonstrates the Senator's practical and prosaic ways of assessing things Karl's reminiscences reveal the characteristic qualities of the creative artist's mode of thought. Sparked off by the immediate situation in the Captain's room the fragments of Karl's memories take on the coherent shape of a fictional account of what, in the uncle's report, remains a string of incidental information. The sentence 'That was all that had happened' is a highly ironic understatement. Much more in fact, or less, happened than is conveyed by the Senator's 'seduced'. One of the functions of the whole passage is to expose the inadequacy of the Senator's concept ('seduced') by revealing something of the complex situation from which he rather conventionally deduced it. Can the events recollected by Karl be called a seduction-scene at all? The logic of the metaphors seems to point in a different direction. Nowhere is there any suggestion of Karl being induced to surrender his chastity. It is rather as if an impersonal force was closing in on Karl's existence, stripping him naked and rendering him helpless and defenceless—'her eyes were devouring him, while his eyes saw nothing at all' is a familiar example of Kafka's attempt to depict his heroes' incomprehension in the face of unknown powers. Now it is the American metropolis that is challenging Karl in a similar way : 'And behind them all rose New York, and its skyscrapers stared at Karl with their hundred thousand eyes' (A, 21). Like most of Kafka's heroes Karl Rossmann too is motivated by both a sense of solidarity with the unseen order of things and the terror of submitting to it. The uncertainty of not knowing where the individual begins and where it ends makes him at times a self-righteous defender of his and others' individuality, at times an easy prey to impersonal forces. When he feels the girl's naked belly against his body he is both repelled by the violent onslaught on his person and seized by a terrible yearning for unity. It is true that the passage quoted retains much of the traditional seduction-scene but the symbolic meaning of parallel scenes in the later novels is already there in embryo. The emphasis is not on the loss of chastity, or whatever seduction-scenes are about, but on the loss of self. After the encounter with powers unknown to him the 'innocent' individual is left in a state of self-abandonment and somatic exhaustion.

It is significant that Karl 'had no feelings for Johanna Brummer'. On the other hand 'it was as if she were part of himself'. Once more the impersonal quality of the whole incident is underlined. The constant opposition of the self and outside forces is a recurrent motif in *America*, as it is in Kafka's work generally. As with Nietzsche, 'physical intoxication' is frequently Kafka's analogy for the self transported into other realms. The difference between Nietzsche and Kafka is that Kafka's heroes resist the temptation to destroy all individual boundaries where Nietzsche recommends us 'to forget ourselves completely'. But this does not mean that Kafka's heroes do not experience the unimaginable yearning for unity which Nietzsche thought was typical of all individuals. Joseph K.'s consciousness of guilt and K.'s irrepressible desire to operate on another plane of being are all expressions of that yearning. In Karl Rossmann's case it is his wide-eyed innocence, the 'spell of individuation' (Nietzsche), which makes him not so much seek as provoke external powers. Above all, his unresolved predicament turns him into a kind of buffer-figure, into somebody who always finds himself 'between' the powers that ultimately matter. Karl has travelled in the '*Zwischen*deck' (steerage), that part of the ship where nothing ever happens, between the decision-making powers above him (the Captain and his officers) and the dynamic forces below him (engine-room and stoker). Sometimes he quite consciously attempts to put his normal position to some good use, as when during the interrogation of the stoker 'he was standing between his uncle and the Captain, and, influenced by his position, thought that he was holding the balance between them' (A, 39).

Karl has to make an important decision. Should he stay with the stoker, whom he trusts and loves, or should he follow his uncle, who is as strange to him as America itself? The stoker is an epitome of the old Europe, i.e. of 'inner-directed' (David Riesman) efforts and energies. Deep down, in the lower regions of the ship, he is a silently working force. His inner withdrawal finds expression in his environment, the twilight atmosphere of the engine-room and the cosiness of his little cabin. Everything is arranged as if part of a natural world-order. Karl instinctively feels at home here : 'He had almost lost the feeling that he was on the uncertain boards of a ship, beside the coast of an unknown continent, so much at home did he feel here in the stoker's bunk' (A, 17). But Kafka does not fail to draw attention to the out-modedness of such an existence. There is also something cramped and stale about the stoker's 'wretched cubby-hole in which a bunk, a cupboard, a chair and the man were packed together, as if they had been stored there' (A, 14). The stoker's mode of existence is ultimately a relic of the past rather than a relevant example for the present. His greatest tragedy is that he can no longer either communicate his inner-directed way of life or absorb the new kinds of realities which are rapidly closing in on him. After his irrational outburst in the Captain's room all there is left of him is a spent force, an old man, from whom everybody turns away in embarrassment. 'I think we have had enough and more than enough of the stoker', as the Senator puts it. Karl has hitherto confidently accompanied the stoker in order to ensure that justice is done in his case. But now he is 'gently yet firmly' led away from him, like a child whose parents can no longer be considered responsible for his upbringing. Before following his uncle Karl 'burst out crying and kissed the stoker's hand, taking that seamed, almost nerveless hand and pressing it to his cheek like a treasure which he would soon have to give up' (A, 41). On a more symbolical level Karl's farewell to the stoker is a forced decision to cut himself loose from his own European past. With him he carries a suitcase, which is filled with his best suit, a piece of Veronese salami, his parents' photographs and other items typical of the closed petty-bourgeois world he comes from. It is a kind of portable old world, which he entrusts to a complete stranger when he goes below deck to look for his umbrella. Karl's absent-mindedness, together with his inability to remember things clearly, is a symptom of disintegration. He finds it increasingly difficult to retain his European past as a determining influence on his actions. In a sense, Karl is a replica of the stoker. The difference is that he is still young enough to adjust his life in the light of new circumstances, and that he has found a mentor who will assist him in his quest for a new world.

The first chapter also contains an indication of the choices open to Karl. They are in fact not so much choices as powerful influences with which Karl has to reckon. First there is the New World, streamlined America, of which the uncle is a perfect representative. Secondly, there is a more sinister and primitive reality, with which Karl, and all men, will have to come to terms. It is symbolised by the strange spectacle which Karl watches from behind the porthole in the Captain's room : 'Here and there curious objects bobbed independently out of the restless water, were immediately submerged again and sank before his astonished eyes. . . . A movement without end, a restlessness transmitted from the restless element to helpless human beings and their works!' (A, 26). Last, but not least, Karl's European past will after all remain the most powerful influence on his life, turning his American adventure into a quest less for the future than for the past. When this happens Karl will be ready, after unsuccessful acts of self-transcendence, to make the final choice. In the meantime, however, he has to be thrown in at the deep end of things. The final sentence of the stoker story points both to the brutality of Karl's separation from his origins and the uncertainty with which he anticipates the future :

It was now as if there were really no stoker at all. Karl took a more careful look at his uncle, whose knees were almost touching his own, and doubts came into his mind whether this man would ever be able to take the stoker's place. And his uncle evaded his eye and stared at the waves on which their boat was tossing (A, 43).

Uncle Jacob

Karl's uncle, business man, politician and spiritual defender of the American dream, immediately creates what he considers to be a sound routine for his nephew. Karl is to make proper use of his time and to devote himself, with moderation to begin with, to such activities as riding and the study of English. Gradually he is initiated into the mysterious world of his uncle's business, a perfect microcosm of the capitalist enterprise at large. The telegraphists' hall alone is larger than the telegraphic office of Karl's native town. But the complete mechanisation of work has led to conditions from which everything human is excluded. In the glaring electric light Karl watches an operator, 'quite oblivious to any sound from the door, his head bound in a steel band which pressed the receivers against his ears. His right arm was lying on a little table as if it were strangely heavy and only the fingers holding the pencil kept twitching with inhuman regularity and speed' (A, 52). The man has hardly any time to speak himself, to raise objections or to ask for more exact information, because 'the next phrase he heard compelled him to lower his eyes and go on writing before he could carry out his intention'. Anyway, there is no need for the man to say anything, as the uncle explains, for the same conversation which this man is taking down 'was being taken down at the same time by two other operators and would then be compared with the other versions, so that errors might as far as possible be eliminated'. The ceaseless activity generated by the complex technical and administrative structure reduces people to automatons, who cannot afford to step out of line: 'Nobody said good-day, greetings were omitted, each man fell into step behind anyone who was going the same way, keeping his eyes on the floor, over which he was set on advancing as quickly as he could, or giving a hurried glance at a word or figure here and there on the papers he held in his hand, which fluttered with the wind of his own progress.' It is a world which is totally alien to Karl's. Though he cannot help expressing his astonishment at such a 'wonderful' set-up, and although he is willing to draw the appropriate conclusions for himself, his innermost self remains untouched by it all. His own ways of doing things are still dominated by the more relaxed and intuitive approaches which his European environment instilled in him. Only two examples need to be given.

His uncle likens the first days of a European in America to a 're-birth', and though Karl is in a better position than an infant coming into the world it is nevertheless essential to him to commit himself to an active life from the start. This is the only way of getting used to things, not, as he might have thought, by passively looking on. His uncle criticises Karl's dreamy and contemplative attitude towards his new environment, his habit of gaping down at the street from the balcony 'like a lost sheep. That was bound to lead to bewilderment! The solitary indulgence of idly gazing at the busy life of New York was permissible in anyone travelling for pleasure . . . but for one who intended to remain in the States it was sheer ruination' (A, 45). Karl is also strongly advised not to use the regulator attached to the huge mechanical writing-desk his uncle has put in his room. By operating the regulator it is possible to produce the most complicated combinations and permutations of the hundred compartments which are built into the desk. Even after one turn of the handle the disposition of the whole is quite changed and the transformation takes place slowly or at delirious speed, according to the rate at which the thing is wound round.

It was a very modern invention, yet it reminded Karl vividly of the traditional Christmas panorama which was shown to gaping children in the market-place at home, where he too . . . had often stood enthralled, closely comparing the movement of the handle, which was turned by an old man, with the changes in the scene, the jerky advance of the Three Holy Kings, the shining out of the Star and the humble life of the Holy Manger. And it had always seemed to him that his mother . . . did not follow every detail with sufficient attention. He would draw her close to him . . . and . . . would keep pointing out to her the less noticeable occurrences, perhaps a little hare among the grass in the foreground, sitting up on its hind legs and then crouching as if to dart off again. . . . The desk was certainly not made merely to remind him of such things, yet in the history of its invention there probably existed some vague connection similar to that in Karl's memory (A, 46f.).

Karl's writing desk is a perfect illustration of what Karl Mann-heim has described as the aspirations of the conservative dream or 'conservative utopia'.[11] According to this dream every element of reality has meaning, that is to say it is part of a higher design or central idea. This idea is either already in us as a subjectively perceived force or as an 'entelechy which has unfolded itself in the collective creations of the community, of the folk, the nation, or the state as an inner form which, for the most part, is per-ceivable morphologically'. If we take Karl's desk as a symbol of existence in general then the use of its regulator illustrates the possibility of an action which is orientated towards the mastery of whole life-situations. However, the principle of regulation is not one that can be arbitrarily chosen and imposed but one that has to be discovered in a world which has already assumed a fixed and inner form. Karl's temptation to use the regulator is not due to any activistic impulses on his part but to an urge to find out about the relations between things. Paradoxically enough, the regulator does not impose a design but discloses one. It discloses how the many compartments of the desk are inter-related. By analogy the human imagination is such a regulator, an instrument for the disclosure of some divine master-design that is supposed to underlie the manifest world. And it is for this reason that the uncle views the monstrous piece of furniture with suspicion, as an archaic and outmoded model of how things work in real life. As the story of Karl's uncle's career reveals, the ideas which 'regulate' his work and life were rationally conjured up and rationally chosen as the best among a number of possi-bilities. Karl's 'European' frame of mind makes him therefore mistrust his uncle's 'American' organisation. To him reality is something prior to human impositions, something that needs to be approached not in a spirit of activism but through sympathetic intuition.

Karl's hope of influencing reality through his intuitive facul-ties finds expression in his love of music. Reluctantly, his uncle buys a piano for Karl, a beautiful instrument which has the immediate effect of dispelling his first discomfort at living in 'a steel house'. And Karl sets 'great hopes on his piano-playing and sometimes unashamedly dreamed, at least before falling asleep, of the possibility that it might exert a direct influence upon his life in America . . . but the street, if he looked down it, afterwards remained unchanged' (A, 48). The hope of having an effect on reality from a distance is no more than a utopian dream. Man's imagination is not, like a magnet, capable of generating a power field to which particles of matter conform. Nor is Karl's dream of becoming an engineer a guarantee for putting man at the centre of things. The technical world soon cuts itself loose from its inventor, like Frankenstein's monster, and becomes a threat to man rather than a liberating force. Already in his first novel Kafka establishes the radical hypothesis central to all his future work, the antinomy of individual existence and the external order of things. Like the K.s of *The Trial* and *The Castle* Karl too will have no choice but to meet this order head-on.

As Karl suffers from the illusion that the external world can be controlled by the individual, his uncle suffers from the illusion that intimate contact is possible between individuals. His desire for a kind of spiritual union with his nephew is motivated by his fear that a meaningful relationship between himself and the technocratic environment he helped to create no longer exists. He is plagued by his own rigorous principles and senses the possibility of his political and economic empire turning one day against him. When Karl is invited by one of his uncle's business friends, Pollunder, to spend a few days at his secluded country estate near New York he is thrown into confusion by the Senator's unwillingness to let him go. It is only under the strange circumstances in Pollunder's house that he arrives at an understanding of his uncle's hesitation to expose him too soon to the social world at large. In the process Karl also discovers his love for his new protector, picturing to himself unique moments of sympathy which would unite him for ever to his uncle. He imagines how after his return he will surprise him in his own bedroom.

True, he had never yet been in his uncle's bedroom, nor did he even know where it was, but he would soon find that out. Then he would knock at the door and at the formal 'come in' rush into the room and surprise his dear uncle, whom until now he had known only fully dressed and buttoned to the chin, sitting up in bed in his nightshirt, his astonished eyes fixed on the door. In itself that might not perhaps be very much, but one had only to consider what consequences it might lead to. Perhaps he might breakfast with his uncle for the first time . . . perhaps that breakfast together would become a standing arrangement; perhaps . . . they would meet oftener than simply once a day and so of course be able to speak more frankly to each other . . . perhaps this unlucky visit would become the turning-point in his relations with his uncle; perhaps his uncle was lying in bed and thinking the very same things at that moment (A, 66).

At the idea Karl is overwhelmed by a vision of unity which includes the very objects distancing him at present from his uncle :

the road leading to his uncle through that glass door, down the steps, through the avenue, along the country roads, through the suburbs to the great main street where his uncle's house was, seemed to him a strictly ordered whole, which lay there empty, smooth, and prepared for him, and called to him with a strong voice (A, 81).

His uncle too has thought of Karl, but not in the way Karl imagines. At the stroke of midnight he is handed a letter by Mr Green, another guest at Pollunder's house and his uncle's 'best friend'. On the envelope is written : 'To Karl Rossmann, to be delivered personally at midnight, wherever he may be found.' Inside it is a lengthy statement from his uncle announcing his decision to ban Karl from his house for ever and urging him not to contact him either by writing or through intermediaries. Why this sudden dismissal? The following sentence in the letter contains the answer :

I am essentially a man of principle. That is unpleasant and depressing not only to those who come in contact with me, but also to myself as well. Yet it is my principles that have made me what I am, and no one can ask me to deny my fundamental self (A, 91).

The Senator is a man of principle before he is an understanding uncle. His desire for love and union is no less strong than is his nephew's, but by treating a human relationship as if it were a matter of rational choice and not a matter of growth and gradual development he offends against a fundamental law of nature. Even so things would not have gone wrong had Mr Green strictly obeyed the instruction on the envelope. Karl's uncle had in fact left a loophole. He did not really expect the letter to be delivered. All the instructions said was that the letter had to be delivered at 'midnight', wherever its addressee might be found. They did not say that Karl was to be detained so that the letter could be conveniently delivered. As it happened Karl had wanted to leave at a quarter-past eleven but was kept on purpose in Pollunder's house by Green until midnight. Had he not been prevented from going the letter would never have reached him. As Karl himself does not fail to notice, Mr Green 'exceeded' his instructions. In doing so he cheated both Karl and his uncle out of an opportunity to establish a harmonious relationship. Green has grossly misused his function as an intermediary. And it is precisely here that Kafka's critique of modern society lies. Real power does not rest with the leaders at the top but with the go-betweens and intermediary devices created by the system. When Green delivers the fatal message he 'took on an almost absurd size'. It is the intermediary who decides the fate even of those in whose service they are. The Senator is thus a victim of his own elaborate system. Both he and Karl were mentally ready for the reunion; all that was between them was the physical distance between New York and Pollunder's house. But it is precisely in the hands of those who control our accidental circumstances that all powers of decision lie.

The Hotel Occidental

Having missed the big chance of his life, initiation into a new world by somebody who combines the advantages of being both a local power and a blood-relation, Karl is left on his own in the difficult task of coming to terms with reality. His experiences on the road to Ramses illustrate once more the differences between the old and the new worlds, and the need for some kind of compromise. In a shabby inn he meets up with Delamarche and Robinson, two rogues who immediately set about exploiting Karl's typically European sense of comradeship. We shall hear more of them later, when Karl is forced to live with them in the sinister commune they set up in a suburb of Ramses. The impressions Karl receives stand in marked contrast to what he has seen in his own country. On the road the traffic moves along as if controlled automatically and from a distance. When it comes to a halt, it does so 'as if governed by a single break'. There are no pedestrians, or market women straggling singly along the road towards town, as in Karl's country, but big lorries filled with people, perhaps market women after all or workers on their way to a factory. Outside town the very landscape lacks organic development. Isolated blocks of tenements are scattered at random instead of being part of any purposeful design. Life itself is chaotic here : 'on all the flimsy little balconies women and children were busy in numberless ways.' The agricultural environment consists of nothing but 'badly tilled fields clustered round big factories'. When the three travellers look back at New York, Brooklyn and Manhattan, everything seems to stand there 'empty and purposeless'. Everything is in such a mess that nothing in particular strikes the eye. A veil of anonymity hangs over everything, discouraging any contact between man and his environment. When the three indulge in 'a little open-air concert', the city at their feet, 'which was supposed to enjoy that melody so much, remained apparently indifferent'. Things always seem to happen mysteriously at a distance, never here and now. The motor-cars on the open road 'flew lightly past one another as they had done the whole day, as if a certain number of them were always being dispatched from some distant place and the same number were being awaited in another place equally distant. During the whole day since early morning Karl had seen not a single car stopping, not a single passenger getting out' (A, 110). The present is a kind of existential vacuum, which is only interrupted by some ghostly object now and then flitting through it.

The very essence of this soulless life is the Hotel Occidental, where Karl finds himself after a quarrel with his two companions. Having cheated him in all sorts of little ways they inflict the greatest suffering on Karl by opening his suitcase and stealing his parents' photograph. With this piece of yellow-stained paper the last visible evidence of his European past is lost. Very soon he will lose the whole suitcase, leaving him more naked and exposed than ever. In the meantime Karl's existence temporarily finds a secure anchor. With the help of the Hotel's master-cook, who also acts as a sort of manageress, he is able to exchange his 'freedom' ('nothing seemed more worthless') for the position of lift-boy. When he searches for food the friendly woman, an ex-Viennese, leads Karl straight to the store-room, explaining to him that the food in the buffet always loses its freshness in the smoke and all the steam. Though the customers seem to be satisfied, it is no more than 'prison fare'. Karl cannot help thinking that his two companions would probably never have reached this store-room, in spite of all their American experience, 'but would have had to be content with the stale food in the buffet'. Robinson and Delamarche are experts in their ways of coming to terms with the surface of existence, but they are unable to penetrate deeper. Karl is no more than a saintly fool in the face of external reality, but his instinct for discovering its inner essence is still strong. His cunning friends would certainly have managed to outwit all other guests in their fight for the stale food in the buffet, but they would have failed to strike up a personal acquaintance with one of the Hotel's influential figures and thus find a guide to the 'vaulted chamber' where the fresh food is kept. In a world of total anonymity this is a great achievement. Not even the lift-boys have ever seen with their own eyes 'either the dynamo in the cellar or the inner mechanism of the lift', though nothing would delight them more than that. Instead they have to satisfy themselves with the monotonous activity of simply pushing buttons and attending to the external mechanism of the lift.

Karl is determined to use his job to the best of his ability. Soon he is one of the most hard-working and reliable lift-boys. As a stranger he is motivated by the feeling that 'the others had gained a better start in life and that he must catch up on them by harder work and a little renunciation' (A, 139). So he neither complains about the absurd conditions in the Hotel nor worries too much about his personal needs, like getting enough sleep or odd moments of relaxation. What he does not realise is that, almost like Gregor Samsa, he is delivering his life into the hands of a system which is there for no other purpose than to get maximum efficiency out of its employees. People have to be cooled off like over-heated engines. When workers are relieved they stretch themselves and then pour water over their hot heads at wash-basins which stand ready for them. When somebody drops out because of exhaustion he is immediately replaced like the broken part of a machine. There is no privacy anywhere; one is always among everybody else. The lack of communication in this huge organisation is exemplified by the chaos at the Porters' Lodge : among those queueing up 'there was often a perfect babel of tongues, as if each were an emissary from a different country. There were always several making inquiries at the same time, while others again carried on a conversation with each other' (A, 180). The porters' answers are automatic reactions rather than clearly formulated information : 'Additionally confusing was the fact that one answer came so quickly on the heels of another as to be indistinguishable from it, so that often an inquirer went on listening intently, in the belief that his question was still being answered, without noticing for some time that his turn was past.' Guests also have to conform to the porters' methods of conveying information rather than expect them to conform to their personal needs : 'You had also to get used to the under-porter's habit of never asking a question to be repeated; even if it was vague only in wording and quite sensible on the whole, he merely gave an almost imperceptible shake of the head to indicate that he did not intend to answer that question and it was the questioner's business to recognise his own error and formulate the question more correctly.' Questions have to be put in a form recognisable to the computer-like brain of those who answer them. It is no use asking personal questions. And only such information can be provided as can be retrieved from the innumerable files and manuals on the shelves by specially allotted messenger boys.

Wherever life is given a chance to regulate itself, as in the dormitories, there is no danger of bureaucratic modes of behaviour coming into existence. The perpetual turmoil in the dormitories could indeed do with some attempt at bringing order into the chaos. But the individual habits of the lift-boys, who are allowed to do what they like in their communal room, are stronger than any rule, even when self-imposed. 'Although the majority agreed in principle that lights should be kept burning only at one end of the room during the night, it was impossible to enforce it' (A, 137). The boys, however exhausted they may be, have a strong desire to give free rein to their personal and social interests. Their social impulses manifest themselves in their playing at dice or cards, their sense of independence in their pipe-smoking. The boys may share the same room but the place where each bed stands remains a sanctuary of privacy. 'Each bed stood in its own smoke.' It is only the over-anxious Karl who is inclined to match the administrative rigmarole of the Hotel with his own ascetic tendencies. He has no pipe, and does not play cards or dice. He either tries to get enough sleep or fill his spare time by reading instructive books.

It would seem that Karl is a model lift-boy. He avoids all temptations which might distract him from doing his job to the utmost satisfaction of everybody. He even manages to stay clear of Therese, the manageress's secretary, who selects Karl as her confidant. At no cost will he allow himself to slip up as far as his job and hard-won reputation are concerned. So far does he push his perfectionism that it becomes an end in itself, a supreme defence-mechanism against external pressures. There is even the expectation of imminent fulfilment in his one-sided pursuits.

One morning, after four o'clock, and having just finished his work, Karl leans wearily against the balustrade beside his lift 'and gazed down into a lighted shaft surrounded by the windows of the store-room, behind which hanging masses of bananas gleamed faintly in the darkness' (A, 148)—a typically Kafkan image of elevated experience. But it is at exactly this moment of affirmation that Karl's dream of a sheltered existence is cruelly shattered. Somebody taps him on the shoulder from behind, as if waking him up. The man is not a guest as Karl instinctively expects, but Robinson. He has been sent by Delamarche to extract money from Karl. To make things worse, Robinson is dead drunk and has to be hidden by Karl in the dormitory to avoid a scandal. Not only is Robinson soon discovered but also Karl's failure to report his temporary absence from duty to the Head Waiter's office. Once suspicion has been aroused, there is no way of stopping the chain-reaction of accusations from all sides. The Head Waiter gives Karl the sack on the spot, whilst the Head Porter is determined to use the occasion for settling old scores. Karl has in the past offended against his dignity by not greeting him 'every time, every single time, without exception'. The Head Porter is a tall bulky man, 'whose splendid and richly-ornamented uniform . . . made him look still more broad-shouldered than he actually was'. His 'gleaming black moustache drawn out to two points in the Hungarian fashion' gives him a particularly sinister appearance. It is again a non-German, as in the stoker's case, who sits in judgment over a German and his way of life. The Slavonic and Eastern is in Kafka frequently a symbol of an archaic and primitive mentality, also of the addiction to conquering what others have achieved. Earlier on it was 'a little Slovak' who had 'cast melancholy glances at Karl's box' on the ship. As in Uncle Jacob's business, so too in the Hotel it is the lower ranks of the hierarchy in whose hands all real powers lie : 'As Head Porter I am in a sense placed over everyone, for

I'm in charge of all the doors of the hotel, this main door, the three middle and the ten side doors, not to mention innumerable little doors and doorless exits' (A, 184).

But Kafka's insights into modern economic conditions go further than this. If the technocratic efforts of modern society are supposed to transcend primitive conditions then the exact opposite has happened. The primitive has once more succeeded in infiltrating our apparently civilised and sophisticated structures. These structures are in fact no more than the contemporary manifestation of a prehistoric collective law of force, a throw-back to barbarity. Ultimately, they are merely a means, in the hands of a small group of people, for inflicting pain and suffering on everybody else. Before any rational attempt is made to establish whether Karl is guilty or innocent the Head Porter tortures him behind a black curtain by crushing and twisting his arm. When Therese tries to intervene, the Porter answers : 'Orders, little girl, orders.' And he affectionately pulls her to him with his free hand, 'while with the other he squeezed Karl with all his might, as if he not merely wished to hurt him, but had some particular and, so far, unfulfilled design upon the arm he was holding' (A, 168). This identity of violence and sexuality is foreshadowed in the novel by the attempt of Klara (Pollunder's daughter) to seduce Karl, a scene which degrades love to a sort of wrestling-match.

Even the sympathetic master-cook is powerless to help. As an ex-European she has taken a great liking to Karl. She particularly enjoys mentioning places to him she remembers, only to be told that they no longer exist. Her Europe is a world of the past which can at best be retained by the faint photographs she keeps on her desk. Though she knows in her heart that Karl is 'a fundamentally decent lad', she gives in to the Head Waiter's way of dealing with the case. It has already occurred to Karl that the cook is probably 'not quite so influential as he thought on the first evening'. But now he is convinced that the women, crumbling pillars of an almost divine kind of justice, have also come under the grip of the new forms of power, as is confirmed by the erotic scene Karl witnesses : 'he saw the Head Waiter surreptitiously seizing her hand and fondling it' (A, 178). We have already considered a parallel scene in *Metamorphosis*, when Gregor's mother rushes towards Herr Samsa loosing all her petticoats on the way.

Karl's mother too is a victim of brutal forces she cannot fight against. The photograph Karl had brought with him to America, and lost, showed a woman whose 'mouth was twisted as if she had been hurt and were forcing herself to smile' (A, 99). Karl's father on the other hand appeared as a lifeless and unreal character on the same photograph. It is he, and his moral code, who have been responsible for driving the son away from his mother and his fatherland.

A refuge?

From Karl's adventures so far we can easily deduce that he is the archetype of an 'innocent' character. For a man who never does anything himself the question of guilt simply does not arise. Everything happens *to* Karl, including his limited sexual experience. Helen Weinberg has written that 'in his innocence, his marginality, his insubstantiality of character, his random, free-floating adventures unguided by any principle of purpose, neither wishing nor needing to prove himself innocent, Karl becomes the hero of a rambling, picaresque story'.[12] This is certainly true though the statement is in need of qualification. The heroes of traditional picaresque novels are activists, not passive characters like Karl Rossmann. The picaresque hero, whose parental and social background normally fails him early in life, is thrown back completely on his own all-too-human resources. Unlike Karl he does not fail to recognise the presence and power of these resources. Instead of learning how to proceed and tackle life by a well-tried external code of conduct—such as is available to everybody who is part of a civilised society—he learns how to rely on himself. His imagination becomes the measure of all things, and an instrument for discovering the loop-holes in the social structure. In comparison with the mental agility of the picaresque hero, society is like a clumsy dinosaur whose weaknesses are quickly spotted, and manipulated. All aspects of a truly picaresque novel are therefore firmly orientated towards a criticism of society and human consciousness. Because the picaresque hero's imagination can conceive of a world in which stealing would be impossible he is inclined to think that it is not his but society's fault if he happens to be a thief. Picaresque novels specialise in pointing out the double-edged aspects of all our actions; they are powerful instruments of social and moral criticism, and quite generally demonstrate the eternal conflict between the human imagination and external systems and categorisations. The hero's pure and precise imagination not only gives him pride (sometimes arrogance) and self-respect but also a powerful sense of identity. If we apply all this to *America* then we cannot fail to see that the exact opposite is true for Kafka's fiction and his hero. Where the picaresque model is in evidence in the novel it is turned upside down. In Kafka it is always society, or some other authority with its motley collection of cunning schemers, which manipulates the individual. There is no way of shielding oneself against outside forces. Just as society cannot defend itself against the onslaught of a lively imagination, so the individual as a self-professed *tabula rasa* cannot prevent society from writing its own 'truth' (quite literally so in *The Penal Settlement*) on his back.

America has also frequently been called a 'Bildungsroman'. Admittedly, quite a few of the formal features of this time-honoured genre are present in Kafka's first novel. But again, the primary intention of the novel of education, to illustrate the growth of a well-integrated individual and the development of all his faculties, is reversed. As an 'innocent' character, to whom life is no more than a chain of rebirths, Karl Rossmann is incapable of growth. The novel burdened with a character of this type can no longer be an examination of the hero's potential for development but a kind of tribunal, an instrument for finding the vanishing point of his existence.

Karl is always on the run, not so much from himself (he has not really got a self) as from reality, in all its shapes and forms. The Sophoclean 'human kind cannot bear very much reality' (in Eliot's version) hardly applies to Karl. As an extreme case of inner withdrawal he cannot bear any reality at all. Where he apparently accepts the challenge the experience merely discloses his sublime egotism. His 'contacts' with the maid, his uncle, and the world of the Hotel Occidental do not lead anywhere but to incomplete visions of an unknown destiny.

Having escaped from the Hotel the eternal fugitive is once more 'rounded up'. Robinson has not only managed to bring back Karl's money but Karl himself. Characteristically enough the scene before Delamarche's flat turns into a kind of tribunal in the street. The unwilling Karl is to be a servant in the sinister household Delamarche has set up in the suburbs of Ramses. The job of breaking Karl's resistance is left to a policeman, who is naïve enough to interrogate the victim rather than those who abducted him. Karl's first instinct is to run away, to hide, to seek anonymity, and to escape all questioning. But it is above all the children who block his way, watching him like a trapped animal. The incident is reminiscent of similar ones in *The Trial* and clearly illustrates Kafka's view of existence as a trap, or a cage, rather than a playground for the free exercise of the human will. The policeman—his questions are no more than a matter of routine—is a strong man whose hair is however already turning white, as if he were no more than the representative of an old order which is on the way out. This impression is confirmed by the 'old woman' who observes the whole scene, and, again, by the children who are more interested in what Delamarche will have in store for Karl rather than in the mechanical interrogation conducted by the policeman. From the way the group behaves it can be seen that the real power is gradually shifting from the policeman to Delamarche, that is to say from an old power of a bureaucratic and reasonably benevolent kind to a new power of a more instinctive, undefined and sinister kind. When Karl decides to make a desperate bid for his freedom he is chased, in Chaplinesque fashion, by two policemen but caught by the clever Delamarche, who now offers him protection from the police. 'Da laufen die Herren' ('There go our fine friends'), Delamarche comments ironically on the passing policemen, whose feet ring 'in the empty street like the striking of steel against stone'. The police are no longer a guarantee of order, their actions are as impotent and hollow as the noise they produce. They will soon be swept away by the new anarchical powers gaining momentum in the narrow streets and back-yards of the suburb. When Karl says how tired the chase has made him, Delamarche answers: 'You had the whole street to career about in like a horse, but I had to double through these accursed passages and courtyards. It's a good thing that I'm a bit of a runner too. . . . A race with the police like this now and then is good practice' (A, 201). On their way back the two come across a weeping girl. 'I ran her down a minute ago,' Delamarche explains, laughing and flourishing his fist at her. In the coming power-struggle it will be the most innocent who will be trodden down first. The following passage ominously evokes the atmosphere of a pre-revolutionary situation :

The courtyards they threaded [*sic*] were also almost completely forsaken. An occasional porter pushed a two-wheeled hand-barrow before him, a postman was quietly making his round, an old man with a white moustache sat before a glass door smoking a pipe with his legs crossed, crates were being unloaded before a despatch agency while the idle horses imperturbably turned their heads from side to side and a man in overalls supervised the proceedings with a paper in his hand; behind the open window of an office a clerk, sitting at his desk, raised his head and looked thoughtfully out just as Karl and Delamarche went past (A, 201f.).

The emptiness of the scene—only the essential services are still functioning—reflects the general sense of imminent danger. In the meantime, the horses, Kafka's symbols of the will to power, stand idle. The administrators simply wait and see whom they will have to serve next.

Though Johann Bauer, in his investigations of relevant documents from the civil and police archives in Prague, has come to the conclusion that Kafka's assumed relations, before the First World War, with the numerous anarchistic and anti-militaristic groups in Prague are probably founded on myth, this does not mean that he was not a witness of the many political factions struggling for power in his native city or even an occasional, unobtrusive participant in their meetings. Young intellectuals were particularly attracted by the activities of the 'Young People's Club', which was a centre of anarchist youth in Prague. In the early years of its existence its members were mainly Czech socialists, but before long the anarchists gained the upper hand. Johann Bauer has described in detail the various activities of the club, particularly the lectures which were organised between about 1903 and 1910 and many of which were broken up by the police. The anarchist Vohryzek lectured on Max Stirner (1902) and on socialism (1907); Michal Kácha, an anarchist and acquaintance of Kafka's, on Kropotkin (1905) and anarchist morality (1908); and Jaroslav Hasek, later to become the author of *The Good Soldier Schweik*, on political economy (1907). The official reports describe the club at this time as 'a society most of whose members belong to the National Socialist party, and which sets out to make young people acquainted with anarchist theories'.[13] And the police regarded the club as the 'Prague anarchist headquarters'. Whatever Kafka's relations to the 'Young People's Club' and similar societies were, he could hardly have failed to take notice of its widely publicised activities. The character of Delamarche is in fact, together with Musil's Reiting (*Törless*), one of the most memorable anarchistic figures in the literature of the period. His brutal tactics, his charismatic personality, and, last but not least, his deceptive charm are all typical features of the new-style demagogue. Since the most celebrated anarchists in Kafka's time were French and Spanish ones, it is only appropriate that Delamarche should have a French name. Like most street politicians he even has a kind of body-guard or servant, a thug with a 'half-eaten nose'.

His faithful companion, the Irishman Robinson, is the exact opposite of Delamarche. He is a dreamer who either longs for his native country or wants to go hunting for gold in California. He is easily possessed by sentimental moods, is frequently drunk, and never properly awake. It is he whose nose gets bloodied whenever Delamarche plays one of his dubious tricks, like snatching Karl away from the Hotel. As a totally spineless and submissive character he is the ideal associate for his scheming friend. In some ways Robinson is comparable to Reiting's companion in Musil's story, Beineberg, though he has none of the latter's imaginative powers. Having no dream of his own, Robinson is made to suffer the nightmarish reality Delamarche has created for all of them.

One day, when searching for a flat, Robinson and Delamarche meet Brunelda, a former singer who has left her weak bourgeois husband because of his almost masochistic devotion to her. She is immediately attracted to Delamarche when she sees him slapping Robinson's face, and decides to live with him. They set themselves up in a luxuriously decorated flat, creating a dense atmosphere of wealth, sex and stupefying whimsicality around them. Robinson becomes the couple's obedient servant and is treated no better than a dog. Karl is also forced to join them in their flat and ordered to help the already exhausted and ill Robinson. The Brunelda chapter is too incomplete to allow the reader to come to any definite conclusions about Kafka's intentions. Emrich has interpreted the Delamarche-Brunelda relationship as a critique of the hidden forces at work in society and of the way these forces pervert individual feelings and emotions:

Because love is here no more than a master-servant relationship, based on pure possession, she must demand to be subjugated by a man who has emerged from the depths, who is characterised by brute force but over whom she at the same time can exert control by means of her wealth and whom she makes sexually dependent on her. However much relations between them may be reversed, it is always a case of mutual possession and subjugation. Her humiliation in front of Delamarche is another form of domination. Delamarche's physical supremacy is at the same time financial and sexual bondage and enslavement. Thus both are fettered to one another in an endless mutual torment and perversion of all feeling. Wealth or poverty, in both spheres the unchanging struggles for power are enacted.[14]

Politzer on the other hand sees in Brunelda's domicile the expression of a natural order as opposed to the restricted and prison-like world outside:

Surrounded by men, Brunelda makes up for her rank flesh, which she cherishes and protects, bathes and scents, nourishes and dresses. She is a relic of tropical primitivity surrounded by the depraved civilisation of a slum street. Neither good nor bad, always eager to sate her never-diminishing appetites, she is reminiscent of Molly Bloom, who, while falling asleep, says yes to the murderously virile world of James Joyce's *Ulysses*.[15]

It is Brunelda's function to awake Karl finally from his Sleeping Beauty existence, to introduce him to the 'reality of human relationships in their grossest and most grotesque form'. Brunelda is to do what Johanna Brummer, and the other women in his life, have failed to do, turn him into a natural man who says 'yes' to himself and existence in general. Kafka's text however makes quite clear that Emrich's and Politzer's readings by no means exclude each other. What we get in the Brunelda chapter is a combination of social criticism and the sketching of some primitive order. As so often in Kafka, perhaps most clearly in *The Penal Settlement*, critical and mythopœic intentions are kept in perfect balance. The resulting ambiguity is not merely a characteristic feature of Kafka's narrative method but expresses a genuine political dilemma. One of Delamarche's neighbours is a student who works by day and studies by night, keeping himself alive by drinking strong black coffee. In his conversations with Karl he calls himself an 'enemy' of Delamarche but at the same time tells him to accept the queer circumstances in Delamarche's flat.

'So you advise me to stay with Delamarche?' asked Karl. 'Absolutely,' said the student, whose head was already bent over his book. It was as if not he but someone else had said the word; it echoed in Karl's ears as if it had been uttered by a voice more hollow than the student's (A, 244).

The student, as so many European intellectuals between the Wars, is both a critic and a prophet of the powers to come. As far as Karl is concerned he is pleased that once more somebody else has decided matters for him. He can now retreat into his old conformist dream of finding a job which will absorb him completely. His 'political opportunism' expresses itself in the thought that 'his prospects of finding a post in which he could achieve something, and be appreciated for his achievement, would be greater if he accepted the servant's place with Delamarche for the time being and from that secure position watched for a favourable opportunity'. The greatest satisfaction his 'bourgeois' imagination can hold out to him is regular office work.

Once he got such a post in an office, he would concentrate his mind on his office work. . . . He would think only of the interests of the firm he had to serve, and undertake any work that offered, even work which the other clerks rejected as beneath them. Good intentions thronged into his head, as if his future employer were standing before the couch and could read them from his face (A, 245).

This is certainly one way of escaping the 'bad dreams' by which Brunelda, for example, is constantly troubled. But there is a price to be paid for such radical self-abnegation. What this price is we know already. It is explored in *Metamorphosis*, the story of a man who has actually done what Karl is merely dreaming of.

The Nature Theatre of Oklahoma

Twentieth-century German novelists have frequently said that one of their most difficult problems is how to end their novels.

One of the reasons for this is probably that the German novel has never known a tradition of what one might call 'natural' endings, that is to say, endings which grow organically out of the plot and thematic structure of the work and are relatively free from contamination with existing models or the influence of a commanding 'sense of an ending'. Before Kafka himself showed a different way the German novel normally conformed to three types of 'fictions of the End' (Kermode): utopia, apocalypse and revelation (a kind of apotheosis of bourgeois existence). More recently, and under the pressure of political events, novelists have become suspicious of all three of them. But in Kafka's time they were powerful ingredients not only of fiction proper but of the current ideologies as well. Utopia and apocalypse in particular were successfully revived by German Expressionism and imbued with existential relevance. It is therefore not surprising that Kafka too should have succumbed, at least once, to the temptation of finishing a work of his with the help of one of the existing models.

The last chapter of *America* is a utopian ending to an essentially non-utopian novel. In this respect Kafka's choice was an unfortunate one. On the other hand the hero of Kafka's first novel consistently betrays states of mind which have more in common with utopian visions of life than realistic quests for personal identity. Karl Rossmann's 'inner-directed' mind prevents him from creating a satisfactory balance between the demands of his own life and the buffetings of his external environment. That is to say he cannot reconcile outward appearances and events with his deeply ingrained inwardness. Let us look at the problem with the help of David Riesman's definition of 'inner-direction': 'the source of direction for the individual is "inner" in the sense that it is implanted early in life by the elders and directed towards generalised but nonetheless inescapably destined goals'.[16] The source of direction in Karl's case is a code of highly general values which was transmitted to him through association with his teachers and parents. The particular parental and educational backgrounds Karl inherits breed a strong sense of conformity in him rather than individuality of character. Since he is cut off prematurely from his background, and left with no chance to develop an individuality of his own, the circumstances of his European milieu not only act as a source of direction ('implanted

94

early in life') but also become his 'destined goals'. What he remembers in America at crucial moments of his new life is a set of gestures, words and actions he observed or heard earlier on, as for example the characteristic sayings and behaviour-pattern of his classics teacher. Instead of committing himself to the business of coming to terms with his American experience, he develops a habit of contrasting the new with the old until his search for the past becomes the distinctive goal of his life. In the absence of any other acquired ways of responding to reality his conformist instincts establish themselves as the dominant motives of all his actions. They even induce in him the kind of self-righteous dreams which are said to be typical of fourteen-year-olds. When he defends the stoker against his accusers, and thinks he is doing a splendid job, he wishes that his parents could witness the proceedings :

If only his father and mother could see him now, fighting for justice in a strange land before men of authority, and, though not yet triumphant, dauntlessly resolved to win the final victory! Would they revise their opinion of him? Set him between them and praise him? Look into his eyes at last, at last, those eyes so filled with devotion to them? (A, 30).

These sentiments not only betray his need and respect for a justice beyond man-made laws but also a craving to have his 'good' actions acknowledged by those nearest to him. In this respect Karl Rossmann is a true brother of Dickensian innocents, like David Copperfield and Oliver Twist. He is the product of an ethics which has declared obedience, devotion and poverty as functions of inwardness.

So it is not surprising after all that Karl's 'utopian' state of mind should bring him to a place which is more unreal than anything else he has encountered so far. The Nature Theatre of Oklahoma is a vast company which admits everybody who applies for membership. On a huge poster Karl reads with his own eyes what he would never have thought possible : 'Everybody is welcome! . . . But hurry, so that you get in before midnight! At twelve o'clock the doors will be shut and never opened again! . . . Up, and to Clayton!' (A, 246). The Cinderella-motif once more expresses the urgency of the decision. But this time Karl is ready to make the choice. And there can't be any snags.

The poster unambiguously says that everybody is welcome, including Karl. When he arrives at Clayton he is welcomed by the noise of many trumpets. The trumpeters are all women who, mounted on pedestals and covered in long robes, blow their instruments 'regardless of each other'. Are they angels (as their wings might indicate) or dead souls (as the dreadful noise they produce and the flowing draperies of their robes also suggest)? Whoever they are, their 'music' appears to confirm the fact that Karl has come to a place where everybody can express himself as he likes. Moreover, the Theatre's admissions officers seem to be more interested in what their enthusiastic applicants tell them about themselves rather than in the objective truth. When Karl says his name is 'Negro', the name Negro is immediately entered on his form. When he says he is an engineer he is taken straight to the 'bureau for technicians'. The Theatre seems to accept as truth what individuals themselves claim it to be and not what is stated on official documents and certificates. But it is relentless in its task of discovering an applicant's real identity. When it turns out that Karl merely intended to become an engineer he is asked to try again. There is no bureau for 'intending' technicians. But there is one for 'intermediate pupils', a bureau which appears to be the proper quarter for Karl's existential problem. Again, he has to be more precise. Since Karl attended a European intermediate school he is referred to the 'bureau for European intermediate pupils' (Bureau für Europäische Mittelschüler). This is an acknowledgement of the fact that Karl's real identity is that of a European intermediate pupil, a state of affairs which his American experience has done nothing to change. It is proven to Karl that his end lies in his beginning. Even the man who now questions him closely resembles a teacher in the school at home : 'the spectacles resting on the man's broad nose, the fair beard as carefully tended as a prize exhibit, the slightly rounded back and the unexpectedly loud abrupt voice held Karl in amazement for some time' (A, 256). This is less a description than a string of metaphors for characteristic attitudes European schoolmasters have adopted towards the acquisition and administration of knowledge. Reality is never seen directly but as if through 'spectacles'; truth is not discovered by processes of reason but wells up from inside, communicating itself in abrupt and unexpected outbursts; if the beard of a 'professor' (as schoolteachers are still called in some European countries) is a sure sign of wisdom and intellectual pride then the 'slightly rounded back' expresses respect and reverence for knowledge.

In being not only reminded of but brought face to face with all this Karl has come full circle. His search for the future has ended where it began, in the confines and vague perspectives of an outmoded past. Karl has indeed reached the vanishing point of his existence. The novel's last paragraph describes the journey to Clayton, with the Tieckian landscape the gay travellers are passing through ominously pointing to the final destiny of our innocent hero :

The first day they travelled through a high range of mountains. Masses of blue-black rock rose in sheer wedges to the railway line; even craning one's neck out of the window, one could not see their summits; narrow, gloomy, jagged valleys opened out and one tried to follow with a pointing finger the direction in which they lost themselves; broad mountain streams appeared, rolling in great waves down on to the foot-hills and drawing with them a thousand foaming wavelets, plunging underneath the bridges over which the train rushed; and they were so near that the breath of coldness rising from them chilled the skin of one's face.

Karl's search for a lost Paradise has brought him to a land of death. This is confirmed by Kafka's own pessimistic interpretation of the end of the novel: 'Rossmann and K., the innocent and the guilty, both executed without distinction in the end, the guiltless one with a gentler hand, more pushed aside than struck down (D2, 132).

Despite its title, *America* is a novel about Europe. The uncle's steel house, the technical hocus-pocus of his business, and the ghostly cars moving through empty space have more to do with the futuristic Europe imagined by many writers and artists of the day than with American realities. The landscape too is recognisably European and bears no similarity with the scenery round New York. It might be argued that the last chapter was inspired by the utopian visions offered by the many sects and religious societies which, to the amusement of a more orthodoxically-minded Europe, have always flourished in America.[17] But the stylised world of the 'Nature Theatre of Oklahoma' is much more readily explained by certain Baroque conceptions of life and the influential 'Good Society' myths of the European intellectual tradition. The peculiarity of Kafka's utopia is that it is a 'journey into the interior' (Heller), a search for the purer roots of a fast-changing Europe. Kafka's America is an image of the drab Europe to come, his innocent hero, like Thomas Mann's Hans Castorp, the symbol of a fatal withdrawal into the Self. The reality thus reached is fixed, sterile, a synonym for death. *America* presents Kafka's ambiguous critique of a static apprehension of reality.

5
The Trial

Tribunal in the Hotel

On August 13, 1912, in Max Brod's house, Kafka met Felice
Bauer, a confidential clerk working for an electrical firm in
Berlin. By the end of 1917 Kafka had twice become engaged to
her, each time breaking off the engagement very shortly afterwards, and left a record of love which Erich Heller in his preface
to the edition of Kafka's letters to Felice has called the songs of
a twentieth-century troubadour. As late as 1922 Kafka writes in
his diary that he had never known the words 'I love you', 'only
the expectant stillness that should have been broken by my "I
love you" ' (D2, 221). The diary entries for 1914 reveal that his
wooing of Felice had taken on the dimensions of an uncanny
quest, not for Felice but for the demon of literary self-justification.
However much 'the expectant stillness' was like waiting for a
ghost, it remained the cherished pre-condition of Kafka's
dialectical acrobatics when attempting to remove, for the sake
of Felice, the discordances ('the lies') between the spiritual and
sensual world, but in the same breath to dramatise these very
discordances for the sake of literature. Logically enough, the
quest had to be conducted ultimately on the level of pure fiction.
Almost immediately after Kafka had broken off his first engagement to Felice, on July 12, 1914, the first prolegomena to *The
Trial* make their appearance in the diary. It is not surprising that
the book, in the course of its composition, mostly during the
second half of 1914, turned into the most elaborate penal fantasy
Kafka was to write. The following pages are devoted to an
analysis of the type of experience, real and fictional, out of which
The Trial grew.

Before Kafka meets Felice for the second time in Berlin (March
23, 1913), they are already on intimate terms as correspondents.
The early letters to the woman who meant most to him are a
written crescendo of self-induced passion. Starting off the
correspondence by using the formal address 'Sehr geehrtes
Fräulein' (September 20, 1912), and variations like 'Verehrtes

Fräulein', 'Gnädiges Fräulein', Kafka soon changes to the less formal 'Liebes Fräulein Felice' (November 1, 1912), intensifying the formula to 'Liebes Fräulein' (November 9, 1912) and 'Liebste, Liebste', until two days later he switches from the formal 'Sie' to the informal and intimate 'Du' half-way through one of the three letters he wrote on that day. In a letter written between the 10th and 16th of June, 1913, he asks Felice to marry him, after having told her many times before that his total commitment to literature will exclude him from ever becoming a married man or a father. Worse than that, Kafka often implores Felice not to write to him any more, or only once a week, because it will be his fate to be 'for ever tied to himself' (November 11, 1912). At the same time he begs her to write to him as often as possible, particularly when distressed by Felice's frequent silences. The story behind the Kafka–Felice correspondence is a story of passionately enacted and equally passionately terminated, and re-enacted, promises of love. When the two actually meet, they never stay together for very long, nor is there very much they can say to each other. [Since Felice's letters to Kafka have not survived we can only deduce from Kafka's own letters, particularly from those in which he analyses the results of their meetings, what Felice's general attitude to her impetuously evasive lover was. There can be no doubt that Felice was an uncomplicated and practically-minded person, who had all the qualities, and the courage, necessary for a successful professional and social life, but who showed little understanding for Kafka's literary ambitions or for the way he conducted the practical and not so practical aspects of their relationship. It is therefore surprising that Felice ever allowed herself to become engaged to Kafka in the first place.

At the beginning of January, 1914, Kafka asks Felice for the second time to become his wife, again putting the question not in person but in a letter. Felice is evasive, and at a meeting in Berlin at the end of February she voices her serious reservations about a marriage with him. Kafka is profoundly disturbed, and in high-pitched letters (which he himself calls 'a whining and baring of teeth') he tries to convince her that his love for her has changed him : 'do try to see what I am, and what I have become through my love for you' (March 17, 1914). Indeed, who *had* he become? The letters Kafka wrote at the time are the gestures of a weaker animal submitting to a stronger one,[1] gestures which also permeate *The Trial* with the persistence of a Wagnerian leitmotif. When Felice asks for a precise answer with regard to Kafka's feelings for her, he replies:

The exact information you want about me, dearest F., I cannot give you; I can give it you, if at all, only when running along behind you in the Tiergarten, you always on the point of vanishing altogether, and I on the point of prostrating myself; only when thus humiliated, more deeply than any dog, am I able to do it (March 25, 1914).

As at the end of *The Trial* the ultimate answer can only be given in terms of a total submission to what has become the final point of support to cling on to. This utmost humiliation is not, however, the supreme sacrifice in a battle of love but the climax of a chain of highly egocentric actions; like the Prince of Homburg's reflections in the face of death (we know that he will not die), it is the imaginary bonfire of the mortal self ignited on paper and for the purpose of 'burning without ashes' (cf. letter to Grete Bloch, April 29, 1914), so that the phoenix of literature can rise once more and, as the same letter shows, simultaneously with the imaginary sacrifice of the self. As Erich Heller has pointed out, *The Trial* contains an echo of another passage from the letter of March 25: 'I have quite definitely reached a dead end. I am not likely ever to forget that it was you who made me realise this.' On the way to his execution Joseph K. once more meets Fräulein Bürstner, or somebody closely resembling her. (In the manuscript Kafka always uses the abbreviation F.B., which are also Felice Bauer's initials). When his two grim companions suffer him to lead the way he 'follows the direction taken by the Fräulein ahead of him, not that he wanted to overtake her or to keep her in sight as long as possible, but only that he might not forget the lesson she had brought into his mind' (T, 247). The same letter also contains the following, tragically self-deceptive, passage:

When you pose that question now [whether he is certain of his love for Felice] I can only say: I love you, F., to the limits of my strength, in this respect you can trust me entirely. But for the rest, F., I do not know myself completely. Surprises and disappointments about myself follow each other in endless succession. What I hope is that those surprises and disappointments will be mine alone; I shall use all my strength to see that none but the pleasant, the pleasantest

101

surprises of my nature will touch you; I can vouch for this, but what I cannot vouch for is that I shall always succeed.

And he invites Felice: 'judge me by my letters and not by your personal experience.' Again the beloved is referred to the cause of her most urgent troubles: the dangerous and nebulous territory of Kafka's continuous self-analysis, where the borderlines between reality and high-flown fiction are thin indeed. If ever there was a vicious circle, this is it.

The letters to Felice are far more impressive as documents of Kafka's quest for a life totally committed to literature than as documents of a love-relationship. Throughout 1912 and 1913 Kafka had imprinted on Felice's mind that all that mattered to him was his writings: 'But when I didn't write, I was at once flat on the floor, fit for the dustbin' (November 1, 1912), like the dead insect in *Metamorphosis*, or, as Kafka put it more aggressively on August 14, 1913, 'I have no literary interests, but am made of literature, I am nothing else, and cannot be anything else'. Indeed 'in matters concerning the realm of the ideal he cannot take a joke', as Max Brod explained to Felice in a letter about his friend. The words 'I love you', as they occur in the ambiguous context of the letter of March 25, 1914, do not signify a plain confession of love but a contrived interruption of that 'expectant stillness' which Kafka admitted to have experienced throughout his life, but most extensively during 1914, and which was tending towards spiritual matters rather than involvement with worldly ones. 'Nothing but anticipation,' he enters in his diary on March 15 of that year.

Had Kafka met the wrong woman in Felice? The answer is no. The pattern was to repeat itself, though in a less acute form, in the course of the few relationships Kafka had with other women after Felice. A more 'intellectual' type of woman than Felice would in fact never have been able to provide him with the kind of challenge he needed in order to define for himself the mental and physical preconditions of his writing. As writers concerned with less intimate matters than Kafka frequently need a profound clash with the social order they live under, Kafka needed a similar clash on a personal level. As it happened, Felice became the splinter in his mind round which the spiritual battle for an absolute world raged.

Kafka once explained to Grete Bloch that he knew in Felice four different, mutually exclusive, persons : (1) the girl he had met in Prague, (2) the girl who corresponded with him, (3) the girl he kept visiting in Berlin, and (4) the girl who knew other people (letter of November 10, 1913). But there was a fifth Felice : the one Kafka had selected to become the living challenge, the opposing principle, to his own spiritual and determinedly ascetic endeavours which found expression in his writing. A tender but also rather clinical letter written after the upsetting events narrated below makes the point provocatively :

You see, you were not only the greatest friend, but at the same time the greatest enemy, of my work, at least from the point of view of my work. Thus, though fundamentally it loved you beyond measure, equally it had to resist you with all its might for the sake of self-preservation. It had to do so in every single detail. I thought of it, for instance, when having a meal one evening with your sister consisting almost exclusively of meat. Had you been there, I would probably have ordered almonds.

And to Max Brod and Felix Weltsch Kafka had written at the end of July :

I have renounced the apparent peculiarity which the engagement instilled in me, eat almost nothing but meat, so that I feel sick, and after a bad night with my mouth gaping open my abused and chastised body feels like someone else's mess in my bed.

Though Kafka was familiar with nineteenth-century ways of dramatising the conflict between the real and the ideal world he had no sense of the possible reconciliation of the two. Instead they became two opposing forces, with their own demands and self-assertive powers. Any battle between the two had to end in a draw, because of a lack of adequate equipment on either side, with the individual who had provoked the fight being doomed to become the vanishing point between the two forces. But these are insights which will come to Kafka only in the course of writing *The Trial*, and after himself engineering a deadly combat between the two sides. He stubbornly imagines himself to be fatally caught up in the claws of the spiritual (exemplified by his writing), with the right to force a sign from heaven, and Felice, 'the gay, healthy, self-assured girl', to be a living example of the world he is prepared to accept as both a judge over his 'inner dream-life' and as a power to be for ever challenged. This is reflected in Kafka's paradoxical urge, fully documented in the letters, not only to humiliate himself before Felice but also to take away the very ground from under her feet. Felice is an object of both love and hatred, and he invites her to view him in the same way.

By the end of February, 1914, Kafka had arrived at a situation which he had predicted almost a year earlier : 'I can't live without her, nor with her either' (May 12/13, 1913).[2] But the deadlock had to be resolved in one way or another. At Easter Kafka travelled to Berlin to become unofficially engaged to Felice. The marriage was planned for September. At Whitsun the Kafkas joined the Bauers in Berlin to celebrate the engagement officially. Anybody who follows the letters to Felice closely will not be surprised to learn that the engagement did not last for very long. On July 2, Kafka decided to discuss the matter once more in Berlin. In the Askanischer Hof (where Kafka used to stay during his visits to Berlin), and in the presence of Felice's sister Erna, her friend Grete Bloch and the writer Ernst Weiss, the engagement was terminated. Afterwards Kafka referred to the discussion in the Askanischer Hof as the 'Gerichtshof im Hotel' ('The Tribunal in the Hotel'), or 'Ansprache vom Richtplatz' ('Speech from the Gallows').

During the crucial period between January and July, 1914 Kafka was writing letters not only to Felice but also and more feverishly to a friend of Felice's, Grete Bloch, who had visited Kafka in Prague at the end of October, 1914, in order to mediate between Kafka and Felice in the matter of their rather strained relationship at the time. But things did not end there. Kafka began a correspondence with Grete Bloch which lasted only for about a year but which in its candid references to Felice and Kafka's mental state forms an integral part of the Felice correspondence. Kafka in fact revealed more about himself and the complex recesses of his mind to Grete Bloch than he did to Felice. The more 'practical' things became with Felice, the more he contemplated his future existence as a fiancé, and indeed husband, of 'the girl in Berlin', the more Kafka was in need of a sympathetic confidante, who could understand his predicament fully and from the outside. At the same time the new acquaintance provided him with the opportunity of starting once more 'from the beginning'. The letters to the two women stand in a contrapuntal relationship to each other. Whilst the letters to Felice are comparable to a symbolic theme that is about to exhaust itself, the letters to Grete Bloch blossom forth like a new musical motif. Kafka himself was aware of this and diagnosed his case as one of acute hypochondria and neurasthenia. He quickly sensed the danger of absurdly complicating his involvement with Felice, and of distorting and falsifying the issue in an orgy of self-deception. In a letter to his sister Ottla (July 10, 1914) Kafka described the blind alley his mind had become in the process of multiplying the channels by which he sought to release himself from his mental agony: 'I write differently from the way I speak, I speak differently from the way I think, I think differently from the way I should think—and so it goes on into the darkest depths of infinity.' No wonder that he imagined himself to be caught in an indestructible cobweb of guilt, and his self-styled intellectual life to be one big lie. These are also themes round which a major discussion will evolve in *The Trial*. In the meantime Kafka allowed himself both unwittingly and knowingly the luxury of conducting a kind of emotional 'Parallelaktion' to the mere 'wedding preparations' his correspondence with Felice was rapidly turning into.

Kafka's letters to Grete Bloch read like an unfinished love-poem. They also bring to the surface the almost feminine empathy of which their author was capable, in addition to his normal icy ritual of self-withdrawal. They not only provide a running commentary on the progress of his relationship with Felice, but are self-contained in their spring-like charm, which stands in tragic contrast to the autumnal remnants Felice received at the same time. But above all they reflect the extraordinarily adventurous quality of Kafka's imagination, when, at the age of thirty-one, he pictures a life which could contain both Felice and Grete Bloch. Kafka often invites his 'liebes Fräulein' to meet him somewhere, in Berlin, Dresden, or Prague. On one occasion he plans a meeting with her in the border-town of Gmünd. Felice is asked whether she would like 'to come to Gmünd for a day', but Grete Bloch is not mentioned. Even after his engagement to Felice Kafka assures Grete Bloch that nothing has changed between them: 'My engagement or my marriage won't change anything in our relationship, which contains for me at least splendid and indispensable possibilities.' 'Is this a fact, and will it remain so?' he asks anxiously. And he makes clear to her that this has nothing to do with what both Felice and Kafka owe to her for mediating between them: 'I repeat, in case it hasn't been made clear already: All this is independent of anything that I and F. (so far as I, the bridegroom, can say this) owe to you in our affairs' (April 14, 1914). On May 8 he enthusiastically suggests that she should come and live with the newly-wed couple, once they found a flat:

. . . we have decided—and on no account must you resist—that once we are married you are to come and live with us for some time (and from the very beginning; since you have no vacation now, you will get it this winter). If I take the apartment I mentioned in my last letter, we would have plenty of room. We shall lead a pleasant life and, in order to test me, you shall hold my hand and I, in order to thank you, must be allowed to hold yours.

When dreams of a honeymoon would have been more appropriate, Kafka puts the clock back and dreams of first moments of love; the holding of hands. And how does this desire for a joint life between the married couple and Grete Bloch tie up with Kafka's distaste for having to deal with more than one person at a time, a distaste which even makes him allergic to postcards signed by two people? It is to Grete Bloch herself that Kafka makes this point vividly enough:

You made a remark recently about jointly written postcards. I thought about it. You are wrong, and right. I am delighted with everything I get from Berlin, but unknown to myself I suppose there must also be a desire to have each one separately rather than together; I love the individual, not so the community (July 1, 1914).

These are the kind of contradictions and hopeless gestures which permeate the correspondence with the two women, and with which Joseph K. will relentlessly fill his head in his self-destructive mood. Kafka and his K.s live in a world they do not really wish to accept, and therefore do not wish to understand. Instead they create a world in their heads, full of contradictions and indecisions, which are then projected back on to the other world, with the explicit purpose of undermining it. It is all done in the name of some other, undefined powers, which are provoked into revealing themselves. The plot against the world was not really meant to succeed (Kafka said in fact once: 'In the duel between yourself and the world, act as the world's second!') and when he finally reviewed the unique protest his life had become, he did so under the image of the 'trial'. Grete Bloch was one of the first to be seen in the light of a 'judge', towering over the accused in the Askanischer Hof. But, Kafka adds, 'it only looked that way, in reality I sat in your place and haven't left it to this day'. Kafka wrote this to Grete Bloch (October 15, 1914) when work on *The Trial*, the unique penal fantasy in which judge and accused are one, was in full progress.

'Ascensio' by writing

Kafka's diary was another means by which he succeeded in giving some shape to the imagined blankness of his life, a shape which was manageable at least from a literary point of view. On the whole the entries for 1914 record and analyse once more what he puts into his letters but they also set out, with increasing ingenuity, to detect and trap the literary possibilities of his dog-like existence. The passage quoted on page 102 is an example of Kafka's attempts to transform the material of his life into literature and to get 'a kind of inkling of the way a life like this is constituted' (October 15, 1914). And there are many similar passages in the diaries. Of greatest interest are the ones where Kafka intimates the metaphysical directions in which his rigorously ascetic life is pointing. However Kafkaesque otherwise, they are 'Steigerungen' in the Goethean sense. Here is a typical passage:

I make plans. I stare rigidly ahead lest my eyes lose the imaginary peepholes of the imaginary kaleidoscope into which I am looking. I mix noble and selfish intentions in confusion; the colour of the noble ones is washed away, in recompense passing off onto the merely selfish ones. I invite heaven and earth to take part in my schemes, at the same time I am careful not to forget the insignificant little people one can draw out of every side street and who for the time being are more useful to my schemes. It is of course only the beginning. But as I stand here in my misery, already the huge wagon of my schemes comes driving up behind me, I feel underfoot the first small step up, naked girls, like those on the carnival floats of happier countries, lead me backward up the steps; I float because the girls float, and raise my hand to command silence.

Rosebushes stand at my side, incense burns, laurel wreaths are let down, flowers are strewn before and over me; trumpeters, as if hewn out of stone, blow fanfares, throngs of little people come running up, in ranks behind leaders; the bright, empty open squares become dark, tempestuous and crowded; I feel myself at the farthest verge of human endeavour, and, high up where I am, with suddenly acquired skill spontaneously execute a trick I had admired in a contortionist years ago—I bend slowly backward (at that very moment the heavens strain to open to disclose a vision to me, but then stop), draw my head and trunk through my legs and gradually stand erect again. Was this the ultimate given to mankind? It would seem so, for already I see the small horned devils leaping out of all the gates of the land, which lies broad and deep beneath me, overrunning the countryside; everything gives way in the centre under their feet, their little tails expunge everything, fifty devils' tails are already scouring my face; the ground begins to yield, first one of my feet sinks in and then the other; the screams of the girls pursue me into the depths into which I plummet, down a shaft precisely the width of my body but infinitely deep. This infinity tempts one to no extraordinary accomplishments, anything that I should do would be insignificant; I fall insensibly and that is best (May 29, 1914).

This little allegory of a frustrated assault upon the heavens anticipates the general scheme of *The Trial*; the attempts on the part of K. to provoke, with all the cunning manœuvres of a game of chess, the invisible powers to reveal themselves. *The Trial* will also demonstrate that it is equally impossible for the heavens to establish contact with the human sphere and that there is therefore corresponding frustration on both sides. The passage quoted concentrates on the absurdity of the plans, involving everything and everybody, whereby the encounter is attempted, and the extravagant pomposity with which the approach is staged, as if the protagonist had exhausted his patience and decided to storm the heavens by an act of supreme art culminating in a gesture of self-humiliation and arrogant exhibitionism. Needless to say, the magic does not work and the bold assailant sinks into a hollow just big enough for his body. Kafka once wrote to Grete Bloch that 'everybody works his own way out of the underworld, I through writing' (June 6, 1914). But *ascensio* by writing was not an unambiguous ritual of self-redemption. Sometimes Kafka felt that literature was on the side of pure truth, more often, however, that it was a pure lie, like the priest's and Joseph K.'s attempts in *The Trial* to interpret the law. Writing was a snake-charming activity, an absurd and gratuitous stage-act, designed to support and enhance an equally absurd and gratuitous quest for salvation.

Often enough Kafka's spiritual quest was not so much a religious quest as an attempt to establish equality between man and the powers beyond. It was not always this, but the passage quoted is an allegorical summary of the more sinister aspects of an absolute quest. Between the traditional *via negativa* and *via positiva* Kafka had mapped out a third path : that of direct confrontation. In doing this he was interpreting Nietzsche's 'God is dead' in his own characteristic way. Unlike more shallow readers of Nietzsche Kafka realised that the cunning philosopher did not mean that God was literally dead—he often indicated that the exact opposite might be the case at some future time— but that the gulf between man and God had become so wide, and man's methods of seeking God so monstrous, that God was for all practical purposes dead. If so, God's and man's chances of coming together again were apparently equal. Moreover, the increasing distance between man and God was liable to raise legitimate doubts that God was probably as powerless to reach man as man was to reach God. Therein lies another reason for Kafka's strong sense of the equality of means on either side. Man and God may just be two different entities who have taken it into their heads to stretch out a helping hand to each other, but for some reason have failed to reach each other. *The Trial* certainly suggests that the Law's attempts to reach K. are just as farcical and still-born as K.'s to reach the Law. Whatever the theological implication of Kafka's extraordinary way of interpreting the curious predicament of both man and God, he had come up with a model which not only served him superbly in the business of understanding the 'noble and selfish intentions' of his life but which was also of supreme interest to French existential writers like Camus.

Another telling, though infinitely more subdued, example of Kafka's desire to meet 'eine ihm geltende Erscheinung' ('a vision disclosed specially to him') is the following one :

Toward evening I walked over to the window and sat down on the low sill. Then, for the first time not moving restlessly about, I happened calmly to glance into the interior of the room and at the ceiling. And finally, finally, unless I were mistaken, this room which I had so violently upset began to stir. The tremor began at the edges of the thinly plastered white ceiling. Little pieces of plaster broke off and with a distinct thud fell here and there, as if at random, to the floor. . . . It was meant for me, there was no doubt of that; a vision intended for my liberation was being prepared. . . . In the dim light, still at a great height, I had judged it badly, an angel in bluish-violet robes girt with gold cords sank slowly down great white silken-shining wings, the sword in its raised arm thrust out horizontally. 'An Angel, then!' I thought; 'it has been flying toward me all the day and in my disbelief I did not know it. Now it will speak to me.' I lowered my eyes. When I raised them again the angel was still there, it is true, hanging rather far off under the ceiling (which had closed again), but it was no living angel, only a painted wooden figurehead off the prow of some ship, one of the kind that hangs from the ceiling in sailors' taverns, nothing more.

The hilt of the sword was made in such a way as to hold candles and catch the dripping tallow. I had pulled the electric light down; I didn't want to remain in the dark, there was still one candle left, so I got up on a chair, stuck the candle into the hilt of the sword, lit it and then sat late into the night under the angel's faint flame (June 25, 1914).

It is a very Rilkean angel under whose wan light Kafka is conducting the business of his art. There are times when the angel is invited to be present, but at other times he is, as we have seen, repudiated with equal determination.

The more direct comments during 1914 on Kafka's mental and physical condition repeat very much the same complaint: insomnia, exhaustion, heart-trouble, acute sense of isolation, inability to write. He calls himself: 'Full of lies, hate and envy. Full of incompetence, stupidity, thickheadedness. Full of laziness, weakness and helplessness. Thirty-one years old' (August 6, 1914), all things he shares with Joseph K. 'I find the letter "K" offensive, almost disgusting, and yet I use it; it must be very characteristic of me', Kafka writes on May 27. Another typical passage reads: 'I am more and more unable to think, to observe, to determine the truth of things, to remember, to speak, to share an experience;

I am turning to stone, this is the truth' (July 28). His only true companion is his favourite sister Ottla : 'How the two of us, Ottla and I, explode in rage against every kind of human relationship' (June 19). Kafka had reached the bottom truly, but in another sense this meant that his creative powers were taking wing again. In a state of utter desolation, and dreaming of Felice 'as though of someone who was dead', Kafka began writing *The Trial* in August, finishing the essential chapters by the end of the year.

The arrest

When reading *The Trial* readers are normally puzzled by three questions : 'Who arrests K.?', 'Why is he arrested?' and 'What is the nature of this arrest?' It is little consolation to them to be told that K. himself does not appear to know, or that the absence of any narrative comment may suggest that knowing the answers may be as unimportant as knowing why Alice runs down a rabbit-hole. Fear of allegorical over-interpreting has prevented recent critics from attempting to explain literary *faits accomplis* of this kind and they have turned to other layers of the work in order to make sense of the novel. But there is a difference between unashamedly imposing allegorical meaning on literary events and determining the aesthetic reasons for and structural significance of such events. A clear understanding of the events described in the first chapter of *The Trial* is crucial for an understanding of the work as a whole. The following pages, then, are devoted to as close an analysis as possible of the plot and conversations of this chapter. This should provide a sound basis for unravelling at least in part what is one of the most labyrinthine books in the history of literature, a book not only pregnant with dire complexities but full of dead ends, contradictions and paths continuously doubling back on themselves.

Though an actual arrest appears to be made, its actuality is quickly undermined. Joseph K. *is* arrested, but this does not prevent him from following his normal routine. As the Inspector tells him : 'You are under arrest, certainly, but that need not hinder you from going about your business. You won't be hampered in carrying on in the ordinary course of your life' (T, 21). Moreover, his warders cannot even confirm that K. is charged with an offence, or rather do not know whether he is.

Instead he is advised to think less about his intruders or about what is going to happen to him, and more about himself. In the very first chapter a correlation is being established between Joseph K.'s state of consciousness and some enigmatic powers responding to it. In fact, 'our officials, as far as I know them', says one of the warders, '. . . never go hunting for crime in the populace, but, as the Law decrees, are drawn towards the guilty and must then send out us warders' (T, 12). Is Joseph K. then guilty? Concrete evidence of anything that could usefully be called 'guilt' is offered neither by Joseph K. nor his prosecutors. But as we shall see later, a particular human predicament, inviting the interference of some impersonal powers, is being evoked, and vaguely hinted at, by the ambiguous metaphor of 'guilt'. Let us first proceed with our present concern. The most pertinent comment on Joseph K.'s 'arrest' comes from Frau Grubach, Joseph K.'s landlady. Trying to seek consolation from a woman about the disagreeable happenings on his thirtieth birthday, Joseph K. receives the following answer:

As you've spoken so frankly to me, Herr K., I may as well admit to you that I listened for a little behind the door and that the two warders told me a few things too. It's a matter of your happiness, and I really have that at heart, more perhaps than I should, for I am only your landlady. Well, then, I heard a few things, but I can't say that they were particularly bad. No. You are under arrest, certainly, but not as a thief is under arrest. If one's arrested as a thief, that's bad business, but as for this arrest—It gives me the feeling of something very learned, forgive me if what I say is stupid, it gives me the feeling of something abstract which I don't understand, but which I don't need to understand either' (T, 27).

This is an extraordinary statement coming from a simple woman, a piece of practical theology such as we can now and then expect from the unassuming characters in, say, Eliot's plays. But the passage goes a long way towards an explanation of Joseph K.'s arrest, pointing to the double meaning of the German 'Verhaftung', which can mean both 'arrest' and something more easily explained by a phrase like 'einer Sache verhaftet sein' ('in the grip of a thing'). Joseph K. is not so much 'arrested' as he is in the grip of something normally not present in his everyday life. Nor is the very fact of being caught out in this fashion anything like a normal state of affairs. As Frau Grubach puts it:

'No, that can't happen again.' Joseph K.'s 'arrest', in the figurative meaning of the German noun, is then a once and for all event. There will be no other arrests, merely consequences of the first and only incisive occurrence in Joseph K.'s life. Moreover, the event is something of a miraculous spectacle, attracting the attention of an elderly couple in a window opposite the one in which the alleged court proceedings take place. They shyly look on, as if hoping for a redemptive effect on their own life, which is much nearer to death than Joseph K.'s, in the event of a positive development in the affair which they have witnessed. By being arrested Joseph K. has met not with disaster but with the possibility of 'happiness', with the bliss of having been granted the special privilege of establishing a line of communication with powers transcending the sphere of ordinary life. 'Will he see the point?', 'Will he behave accordingly?', 'Will anything useful come out of this for ourselves?', the coy but inquisitive faces at the window (frequently a symbol of expectation, of a new beginning, in Kafka's work) seem to ask.

Joseph K.'s response

Joseph K. is an undistinguished member of what has been called the 'petty bourgeoisie'. As a bank official he has a regular job, he never does anything out of the ordinary, and he is meticulously looked after by his landlady, who considers him as her 'cleanest' and favourite lodger. After work he normally takes a short walk, alone or with some of his colleagues, and then goes to a pub, where until eleven he sits at a table occupied mostly by elderly regulars. Occasionally the manager of the bank, who values Joseph K.'s diligence and reliability highly, invites him for a drive or for dinner at his villa. As is the custom in his kind of society his average sexual drives are gratified on the quiet at regular intervals. 'Once a week K. visited a girl called Elsa, who was on duty all night till early morning as a waitress in a cabaret and during the day received her visitors in bed' (T, 24). He is not a pillar of his society, but a perfect replica of it. How does a man like this respond to the extraordinary events in which he, paradoxically the least striking of his kind, has become involved? It is important to study Joseph K.'s behaviour carefully. Later on he will get more deeply involved, he will intensify his defensive and offensive tactics, he will cunningly vary his strategy, but the main reflexes of his initial response will not change. In this respect too the first chapter contains embryonically what is to come later.

More telling than anything K. has to say are the poses and gestures by which he, quite literally, tries to brush aside the physical and mental consequences of his arrest. When one of the warders enters his bedroom K. adopts a characteristic pose which is not adequately described in the standard English translation ('half raising himself in bed'). The German 'sass gleich halb aufrecht im Bett' ('reared half upright in bed') underlines the snake-like movement leading to a posture which expresses at once threat and fear. Joseph K. is both shaken by the intrusion and ready to defend himself, as if unconscious guilt and the knowledge that he has the right and the means to defend himself were equally powerful causes of his abrupt movement. The posture is symbolic of Joseph K.'s subsequent behaviour. He will partly threaten his strange intruders and partly submit to their persistent demands, hoping to beat them on their own ground with his 'Bürgerschlauheit'. He is quick to suggest that the whole thing is a practical joke, which he is prepared to play along with as long as this will help to neutralise the seriousness of the situation. Joseph K.'s play-acting at this point is reminiscent of those famous situations in which Charlie Chaplin (whose acting-style is known to have influenced Kafka's writing) pretends to be on the side of his pursuers in order to appease them. When the trick does not work Joseph K. decides to transfer the fight to more familiar territory, remembering that he 'lived in a country with a legal constitution, there was universal peace, all the laws were in force', and triumphantly producing his legal papers. But this does not work either, the gesture leaving his warders in a state of incomprehension and bewilderment, as if totally disconcerted by K.'s stubbornness. When K. begins to shout, they grow 'quite calm, indeed almost rueful'. 'Rueful' ('traurig') is one of Kafka's favourite words. He uses it whenever he wants to describe an utterly hopeless state of affairs, a deadlock which is in the nature of things rather than anybody's fault. A sadness befalls the warders whenever Joseph K. shows signs of serious incomprehension, the kind of sadness Christ is said to have suffered in the face of uncomprehending crowds. We shall see that *The Trial* can easily be read if not as a systematic then at least as a partial revaluation of the doctrines of salvation offered by the Old and New Testament. Subdued religious symbolism occurs already in the first chapter of the book. When the warders deprive K. of his own breakfast (lovingly prepared by Frau Grubach, the guardian angel of K.'s mediocre but nevertheless, on one plane, potentially redeemable life)

he flung himself on his bed and took from the washstand a fine apple which he had laid out the night before for his breakfast. Now it was all the breakfast he would have, but in any case, as the first few bites assured him, much better than the breakfast from the filthy night café would have been, which the grace of his warders might have secured him (T, 14).

Having eaten from 'the tree of knowledge' he is momentarily able to view his situation from 'the warder's point of view' and 'from his own point of view'. But there is no sense in which he generally enters the minds of his warders. His mental acrobatics do not transcend the level of guess-work, of the cynical manipulation of the demands of powers whose presence he cannot comprehend. But, significantly, K. has gradually come round to recognise, and partly accept, that he is no longer alone, or securely anchored in the established normality of his life. The tragedy is that he appears to have no special equipment, mental or physical, to communicate effectively with the powers which have elected him. The special privilege granted to Joseph K. amounts to little more than the fact that the Law puts in an appearance on his thirtieth birthday, the significant watershed in his life. If prepared at all to take up the challenge, K. will have to do so, like Judith in her fight against Holofernes, on the basis of his own all too human resources. And he behaves accordingly. What in Frau Grubach's opinion is potentially a happy event in K.'s life he opposes with all the meanness his native and 'official' intelligence can command.

It would be wrong to blame K. for this. Kafka poses a general problem here : is it in the power of human beings to lift themselves up by their own boot-straps, when a 'chance' of some kind is apparently provided but no further help given? Critics have accused K. of living, and of continuing to live, 'in bad faith' (in Sartre's sense). They miss the point. Kafka is not interested in the metaphysics of particular paths of salvation, however much the feverish meanderings of K.'s subsequent quest may suggest this, but in the possibility of salvation itself. The problem posed is of a terrifying simplicity: can we reach those powers which so authoritatively stretch out a helping hand towards us, and, indeed, can these powers themselves ever quite reach us? And of course, there is always the awful question of whether these other powers have any real existence at all. Is their appearance a mere illusion, tragically distracting our attention from this world and its concrete demands? Again this is not a problem Kafka is very interested in as such, at least not in this form. *The Trial*, like some of his other works, quite clearly testifies to the reality of a natural and a supernatural world, but also to their mutual exclusiveness. The two are unable to meet. In their mutual desire to come together they merely become interlocked in mortal combat. As a piece of modernist metaphysics, quite clearly fore-shadowing subsequent existentialist thinking, this is, in itself, an interesting, very Nietzschean version of a well-established dualism in the Western mind. But Kafka goes even further than that. He brings the scheme, in its abstract or metaphysical form, into strict correspondence with human psychology, and succeeds in devising an essentially explorative model for the analysis of genuine human predicaments, but not for the purpose of engineering a metaphysical tug-of-war, the kind of thing we get in Eliot's plays or in the loftier philosophising of Sartre. The spotlight in *The Trial* is always on this world, represented by Joseph K. The other world, or our unworldly instincts, represented by the Law, are highly ambiguous forces. They can both absurdly violate the world and warn it when it is in need of corrective punishment. We shall see how the later chapters of the book bring out this point. What we get in the first chapter is a preliminary to all this, a demonstration of how Joseph K. discovers, in the course of his encounter with the Law, a level of consciousness different from the one he is normally accustomed to.

The two levels of consciousness

The first chapter of *The Trial* contains one of the most skilful attempts in literature to suggest how two different planes of reality are superimposed on each other, and how this affects the protagonist's consciousness when he switches from one to the other. The passages in question emphasise the incompatibility of the officials from the court with things and characters from K.'s everyday life, and the confusion resulting for K. The first hint of this comes when Frau Grubach almost enters the room where K. is talking to the warders :

As he was re-entering the next room the opposite door opened and Frau Grubach showed herself. He saw her only for an instant, for no sooner did she recognise him than she was obviously overcome by embarrassment, apologised for intruding, vanished, and shut the door again with the utmost care. 'Come in, do,' he would just have had time to say. But he merely stood holding his papers in the middle of the room, looking at the door, which did not open again, and was only recalled to attention by a shout from the warders, who were sitting at a table by the open window and, as he now saw, devouring his breakfast (T, 11).

K., although he has the opportunity, finds himself incapable of asking Frau Grubach to come in. He cannot bring someone from his normal everyday life into contact with officials from the court. It is also implied that the appearance of Frau Grubach drives the presence of the warders from his mind, since he is left standing in a state of stupor until he is 'recalled to attention by a shout' from them.

The exact nature of this incompatibility is made even clearer in another episode. While Joseph K. is being interviewed by the Inspector, three employees from his bank (the counterparts of the three representatives of the Law) are also present in the room. K., although aware that they are there, does not recognise them until the Inspector brings their identity to his notice. Mortified by their presence, he immediately switches his attention to these three young men, but in doing so, and this is the significant fact, he forgets about the officials from the court and they depart unnoticed. K. realises this himself a few minutes later : 'Then K. remembered that he had not noticed the Inspector and the warders leaving, the Inspector had usurped his attention so that he did not recognise the three clerks, and the clerks in turn had made him oblivious of the Inspector' (T, 23). The implication here is that the incompatibility of these characters is, despite their differences, not inherent in them, but results from an inability on K.'s part to incorporate them both into his consciousness at any one time. The bank clerks and the court officials do exist in the same room; it is just that Joseph K.'s awareness of the one precludes an awareness of the other.

Joseph K. has then a kind of double consciousness, which is to say he has to process reality into two separate worlds. The general nature of these two worlds is to some extent clear. The first is that of K.'s everyday practical existence. His work at the bank, Frau Grubach, his visits to the pub all belong to it. It is a world of carefully established and closely kept routine. The second world is one where totally different values and patterns of behaviour are valid—it is the world to which, for K. at least, the court belongs. If salvation is to come at all at this significant moment in his life (his thirtieth birthday) it will come not as 'deliverance' or as 'resurrection' but as 'judgment'. That the world of the court is a world which is at best complementary to K.'s own can be assumed from the fact that K. cannot combine the two, and by the fact that the world of the court can only claim K.'s attention at times when he is not deeply involved in his own —for example, on waking first thing in the morning. Joseph K. himself suggests this when discussing his arrest with Frau Grubach:

'In the Bank, for instance, I am always prepared, nothing of that kind could possibly happen to me there, I have my own attendant, the general telephone and the office telephone stand before me on my desk, people keep coming to see me, clients and clerks, and above all, my mind is always on my work and so kept on the alert; it would be an actual pleasure to me if a situation like that cropped up in the Bank' (T, 27).

When K. reflects in the evening on what has happened earlier in the day, it seems to him that the whole

household of Frau Grubach had been thrown into great disorder by the events of the morning and that it was his task alone to put it right again. Once order was restored, every trace of these events would be obliterated and things would resume their old course. From the three clerks themselves nothing was to be feared, they had been absorbed once more in the great hierarchy of the Bank, no change was to be remarked in them.

Characteristically enough, people uninvolved in these events, like Fräulein Bürstner, K.'s co-lodger, cannot find any 'trace of disturbance' at all. What kind of world is it that our normal routine prevents from taking hold of us? One thinks of Conrad's Marlow steaming up his river in Africa:

I had to keep a look-out for signs of dead wood we could cut up in the night for next day's steaming. When you have to attend to things of that sort, to the mere incidents of the surface, the reality —the reality I tell you—fades. The inner truth is hidden—luckily, luckily. But I felt it all the same; I felt often its mysterious stillness watching one of my monkey tricks. . . .[3]

The 'reality', 'the inner truth'—these are simply Marlow's metaphors. What is watching Marlow is the world of man's irrational and metaphysical desires and ambitions. The same is the case with Joseph K. The difference between Marlow's 'inner truth' and K.'s court is a result of the difference between Marlow the sailor with mystical tendencies and K. the rationalist bank clerk. K., with his deep bourgeois roots, feels guilty about involvement with the other world, and therefore when this other world does intrude on his consciousness, it comes in the form of an arrest. The passage has already been quoted in which the warders point out to K. that the Law does not seek out its victims but rather is attracted by their own sense of guilt. Let us note again that Kafka is content, for his part, to leave the essence of the 'Law' fairly indeterminate. That he does so suggests anyway that the important question is not what the Law is, but why Joseph K. is arrested by it, put on trial, and finally put to death. The answers to these questions lie within K. himself. In other words what K. finds in the other world—arrest and trial—is determined by his own attitude towards it. Hence the warders' advice to K. to think more about himself than about them. Readers do well to bear this point in mind at all times. They are invited, not to speculate about the nature of the supernatural, with the attendant danger of imposing their own views upon it, but to concentrate on Joseph K.'s existential dilemma. That much we learn already from the first chapter: the reason for Joseph K.'s arrest is a totally subjective guilt (in the most general sense of the word)—if he didn't feel guilty he would not be arrested. Hence the irony of the first sentence of the novel, where an apparently contradictory reason for the arrest is stated: 'Someone must have been telling lies about Joseph K., for without having done anything wrong he was arrested one fine morning.' 'Someone' is K. himself, for it is K. who, in feeling guilty, has wrongfully accused himself.

Seekers and sex

Literature right down to D. H. Lawrence, not to speak of the apocalyptic erotica of the Sixties, is full of examples of religious or semi-religious quests which involve one or more women. K.'s quest is no exception in this respect. But Kafka is of course totally free from the exuberance of Romantic or Lawrentian erotic mysticism. He does not draw a simple equation between the emotions of spiritual and sexual fulfilment. He is much nearer to turn-of-the-century literature and psychology, which is full of examples of erotic feelings acting as a temporary substitute for more spiritual concerns. The best illustration we find in Musil's *Young Törless*. Having left his home for an educational institution Törless discovers a curious phenomenon in himself: an as yet undefined spiritual force which flowers in him under the guise of such substitute feelings as homesickness, the 'borrowed emotions' extracted from classical literature, friendship and, of course, unattached sexuality. Only much later on Törless will be able to identify all these things as remarkable conjuring tricks of the soul devised to further the development of his personality—preliminary substitutes for a purer, more spiritual quest. For the time being he has to go through it all. He is plagued and fascinated by childhood memories, akin to certain old paintings he has seen without fully understanding their significance :

Almost naked children tumbled about in the mud of the yards; here and there as some woman bent over her work her skirt swung high, revealing the hollows at the back of her knees, or the bulge of a heavy breast showed as the linen tightened over it. It was as though all this were going on in some quite different, animal, oppressive atmosphere, and the cottages exuded a heavy, sluggish air, which Törless eagerly breathed in.[4]

Only the experiences with a prostitute will free his mind from such visions and prepare him for the next stage in his spiritual development.

It is significant that the investigations into Joseph K.'s 'case' take place not in his own room but in the bedroom of Fräulein

Bürstner, to whom he feels sexually attracted. If we believe the warders, then they were not sent on the Law's own initiative but 'attracted' by a significant change in the bank clerk's consciousness. This change however does not manifest itself, initially, as a breakthrough to more spiritual matters in the life of a hitherto unaware ordinary citizen, but in a recent outburst of erotic feelings. As is made clear in the final paragraphs of the first chapter Fräulein Bürstner's bedroom has already been an object of K.'s erotic fantasies before the Law appears. In the course of his first official interrogation the Examining Magistrate repeatedly but mistakenly refers to K.'s profession as that of 'Zimmermaler' (lit. roompainter), a word containing an important ambiguity. K. has 'decorated', i.e. rearranged, Fräulein Bürstner's room with his erotic fantasies. (Kafka has coined the word 'Zimmermaler' by analogy with such expressions as 'mit seinen Phantasien ausmalen,' or 'Phantasiemalerei' : 'to indulge [lit. to paint] in fantasies'.)

When Joseph K. talks to Fräulein Bürstner late in the evening, he insists on re-enacting, with her, the events that took place that morning. He is particularly keen to talk about the photographs standing on the lady's bedside-table, angrily remembering that one of the three bank clerks has meddled with them in the morning (i.e. partly intruded into K.'s intimate feelings and partly mocked his childish way of approaching the woman he is attracted by). When Fräulein Bürstner walks away from the photographs, 'where they had been standing together for a long time' ('standing united' would be more accurate for the German 'vereinigt gestanden'), K. is disappointed. The scene comically reveals the nature of K.'s involvement with the woman. He cannot really be united with her personally, at best with objects and lifeless photographs belonging to her. Since Joseph K.'s approach to Fräulein Bürstner is essentially meaningless displacement-activity, his fantasies about the woman are as much on trial as all the other mental aberrations we shall hear of in the later parts of the novel. The scene in Fräulein Bürstner's bedroom reaches its predictable sordid conclusion : he 'rushed out, seized her, and kissed her first on the lips, then all over the face, like some thirsty animal lapping greedily at a spring of long-sought fresh water. Finally he kissed her on the neck, right on the throat, and kept his lips there for a long time' (T, 37f.). Back in his own room, 'he thought for a little about his behaviour, he was pleased with it, yet surprised that he was not still more pleased'. It dawns on K. that the episode with Fräulein Bürstner was after all a dead end, the first distraction from what is a personal quest of an altogether different kind.

But there is something else we learn from the episode. Why K.'s involvement with the other world comes in the form of an arrest rather than of inconspicuous deliverance is made clear by the way Fräulein Bürstner views her own relationship to the Law. To our surprise we find out that she too is attracted by it, but in a more positive and practical way. Commenting on her experience in legal matters she confesses to K.: 'I would like to know everything there is to know, and law courts interest me particularly. A court of law has a curious attraction, hasn't it?' (T, 33). She in fact soon intends to remedy her ignorance in that respect, by joining the clerical staff of a lawyer's office. Characteristically enough Kafka again describes what are the beginnings of a spiritual quest in terms of eroticism. As Frau Grubach reports: 'This very month I have met her twice already in outlying streets, and each time with a different gentleman.' Joseph K. furiously dismisses Frau Grubach's implications of scandalous behaviour. In a sentence which does not quite fit the context, as if Kafka had intended it for Felice, he cries out: 'if you want to keep your house respectable you'll have to begin by giving me notice.' But the main point is clear. Whereas F.B. will quietly find a way of co-operating with the Law, i.e. of successfully incorporating the other world into her consciousness, K. will rebel by repeatedly falling back on precisely what now stands arraigned: his narrow, unredeemed bourgeois way of life and thinking. Only shortly before the end will he realise that he could have done better, by following Fräulein Bürstner or a woman like her:

The important thing was that he suddenly realised the futility of resistance. There would be nothing heroic in it were he to resist, to make difficulties for his companions, to snatch at the last appearance of life in the exertion of struggle. He set himself in motion, and the relief his warders felt was transmitted to some extent even to himself. They suffered him now to lead the way, and he followed the direction taken by the Fräulein ahead of him, not that he wanted to overtake her or to keep her in sight as long as possible, but only that he might not forget the lesson she had brought into his mind (T, 247).

First interrogation

Significantly enough a Sunday has been chosen for Joseph K.'s first interrogation. On that day he is free from his normal business and can bring a fresh mind to the matters concerning his arrest. Because K. is not informed of the exact time he assumes that he is wanted at nine in the morning, 'since that was the hour at which all the law courts started their business on week-days'. From the very start K. is, more or less consciously, determined to stick to the routine of the urban life and society to which he belongs. And he has good reasons for doing so, if he does not want to lose his identity from the outset. Not only are the practices of the Law far removed from anything Joseph K. is used to, but also its locality. The courts are to be found on the very outskirts of the city, in the shabby suburban parts which K. has hardly ever visited before. On his way to them he comes across a familiar, yet to him unfamiliar, scene :

This being Sunday morning, most of the windows were occupied, men in shirtsleeves were leaning there smoking or holding small children cautiously and tenderly on the window-ledges. Other windows were piled high with bedding, above which the dishevelled head of a woman would appear for a moment. People were shouting to one another across the street; one shout just above K.'s head caused great laughter. Down the whole length of the street at regular intervals, below the level of the pavement, were planted little general grocery shops, to which short flights of steps led down. Women were thronging into and out of these shops or gossiping on the steps outside. A fruit hawker who was crying his wares to the people in the windows above, progressing almost as inattentively as K. himself, almost knocked K. down with his push-cart. A phonograph which had seen long service in a better quarter of the town began stridently to murder a tune (T, 42).

Joseph K. is like a fish out of water, the polished bank official now suddenly behaves clumsily and without care, like E. T. A. Hoffmann's Anselmus who, when plagued by his fantasies and about to be claimed by the supernatural, stumbles head first into an egg-basket. Whenever Kafka wants to characterise the breakdown

of K.'s normal behaviour-pattern when exposed to things belonging to the Law, he uses the Anselmus-motif with ironic effect.
Penetrating deeper into the heart of suburbia K. suffers the
full impact of a life with a movement and density of its
own :

almost all the doors stood open, with children running out and
in. Most of the flats, too, consisted of one small single-windowed
room in which cooking was going on. Many of the women were
holding babies in one arm and working over the stove with the arm
that was left free. Half-grown girls who seemed to be dressed in
nothing but an apron kept busily rushing about. In all the rooms
the beds were still occupied, sick people were lying in them, or
men who had not wakened yet, or others who were resting there
in their clothes (T, 44).

This contrast with Joseph K.'s own milieu makes it clear that
not only Joseph K. is on trial but, with him, a whole mode of
life : the stream-lined and rationalised conduct suggested by the
life and institutions of our urban communities. Kafka is not the
first to invite comparison between conditioned civilised society
and more primitive forms of life. Nineteenth-century literature
is in fact full of such comparisons, which became fashionable at
the turn of the century, when under the influence of Nietzsche,
Dostoyevsky and Tolstoy the critique of European culture reached
its peak in the novel. But nowhere do we find an economical
and unsentimental treatment of the matter to match Kafka's.
With uncanny precision, and without a trace of moralising, he
points to a life with its own order, chaos, and inbuilt salvation.
The people K. meets have no notion of punctuality, cleanliness,
or of a routine measured by the clock. But they do what needs
doing. They attend to their babies, cook their meals, and wash
their dirty linen. And they appear to be doing everything at the
same time. Life is an integrated affair with them. The old and
the young, the healthy and the sick live alongside each other. And
there are no 'lodgers'. It is also a life that has no need to defend
itself. All the doors are wide open. 'Against his usual habit', K.
stops and studies these unfamiliar appearances with close attention, like Törless who 'eagerly breathed in' his uncommon
experiences. What K. encounters is a life uncontaminated by
rational structures and self-conscious habits, a kind of pre-

conscious affair. It is a life with its own unshaken confidence and capacity for duration; a bit of a mystery and something that has its effect on K., by tiring him and distracting him from the pre-planned strategy which he has prepared for his first encounter with the court.

Joseph K.'s approach to the court rooms is related in typical Kafkaesque fashion. He finds himself crossing yards, climbing staircases and walking down corridors, all of which seem to run into each other. Again, K. was not informed of the precise location of the Interrogation Chamber. But after a quick piece of ingenious reasoning he finally finds it: 'his mind played in retrospect with the saying of the warder Willem that an attraction existed between the Law and guilt, from which should really follow that the Interrogation Chamber must lie in the particular flight of stairs which K. happened to choose' (T, 43). To K.'s surprise what he finds in the Chamber looks more like a local political gathering than a court in session. The audience appears to be divided into two different factions, with a noisy mob occupying the gallery. Whilst the 'party' on the right seems favourably inclined towards the accused, the party on the left watches him in deadly silence. K. is quick to exploit the situation. After the rather clumsy opening by the Examining Magistrate he delivers a speech worthy of any experienced political dema-gogue. With extraordinary skill he distorts the events on the morning of his arrest in his own favour. When he is about to score his final victory, by shifting the audience's attention from himself to the corruption of the court, he is, as so often in the course of his defensive moves, distracted by a strange occurrence at the far end of the room:

K. was interrupted by a shriek from the end of the hall; he peered from beneath his hand to see what was happening, for the reek of the room and the dim light together made a whitish dazzle of fog. It was the washerwoman, whom K. had recognised as a poten-tial cause of disturbance from the moment of her entrance. Whether she was at fault now or not, one could not tell. All K. could see was that a man had drawn her into a corner by the door and was clasping her in his arms. Yet it was not she who had uttered the shriek but the man; his mouth was wide open and he was gazing up at the ceiling. A little circle had formed round them, the gallery spectators nearby seemed to be delighted that the seriousness which

125

K. had introduced into the proceedings should be dispelled in this manner (T, 55).

The scene has the effect of a Dionysian happening in the face of Apollonian play-acting. Later we learn that the washerwoman, the wife of a law-court attendant, is being followed and harassed by a student, a 'bandy-legged twiddle-beard', a satyr-like figure whose main job it is to deliver the woman into the hands of the Examining Magistrate whenever he wants her. She explains the matter to the perplexed K.: 'The man you saw embracing me has been persecuting me for a long time. I may not be a temptation to most men, but I am to him. There's no way of keeping him off, even my husband has grown reconciled to it now' (T, 59). The relationship stands in curious contrast to K.'s own affairs with women. Whereas K. has incorporated such affairs into his life as yet another routine, the sexual involvements amongst the law-court staff are based on genuine attraction. They are 'arrested' in their own way, that is to say, in the grip of a powerful force which is one of the big challenges to K.'s existence. Another such challenge is the way of life in the suburbs, of people who are tied down to the ground, as if in the grip of life itself. Since the law-courts are practically manned by these people, they are the actual prosecutors of Joseph K. and his way of life and thinking. Compared to K.'s own society they form a community beyond good and evil, a tightly-knit unit which is not so much governed by imposed 'laws' as by inexplicable 'practices'. They are replicas of nature in its strongest tendencies, and heralds of a life whose wisdom and mystery are, however absurd to 'civilised' K., unfathomable. K. will feel its pull throughout his quest, not knowing to the end whether he wants to keep himself free from its grip or whether he wants to plunge right into it. It is in fact K.'s tragedy that he wants to have it both ways.

Driven by curiosity Joseph K. accepts an opportunity of being shown round the labyrinthine building of the court. He is puzzled by the way the law-court offices appear to be telescoped into the living-space of the people. And there are rooms which can instantly be transformed from a living-room into an office. In one corridor K. finds other accused men, all of whom are humbly waiting without any apparent purpose. They too belong to a class different from the one the law officials represent: 'All of them were shabbily dressed, though to judge from the expressions of their faces, their bearing, the cut of their beards, and many almost imperceptible little details, they obviously belonged to the upper classes' (T, 73). Asking one of the men why he is there, K. receives a confused answer, which is the more embarrassing as 'he was obviously a man of the world who would have known how to comport himself anywhere else and would not lightly have renounced his natural superiority'. Though K. does not intend to surrender any of *his* superiority he is soon overcome by the dull and heavy air around him which makes him experience a spell of dizziness. The next moment he is in serious danger of losing control over himself :

He felt as if he were seasick. He felt he was on a ship rolling in heavy seas. It was as if the waters were dashing against the wooden walls, as if the roaring of breaking waves came from the end of the passage, as if the passage itself pitched and rolled and the waiting clients on either side rose and fell with it (T, 83).

K. has just enough strength left to resist the temptation of sitting down and resting, for in that event the powers to which he has in a moment of curiosity and carelessness exposed himself might claim him for ever. This might not be a bad thing, since drawing him into its orbit appears to be the purpose of the Law's bustling activities. But he is determined to fight what to him is an absurd and barbarian state of affairs to every inch. Ironically enough, he decides that all he needs to do, in order to cure himself of his troubles, is to leave the place quickly, see a doctor, and start all over again. He does not realise that his dizziness is none other than a reflection of the crumbling edifice of his 'unarrested' life and concepts.

Three possibilities of acquittal

In the first three chapters of *The Trial* Kafka has skilfully solved an intractable problem : how to give concrete expression to events originating in the supernatural rather than in the natural sphere. His method of manipulating the two is based on two typical modernist assumptions, as inherited from Romanticism : firstly, the antinomy of rational and irrational forces in man, and secondly, the undifferentiated unity of the perception of the real and the structure of our experience. From the latter point it is only a short step to Kafka's acute sense of the identity of reality and experience. The K.s are imbued with this sense, but unfortunately they also have a rather limited notion of what experience means. To Joseph K. it means hardly anything but the life, thoughts and feelings of a bank official. Other areas of human experience, such as sex, religion and matters of the spirit, Joseph K. instinctively distrusts. When confronted with them, he either temporarily submits to them (ascribing the matter to exhaustion and forgetfulness) or he quickly thinks of ways of using them to his own advantage. Hence K.'s cunning game with the women who so easily fall in love with him, or his harsh dismissal of the Advocate who so eagerly offers his help.

Kafka's emphasis on the unity of reality and experience, as his letters and diaries also amply prove, leads him straight into a curious paradox. The quests of his heroes are no longer simple and primitive functions of their existence but intellectual constructions of great complexity. As such they are totally alien to the nature of the powers they are designed to appease. Worse than that, quests conceived in this way must appear to these powers as a Luciferian rebellion. If the 'limping motion' of the verger who with ambiguous signs and gestures directs K. to the pulpit of the cathedral left us in any doubt as to the real identity of the figure, his grim enjoyment of K.'s discomfiture when arguing with the priest confirms that K. is caught in an awkward spot, with the priest before and the devil behind him. The scene is symbolic of Joseph K.'s quest as a whole. His enquiring mind ('there were so many questions to put. To ask questions was surely the main thing') produces devilish fireworks of contradictions and incongruities instead of a trustworthy basis for further communication. Meaningful communication becomes more and more clearly the main problem, both for K. and the Law, the longer the trial lasts. To state his case is a sheer impossibility for K.: 'because to meet an unknown accusation, not to mention other possible charges arising out of it, the whole of one's life would have to be passed in review, down to the smallest actions and accidents, clearly formulated and examined from every angle' (T, 142f.). This would be not only a dreary but also a hopeless task. In Chapter 2 we found that writers like Joyce and Musil too, for different reasons, felt the need to make the process of writing a continuous and life-long one. Their way of escaping this impossible task was to devise narrative formulae and strategies which put the onus squarely on the reader. *He* it was who had to approach the modern work of art in a spirit of 'life-long' (Joyce) and continuous exegesis. In this sense he, the reader, is the real hero of modern fiction. Kafka repeatedly refused to grant literature this elevated status and turn it into what is practically a substitute for personal quests, or, depending on the nature of such quests, for religion. Instead he burdened his heroes with the agony of self-defensive fiction-building, thereby not only demonstrating the futility of it all but also exposing an apparently genuine quest for salvation, bearing the stamp of moral honesty and intellectual rigour, as a system of lies. K. senses this when he encounters the priest's review of possible interpretations of the 'Türhüterlegende' (Doorkeeper Legend) with the lapidary statement: 'Lying is turned into a universal principle.' But as usual Joseph K. is too tired and exhausted to follow up the implications of his insight. Anyway, in his addiction to logical tidiness he has missed the main point of the priest's reasoning: 'it is not necessary to accept everything as true, one must only accept it as necessary.' This paradox will remain the supreme stumbling-block in Joseph K.'s desperate attempt to free himself from the impositions of the Law. The problem is exemplified in the Titorelli episode.

Like the Advocates and the motley collection of women Titorelli is one of the 'helpers' K. gradually gathers round him. He is one of the figures who have no real access to the Law (nobody has, we are told) but who can be effectively employed 'behind the scenes; that is, in the consulting rooms, in the lobbies or, for example, in this very studio'. Though a painter by profession Titorelli's functions are more those of a psychoanalyst. As soon as K. arrives he is urged to take off his coat and pushed 'deep down among the bedclothes and pillows'. The ensuing conversation is one that might occur between an analyst and his patient. The cramped conditions of the box-like room ('with cracks showing' between the bare wooden planks), its sultry heat and the window that cannot be opened, all symbolise the claustrophobic privacy of the analytical situation. K. is intensely aware that he has become the prisoner of his own consciousness. 'Mouthfuls of fog' (the blankness and nothingness outside) would be preferable to being thus exposed to his inner darkness. Characteristically Kafka does not press the analogy with psycho-analysis too far. He almost dissolves the symbolic content of the scene, by shifting the conversation from analytical chat to a curious mixture of scholastic and existential theology. Titorelli now explains the three possibilities of acquittal open to Joseph K.: 'that is, definite acquittal, ostensible acquittal, and indefinite postponement' (T, 169). The first possibility, being available only to the completely innocent, is extremely rare and Titorelli cannot recall having encountered a single case, though such acquittals have most probably occurred in the past :

'Such acquittals . . . there must certainly have been. Only it is very difficult to prove the fact. The final decisions of the Court are never recorded, even the Judges can't get hold of them, consequently we have only legendary accounts of ancient cases. These legends certainly provide instances of acquittal; actually the majority of them are about acquittals, they can be believed, but they cannot be proved. All the same, they shouldn't be entirely left out of account, they must have an element of truth in them, and besides they are very beautiful. I myself have painted several pictures founded on such legends' (T, 171).

We should be disregarding the extraordinary economy of the allusions in this passage if we understood Titorelli as saying that all Joseph K. had to do was to entrust himself to the religious wisdom transmitted to us by our legends, sacred books and stories about exceptional men. But the point is made that faith rather than the application of reason is called for when dealing with the Law. Predictably enough the way of faith is not Joseph K.'s way. 'Mere legends cannot alter my opinion', he replies, 'and I fancy that one cannot appeal to such legends before the Court'. As usual he is both right and wrong. He is right in his belief that the 'legends' which have grown up around the Law, like the religious tradition we have ourselves inherited, cannot be used in evidence against the will and purpose of the Law. But he is wrong in assuming that these legends, or our sacred books and stories, have no cognitive value at all. Hoping that the second possibility of acquittal may serve him better than the first, he asks Titorelli to explain it. Ostensible acquittal is a state of provisional freedom. If K. agrees, Titorelli is prepared to write down on a sheet of paper an affidavit of K.'s innocence and take it to the judges he knows. These judges do not have the power of absolving K. from guilt, 'but they do have the right to take the burden of the charge off your shoulders'. The procedure resembles, say, the Catholic absolution after confession. But acquittal is only possible on a temporary basis. Whilst in the case of definite acquittal all records and charges relating to the investigation are destroyed, in this case the whole dossier plus the affidavit continues to circulate. 'One day—quite unexpectedly —some Judge will take up the documents and look at them attentively, recognise that in this case the charge is still valid, and order an immediate arrest' (T, 176). Though a second acquittal is possible, an arrest may soon follow again, and so on. Clearly, K. is not in a mood to satisfy himself with half-measures like this. He now wants to know all about the third possibility, indefinite postponement. 'Postponement', his would-be agent explains, 'consists in preventing the case from ever getting any further than its first stages' (T, 177). This can be achieved by restricting the case artificially to a small circle of lower judges, who can be appeased by showing up more or less casually but at regular intervals. Interrogations would only be short ones, and a mere formality. It would be like going to church on Sundays only, or like putting in a routine appearance at a psychoanalyst's. Whilst one would acknowledge one's status as an accused man, there would be no sudden arrests and one would be free from the strain and agitation inevitable in the achievement of ostensible acquittal. It appears that 'postponement' is the most mediocre and average way of securing a freedom which is no freedom at all.

In his own way Titorelli in fact highlights a paradox which Joseph K. is not yet ready to accept: whereas we shall never be free it is necessary for us to find ways and means of striving for freedom, lest we perish in the knowledge of the impossibility of freedom. The value of our 'phony' rituals of achieving freedom is analogous to the value which the Olympian world had for the Greeks. 'The Greeks were keenly aware of the terrors and horrors of existence', Nietzsche explains in *The Birth of Tragedy*: 'in order to be able to live at all they had to place before them the shining fantasy of the Olympians. . . . The gods justified human life by living it themselves—the only satisfactory theodicy ever invented.'[5] Likewise we moderns shall have to commit ourselves to the penal fantasy of God as Supreme Judge, if we want to take cognisance of both our imprisoned existence and our need for freedom. K.'s tragedy, indeed that of modern man, is that he has lost the ability to live by fictions, which admittedly would not secure his freedom but which would at least meaningfully dramatise his paradoxical predicament. Instead we stake everything on manipulating our own consciousness, until we gradually discover that this is the very evil we tried to exorcise in the first place. So the priest is right when he says to K. in the cathedral: 'The verdict is not so suddenly arrived at, the proceedings only gradually merge into the verdict' (T, 232).

'Before the Law'

One of Kafka's favourite pieces was a short parable, entitled 'Before the Law', which was printed no less than three times: in the almanac *Vom Jüngsten Tag,* in the Jewish weekly *Selbstwehr,* and in the ninth chapter of *The Trial.* Critics, including Kafka himself, have ever since busied themselves with making sense of this paradoxical story. 'Making sense' can only mean to state what can be expressed rationally. But to transcend reason, to give a symbolic account of a complex situation, is precisely the job of a parable. All interpretations, as the priest who preaches the parable to K. is eager to prove, are therefore partial, contradictory and inconclusive. The parable demonstrates, as it were, the impossibility of its own interpretation. Moreover, while the scriptures are unalterable, 'the comments often enough merely express the commentator's bewilderment'. But what, then, is the point of having parables? This is indeed K.'s main problem. What is the point of all these images, metaphors, and vague similes which his helpers appear to use in place of discursive language, K. repeatedly asks himself. What is the point of the verbal fragments, rhetorical debris, and legendary material offered to K. instead of rational analysis? Childish chit-chat, Joseph K. decides, thus revealing his failure to accept any form of communication other than that of discursive argument. In that sense *The Trial* is ultimately about the problem of language, as Professor Thorlby has pointed out in his recent book.[6] The interpolated parable in the novel confirms this impressively.

Here is a summary of the priest's story. A man from the

country comes to the door of the Law, begging for admittance. But the door-keeper says that he cannot admit the man at the moment. Hoping to gain admission later he sits waiting for days and years. In order to speed up matters the man decides to wear out the door-keeper's nerves by incessant begging. But nothing helps, not even the bribes he offers. The answer is always the same, not yet, perhaps later. In the end the man grows old and childish, 'and since in his prolonged watch he has learned to know even the fleas in the door-keeper's fur collar, he begs the very fleas to help him and to persuade the door-keeper to change his mind'. This sentence beautifully demonstrates Kafka's favourite method, that of reduction. To begin with, the man from the country came with a clear purpose in his mind. With the passing of time he undermines this purpose by opportunist behaviour, bribery and undue argumentation. You cannot make a deal with the Law: you can only come and wait. In the end the man's horizon of vision is as narrow as that of the fleas in the door-keeper's fur. Physically the man is as near to the Law as he can get, mentally he could not be further away from it. The language and method of the opportunist attitude has caused the man's spiritual vision to dwindle to nothing. Not until shortly before his death, when his consciousness is at the point of being eliminated, does he perceive the radiance that streams immortally from the door of the Law. He has just enough strength left to ask a question he should have asked a long time ago: 'how does it come about . . . that in all these years no one has come seeking admittance but me?' The paradox of the matter is, as the door-keeper puts it: 'No one but you could gain admittance through this door, since this door was intended only for you. I am now going to shut it' (T, 237). Could the man have done anything at all to secure his entry into the Law? The answer must be a firm no. The parable does not allow any moralising about it, it simply confirms the incompatibility between the Law and human consciousness. The sum-total of our experience makes us uniquely unprepared for entry to the Law. Though we may get a glimpse of the light inside, we cannot do anything further about it. That is our predicament. And the purpose of the parable is to demonstrate it. K. lives in delusion about the Law. When he encounters the priest, he puts too much hope in him:

'You are very good to me,' said K. '. . . you are an exception among those who belong to the Court. I have more trust in you than in any of the others, though I know many of them. *With you I can speak openly.*' [My emphasis.] 'Don't be deluded,' said the priest. 'How am I being deluded?' asked K. 'You are deluding yourself about the Court,' said the priest. 'In the writings which preface the Law that delusion is described thus' (T, 235).

And now the priest quotes the parable to prove his point. So the man's story is really about the impossibility of reasoning with the Law in the open, of approaching it with our arguments and appeals. *The Trial* (itself a 'petition', a 'Bittschrift', as Professor Thorlby has appositely remarked) is the trial of language and human consciousness, not of anything K. has or has not done. 'The mind's situation before the law of existence is hopeless', our problem results from 'existing consciously at all'.[7] What is there left for K. to do?

The end

In the diaries for 1914 Kafka twice recorded the observation that his best creative efforts were not made 'in order to live quietly, but rather in order to be able to die quietly' (D2, 73, 102). This is the spirit in which Joseph K. meets his death after the long process (one of the meanings of the German 'Prozess') of futile striving, and which is the message, if there is any, with which the novel concludes. After brief resistance to the two 'pallid and plump' characters sent to collect K. he follows them willingly. 'The only thing for me to go on doing is to keep my intelligence calm and discriminating to the end,' he reflects. He is not going to allow people to say of him that at the beginning of his case he wanted it to finish, and at the end of it to begin again. It is K. rather than his companions who is eager to reach the place of execution as quickly as possible. When they kill him, 'like a dog', it is only because K. has not enough strength left to seize the knife himself. The point is important. To the very end the Law will not do what K. does not want to do himself. And there is something else : K.'s end is both one of the most violent and one of the most peaceful deaths in literature. Its peaceful accept- ance is a measure of the insight K. has gained after all from his way of contacting the Law, a human way and the only way available to us; its violence is the result of the frustration which accompanies both the Law's and K.'s attempts at communication. The incompatibility between the material and the spiritual world is the predominant leitmotif of the novel. Just as K.'s consciousness fails him utterly in the face of the Law, so the court officials lack all ability to reach K.

Their remoteness kept the officials from being in touch with contemporary life; for the average case they were excellently equipped, such a case proceeded almost mechanically and only needed a push now and then; yet confronted with quite simple cases, or particularly difficult cases, they were often utterly at a loss, they did not have any right understanding of human relations, since they were confined day and night to the workings of their judicial system, while in such cases a knowledge of human nature itself was indispensable (T, 132).

Hence the muddle (one of the overtones of the German 'Verfahren', which Kafka uses frequently for 'Prozess') of the whole case, which, because no other outcome is possible, grinds to a halt.

Kafka's attitude to man's predicament is admittedly a nihilistic one. In metaphysical terms K.'s death, however peaceful to him, is without meaning, a brief but violent explosion to restore the nothingness which K. attempted to invade and conquer with his mind. Once more, towards the end, the judgment is repeated in terms of a paradox: 'Logic is doubtless unshakable, but it cannot withstand a man who wants to go on living.' Against this background of the collapse of all higher meaning the image of man shines the more brightly: 'With a flicker as of a light going up, the casements of a window there suddenly flew open; a human figure, faint and insubstantial at that distance and that height, leaned abruptly far forward and stretched both arms still farther' (T, 250). This is the modern gesture of spiritual hope, the equivalent of medieval man kneeling before the altar. It is a gesture both of absolute terror and intense beauty, the only consoling image rising above the horizon of the human enterprise. It is like the absolution given to the penitent sinner at the stake.

6
The Castle

If Goethe's works are, in his own words, 'the fragments of a great confession', then Kafka's are the fragments of an infinite quest. In *The Castle* Kafka once more explores the grand theme of *The Trial,* but in a less solemn mood and in a less trumpet-sounding manner. Whilst the essential elements which make up Kafka's last novel clearly come from the same quarry as the ones we find in *The Judgment, Metamorphosis* and *The Trial, The Castle* shows a more relaxed design and distribution of its fictional and thematic material. Joseph K.'s metamorphosis at the end of *The Trial* is after all a somewhat sudden and contrived affair, the hasty acceptance of an admittedly inescapable plight endowing K. with the pathos of a sacrificial victim rather than with the strength to bear witness. The K. of *The Castle* arrives basically at the same truth as his radical double, but salvation (if the modest achievement open to the K.s deserves this label) does not come to him in the form of judgment but in the form of deliverance. His head-on clash with the authorities resolves itself by his hard-won acceptance of the primary condition of human existence : its inevitable end in death. K.'s survival, his spiritual gaiety after the fight is over, is only possible on the basis of his newly achieved insight, his active knowledge of death.

Landscape of death

In *The Castle* K.'s quest is, traditionally enough, associated with the exploration of a particular locality. The predominant images are appropriately spatial and geographical ones. K. has come with the explicit intention of 'surveying' the land. Which land? Through an apparently mimetic representation of external reality, the village K. has strayed into, Kafka establishes in uncompromising fashion the true nature of the Castle-territory : a geography of death, 'a still-life, a *nature morte* which precludes any hope of regeneration'.[1] The ground is covered in frost and snow, spring and summer are hardly in evidence, with snow sometimes falling even during the most beautiful day. It is difficult to move about in this wintry landscape, hearse-like sledges being the only sensible means of transport. Life is reduced to a minimum in this condition, the grotesque imprints in the snow merely testifying to the futility of all human effort. K.'s entry into the village is both a home-coming, the return of a straying soul, and an attempt to postpone this return, by way of a fantastic invasion, as a living person, of the realm of death. Every major figure, situation and event in the novel is therefore presented through images of death. The man who challenges K.'s right to spend the night at the Brückenhof, in the vicinity of the Castle, is called 'Schwarzer' (a name which is also an Austrian expression for both the devil and death). He wears close-fitting black clothes, the standard dress of the Castle's officials, as if dressed up for a funeral. K.'s assistants seem to be bustling with life and activity. But they are no more alive than puppets are. K. is repelled by Jeremiah, 'this flesh which sometimes gave one the impression of not being properly alive'. Jeremiah quite generally looks as if he were 'in a state of decomposition, a corpse escaped from the grave'. Sortini, a minor official who plays however a crucial role in Olga's story (see the section 'Amalia and Olga' later in this chapter), is another death-figure: 'one thing about him struck all the people who noticed him at all, the way his forehead was furrowed; all the furrows—and there were plenty of them although he's certainly not more than forty—were spread fanwise over his forehead, running towards the root of his nose' (C, 177). About Klamm himself, the highest official who is ever seen by ordinary mortals, Sebald writes this: 'When Frieda lets K. peep through the spy-hole into Klamm's room, the latter is sitting completely immobile at his table. The only sign of life is a cigar smoking in his motionless hand and the glint of the pince-nez which hides his eyes—the most vital part of a man. Immediately afterwards K. wonders if Klamm is disturbed by the rowdiness of the servants.

'No,' said Frieda, 'he's asleep.' 'Asleep?' cried K. 'But when I peeped in he was awake and sitting at the desk.' 'He always sits like that,' said Frieda, 'he was sleeping when you saw him. Would I have let you look in if he hadn't been asleep? That's how he sleeps, the gentlemen do sleep a great deal. . . .'

Sleep is a brother of death and is assiduously cultivated by the inhabitants of the Castle. When they leave their bureaux to attend a hearing, they prefer to do it at night and even then they like to settle themselves in bed like Bürgel, that image of a regressive existence to which K. so fervently longs to return.[2]

The master of the Castle is Count Westwest, a name suggesting a domain beyond the point through which the traditional passage of death leads. It is therefore not surprising that K. is severely criticised, in French, by the teacher, of whom he has asked indiscreet questions about the Count in front of the children: 'Please remember that there are innocent children present' (C, 16). One does not mention death in the presence of the very young. Heinz Politzer has suggested that the name Westwest could be taken as an ingenious pun on the double syllable 'West'. If West means death, then Westwest, i.e. West of West, means death of death, i.e. life, a new beginning. 'Then Kafka would have alluded here to eternal life, would have attempted to say in his opaque way what a more believing soul, the Dean of St Paul's, John Donne, expressed in the line: "And Death shall be no more; Death, thou shalt die." '[3] We are of course equally justified in interpreting the Count's name as an intensification meaning total, absolute death. Nothing in fact. If Kafka intended an ambiguity here it is of such a radical kind that the result is irony rather than a positive interaction of the two meanings suggested. The point is precisely that the strength of belief characteristic of earlier ages would be required to make the pun work in Politzer's sense, or in the sense of Metaphysical poetry. Without this strength of belief the expression is reduced to the kind of doubling-up (e.g. 'bestest') children use when they want to achieve, in their comic linguistic games, the highest degree of affirmation. There is no evidence in *The Castle*, or in most of his other works, that Kafka intimates the existence of a supernatural order that human beings could rely upon. On the other hand, he does little against the reader's inclination to imagine such an order if he wishes to do so. We must not forget, however, that the reader knows nothing, as critics are at pains to point out, he does not learn through exposure to K.'s actions and reflexes. In that sense the reader is really K.'s double. It would therefore be naïve of the reader to identify arbitrarily with certain aspects of K.'s quest but otherwise refuse to accept K.'s predicament which is that of post-Christian man. The reader is then likely to accuse K. of 'blindness', and of other crimes of 'faithless' man, rather than accept Kafka's portrayal of the human condition. The following scene exemplifies the problem.

On his first walk through the village K. is rescued from the snow by peasants and briefly admitted to their house. He stumbles into a dark, steamed-up room, in which children are playing about, a woman is doing the washing, two men are having a bath in a large wooden tub and an old man is sitting on a chest (the Muirs' 'settle' for the German 'Truhe' is not only incorrect but misses an important ambiguity : 'Truhe' in Austrian means both chest and coffin).

But still more astonishing, although one could not say what was so astonishing about it, was the scene in the right-hand corner. From a large opening, the only one in the back wall, a pale snowy light came in, apparently from the courtyard, and gave a gleam as of silk to the dress of a woman who was almost reclining in a high armchair. She was suckling an infant at her breast (C, 18).

Lying in her chair as if lifeless the woman is 'staring at the roof without even a glance towards the child at her bosom'. K. is asked to sit down on the chest, where 'the old man . . . was already sitting, sunk in vacancy'. Like Mann's Aschenbach in the coffin-like gondola K. is overcome by a sweet tiredness and falls asleep. On awakening he finds that his head is lying on the old man's shoulder, as if death had already claimed him. But refreshed by his sleep he is his old, energetic self again. 'He felt less constrained, poked with his stick here and there, approached the woman in the armchair, and noted that he was physically the biggest man in the room', reducing the others to the state of suddenly shrunken people who are only partly alive. Before he departs,

'taking them all by surprise he made an adroit turn and stood before the reclining woman. Out of weary blue eyes she looked at him, a transparent silk kerchief hung down to the middle of her forehead, the infant was asleep on her bosom. ('Who are you?' asked K., and disdainfully—whether contemptuous of K. or her own answer was not clear—she replied : 'A girl from the Castle.'

Ronald Gray has commented on this passage at length, using it as an example of what he calls Kafka's 'Vexierbild' technique, 'the name deriving from those pictures, originally so popular in the seventeenth century, where a given set of lines and shading can be interpreted in two entirely different ways, according to the way in which they are sized up by the eye. The same idea is employed today in those psychological tests where the subject is presented with a picture representing equally well the face of an old hag or the figure of a luscious blonde. Neither interpretation is *the* correct one, both are possible.'[4] In a general sense this is a most helpful comment on Kafka's method. But Dr Gray also implies that it is up to the reader to decide how to interpret the 'picture'. Pointing out that what K. sees in the room is a sort of nativity scene with the Virgin Mary he goes on to say : 'But you are in doubt. Nowhere is it said that this is a picture of a girl who resembles the Virgin Mary. Why is she almost lying down? Why does she not look at the child? Why does she speak with contempt? If there is any symbolical intent, what does this meeting signify? The suggestive overtones tempt one to extend the parallel beyond justifiable limits. As soon as any equivalence is asserted it needs to be withdrawn. It is left to the reader to discover for himself wherein the surprise lay.'[5] Dr Gray is here playing into the hands of those readers who are in a habit of 'deciding for themselves' instead of answering the kind of pertinent questions Dr Gray himself asks, without answering them. A reader with a pronounced interest in Christian messages will probably come to the conclusion that he is dealing here with a nativity scene, and pity K. for asking a stupid question. It is not easy to say what a non-Christian reader might do with this scene (provided that he recognises the allusion to the Virgin Mary in the first place) : he might either consider the allusion as a rhetorical accident or satisfy himself with admiring Kafka's technique of 'ambiguity'.

Let us now try to answer Dr Gray's questions and see what conclusions we can draw from what is quite clearly a *dislocated* nativity scene. The woman is almost lying down because this is the general posture in which most of the Castle's inhabitants can be found for most of the time. The Castle is inhabited by people who are 'partly living and partly not living'. All the images point to a world from which all signs of genuine life have disappeared. The woman does not look at the child because what she has on her breast is not a potential messiah but one more newcomer to the shadowland they all inhabit. And she speaks with contempt because she understands the full meaning of what it means to be 'A girl from the Castle', despising herself for not being able to give a better answer, and K. for having come at all and being on the point of succumbing to yet another of his delusions. The encounter therefore appears to signify that K.'s world, and by implication ours, does not offer any clues to or confirmation of the transcendental. It is a closed world, secured by a powerful lock (the other meaning of the German 'Schloss'), in which man is trapped. It is not K. who is impotent—he is after all one of the most active questers the religious imagination has invented. It is the world and its images which are impotent and sadly lacking in revelatory content. The woman 'made a beautiful, sad, fixed picture', and the longer K. looks at her the more powerfully the positive image of the 'Vexierbild' is contradicted. The woman resembles a statue of the Virgin Mary, but one that has toppled over and disintegrated. K. is looking at the debris of our futile attempts at religious myth-making. The woman's candid answer confirms the negative aspects of the whole scene, the postures of lying down, of appearing to be lifeless, of looking impotently upwards, away from the newborn baby which is just as trapped in the Castle's world as anybody else. The parallels we are tempted to establish between K.'s vision and a nativity scene are cruelly withdrawn by Kafka himself. The reader has no choice as to what he wants to see, if he takes the text seriously. It is quite generally the case that Kafka's ambiguities are dissolved by the metaphors of disconfirmation contained within them. The scene in Lasemann's house demonstrates once more Kafka's own version of the human predicament: 'Sometimes I feel I understand the Fall of Man better than anyone.'

As soon as K. is recognised as the new surveyor by the people in Lasemann's house it is made clear to him that he cannot stay for too long. The underworld-like communities of the Castle-territory do not cultivate human contacts, particularly when the intruder is as unqualified as the activist K. 'We have no need for visitors', as one of the men puts it. Appropriately enough, K. is transported back to the inn by another unmistakable death-figure, the Charon-like coachman Gerstäcker, who answers all questions with a bad bout of coughing. The Castle, which K. had hoped to reach that very day, retreats again into the distance, as if it had found its impetuous petitioner not yet worthy of admittance. 'But as if to give him a parting sign till their next encounter a bell began to ring merrily up there, a bell which for at least a second made his heart palpitate for its tone was menacing, too, as if it threatened him with the fulfilment of his vague desire' (C, 22). If the Castle is an image of redemption and grace, as is so often said, then it is peculiar that the prospect of entering it should have any threatening overtones. If it is above all an image of Death, as the novel's very texture seems to suggest, it is of course understandable that K. should feel the terror of his secret intentions. He has come to satisfy his death-wish, to enter the dominion of Death; but not as a humble person, 'ripe for death' (as the bitter-sweet phrase resounds through the poetry of Rilke and others), but as a conqueror, as a person who is still very much alive. The sound of 'the great bell' both fascinates and terrifies K., as does his desire for death, of which he is half-conscious. The bell's ring reminds us of another intriguing sound the Castle emits. 'It is from the telephone that K. hears the same eleusinian humming which many of us remember from childhood walks beside the telegraph wires,'[6] and which has since been used in many plays and of course in Bergmann's films. As Gerstäcker's sledge moves further away from the Castle, the bell's sound changes into 'a feeble monotonous little tinkle which might have come from the Castle, but might have been somewhere in the village' (C, 22). This is the traditional funeral-bell, accompanying mortals on their last journey. The irony however is that K., in the hands of his 'inexorable driver', journeys away from the Castle, not towards it. What we have here is the uncanny scene of a mock-funeral.

K.'s urge to conquer death is made explicit through the description of a significant childhood experience. Walking aimlessly through the village with Barnabas, the Castle's ambiguous messenger, K. remembers the following scene:

There, too, a church stood in the market-place, partly surrounded by an old graveyard which was again surrounded by a high wall. Very few boys had managed to climb that wall, and for some time K., too, had failed. It was not curiosity which had urged them on. The graveyard had been no mystery to them. They had often entered it through a small wicket-gate, it was only the smooth high wall that they had wanted to conquer. But one morning—the

142

empty, quiet market-place had been flooded with sunshine, when had K. ever seen it like that either before or since?—he had succeeded in climbing it with astonishing ease; at a place where he had already slipped down many a time he had clambered with a small flag between his teeth right to the top at the first attempt. Stones were still rattling down under his feet, but he was at the top. He stuck the flag in, it flew in the wind, he looked down and round about him, over his shoulder, too, at the crosses mouldering in the ground, nobody was greater than he at that place and that moment. By chance the teacher had come past and with a stern face had made K. descend. In jumping down he had hurt his knee and had found some difficulty in getting home, but still he had been on the top of the wall. The sense of that triumph had seemed to him then a victory for life, which was not altogether foolish, for now so many years later on the arm of Barnabas in the snowy night the memory of it came to succour him (C, 34).

The episode has a narrative function similar to that of the parable 'Before the Law' in *The Trial*. The parallels to events in *The Castle* itself are obvious. It is again the teacher who brings K. back to reality from his aggressive fantasies. Later on, when attempting to enter the Castle, K. will hurt himself in a similar fashion. The motif of feeling 'great' and of gaining in size (reminiscent of Alice's rapid transformation in *Alice in Wonderland*) is a favourite one in Kafka's works, not only in *The Castle* but above all in *The Judgment*. The most significant aspect of this childhood incident is that K. recalls it at a time when the business of challenging death is about to become his main pre-occupation. Images of home flit through K.'s mind at the very beginning of the novel, when he embarks on his first approach to the Castle. Looking at the buildings he cannot help comparing them with his home-town. What he sees is not so much a castle as 'a wretched-looking town, a huddle of village houses, whose sole merit, if any, lay in being built of stone, but the plaster had long since flaked off and the stone seemed to be crumbling away' (C, 15). The church tower of his town, though it too looked like 'an earthly building—what else can men build?'—reflected at least a loftier goal than the humble dwelling-houses, and a clearer meaning than the muddle of everyday life. But the tower up there is merely 'the tower of a house', and 'uniformly round', as if stubbornly enclosing a shabby world of its own rather than attempting to provide a bridge to a better one above. It is pierced by small windows that glitter in the sun and topped by what looks like an attic, 'with battlements that were irregular, broken, fumbling, as if designed by the trembling or careless hand of a child, clearly outlined against the blue'. And now comes the magnificent if indirect reference to the Castle's occupant himself, who can be none other than the Count. 'It was as if a melancholy-mad tenant who ought to have been kept locked in the topmost chamber of his house had burst through the roof and lifted himself up to the gaze of the world' (C, 16). The passage is clearly reminiscent of the ending of *The Judgment*, where the gigantic father appears to fill every room and the universe itself. Just as the trapped light in the little windows of the tower produces 'a somewhat maniacal glitter' there the Castle's occupant asserts his presence by maniacal exhibitionism. He can grow to any size but he cannot outgrow his own prison. Like the demiurge Patera in Kubin's *The Other Side* he permeates his strange domain at every point but is incapable of transcending it. All other inhabitants of the Castle and the surrounding village are in exactly the same situation. They are cut off from any other, more agreeable world, if, indeed, such a world existed. It is significant that Kafka presents a possible alternative to the barren Castle-world merely in the form of K.'s vague memories, as if the idea of a redeemed world were no more than the product of our frustrated hopes, and of the memory of such hopes. In this way Kafka establishes the universality of the conditions portrayed in *The Castle*, revealing himself as an extreme representative of the type of Marcionism we have briefly sketched in the second chapter.

K. and Klamm

K.'s importunate attempts to gain access to the Castle are soon answered by the following ambiguous and bewildering letter from Klamm :

My dear Sir—As you know, you have been engaged for the Count's service. Your immediate superior is the Superintendent of the village, who will give you all particulars about your work and the terms of your employment, and to whom you are responsible. I myself, however, will try not to lose sight of you. Barnabas, the bearer of this letter, will report himself to you from time to time to learn your wishes and communicate them to me. You will find me always ready to oblige you, in so far as that is possible. I desire my workers to be contented (C, 28).

As the Superintendent explains to K. later, this is not an official, but a private letter. Moreover, the onus of proving that K. has been taken on by the Castle is laid on himself, as the phrase 'As you know' indicates. K. himself is aware of the essential ambiguities in the letter. In part the document deals with him as with a free man whose independence is acknowledged. But there are sentences in which he is directly or indirectly treated as a minor employee. K. responds in a characteristic fashion to these inconsistencies. Instead of shelving the problem

he was much more inclined to read into them a frankly offered choice, which left it to him to make what he liked out of the letter, whether he preferred to become a village worker with a distinctive but merely apparent connection with the Castle, or an ostensible village worker whose real occupation was determined through the medium of Barnabas (C, 29).

The choice reminds us of the one offered by Titorelli in *The Trial*. But in *The Castle* the problem is not one of finding the best way out of an existential dilemma but one of making the best choice so as to avoid this dilemma in the first place. The protagonist of *The Trial* is striving to keep the ground of his existence (as symbolised by his profession) uncontaminated by the alien order of the Law, in order to seek out the Law on his own terms. The protagonist of *The Castle* is concerned with making the right kind of existential choice, in order to secure total success for his intention of *conquering the Castle* (also symbolised by his profession).

What is the difference between a real village worker and an 'ostensible' village worker? The distinction is best understood if seen from both a social and a religious point of view. A real village worker is one who is fully integrated into his community, one who is indistinguishable from anybody else in that community. His job and the customs and practices of his fellow-beings are the basis of his existence. His relationship with anything transcending this existence will be a 'distinctive' one, because the mode of his existence will differ in kind from the mode of existence transcending it. For the very same reasons the relationship between the two will only be an 'apparent' one. Since the two modes of existence are mutually exclusive all contacts between them are based on illusion. This point is emphasised throughout *The Castle*, as it is throughout *The Trial*. An ostensible village worker has the advantage of having his existence defined by the transcending powers themselves, i.e. of enjoying a genuine and intimate relationship with them, but the disadvantage of losing his human freedom in the process. The option is utopian anyway, since a human being without the will to act, to obey or disobey, cannot be imagined. Human life can only be conceived of in terms of 'achievement', moral or otherwise, and not in terms of a total absorption by other powers. K. understands immediately that only as a village worker amongst others will he be able 'to achieve anything in the Castle itself'. He also realises that the decision to become a worker would have to be taken in grim earnest, 'without any other prospect'. But the undertaking would not be without dangers of its own. Sinking completely to the workmen's level would expose K. to 'the pressure of a discouraging environment, of a growing resignation to disappointment, the pressure of the imperceptible influence of every moment', and so distract him from his higher aims. What he is afraid of is the predicament of the Samsa family and of similarly poor and enslaved people, to which the *Metamorphosis* refers. So K. has a double fight on his hands, against the dangers of succumbing to a rigid impersonal discipline and against the restrictions imposed on him (and everybody else) by the Castle. So far so good. What K. misjudges is his own inability to act according to the logic of his chosen situation. As we shall see later he makes an admirable attempt to become an integrated member of the village community, but at the same time he is unable to accept that illusory nature of his relationship with the authorities, an illusion on which, as K. himself concludes, ordinary existence is necessarily based. His continuous attempts to reach the Castle merely have the effect of alienating him from the village community. In terms of his own analysis of the situation, K. is the unacknowledged 'ostensible' village worker. Depending on the degree of absurdity K. displays by his various actions he enacts both the crime of a self-styled Prometheus and the comedy of a utopian quester.

But what is it K. is looking for in the Castle? Does the novel, apart from generating an aura of mystery and death, tell us something about the more specific aims and purposes of K.'s quest? These questions are best answered by an examination of K.'s relationship to the most enigmatic of the Castle's representatives, Klamm.

Who is Klamm? Some of the details are clear enough. He is the man who has played an important role in the lives of Frieda, the girl who emerged from the chthonic depths of the Brückenhof Inn to become a barmaid in the Herrenhof, and of Gardena, K.'s landlady at the Brückenhof. He is also the official who through Barnabas sends messages to K. and who encourages him to keep up his quest. In other respects Klamm's identity is a mystery. Olga, K.'s confidante, says of him:

'His appearance is well known in the village, some people have seen him, everybody has heard of him, and out of glimpses and rumours and through various distorting factors an image of Klamm has been constructed which is certainly true in fundamentals. But only in fundamentals. In detail it fluctuates, and yet perhaps not so much as Klamm's real appearance. For he's reported as having one appearance when he comes into the village and another on leaving it; after having his beer he looks different from what he does before it, when he's awake he's different from when he's asleep, when he's alone he's different from when he's talking to people, and—what is incomprehensible after all that—he's almost another person up in the Castle. And even within the village there are considerable differences in the accounts given of him, differences as to his height, his bearing, his size, and the cut of his beard: fortunately there's one thing in which all the accounts agree, he always wears the same clothes, a black morning coat with long tails. Now of course all these differences aren't the result of magic, but can be easily explained; they depend on the mood of the observer, on the degree of his excitement, on the countless graduations of hope or despair which are possible for him when he sees Klamm, and besides, he can usually see Klamm only for a second or two' (C, 167).

Klamm's identity depends on the existential situation of the people who look at him. He is at the centre of an infinite number of concentric circles, each of which represents the particular destiny of a particular individual. If for the time being we forget about the one constant in Klamm's appearance, his clothes, then we can say that everything else about Klamm is constantly being redefined by those who observe him. Moreover, what they see in Klamm they see only 'for a second or two', the brief encounters living on in people's memory, as in Gardena's case, as significant moments in their lives. K.'s own complex relationship to Klamm is exemplified in the novel by an extensive analysis of a fundamental human emotion, the experience of love. Before we can clarify the matter in K.'s case, we must first examine Gardena's and Frieda's involvement with Klamm.

K.'s incessant talk of Klamm, and of marrying Frieda, has a disturbing effect on his landlady, to the point of making her physically ill. When she receives K., to settle the matter with him, all normal activities are temporarily suspended. Even the maids in the kitchen are commanded to leave. The more curious, including the assistants, gather near the hatch in order to pick up some fragments of the conversation inside. Kafka has set the scene perfectly for a timeless moment in time, when Gardena interrupts the ordinary business of her life and reminisces about her past relationship with Klamm. Lying in bed with a nightcap of delicate lacework she looks much younger than her actual age. She asks K. to hand her the wrap Klamm had once given her, and the otherwise completely unconceited woman raises herself up for a moment to rearrange her coiffure round the nightcap. It is as if all physical imperfections have to be eliminated in order to lend dignity to the memory of a significant moment in her life. Gardena recalls the happy and sad time when Klamm had sent for her three times, but then had forgotten her. This was a shattering experience for the deserted girl, making her unfit for work and causing her to sit in the front garden all day. 'There Hans saw me, often sat down beside me. I didn't complain to him, but he knew how things were, and as he was a good young man, he wept with me.' He also married her, a woman who later will be faithful to her perplexed husband but at the same time unable to forget the experience of her first love. 'Klamm once chose me as his mistress, can I ever lose that honour?', as she puts it. Even now she would go to Klamm if he decided to summon her. But Gardena is one of those women whom Klamm has 'forgotten completely', as she says, that is to say who will never be able to regain access to the experience of overwhelming love, only to the memory of it. K. is quick to point out that her distinction between periods of Klamm's presence and Klamm's absence is fallacious. As K., the cunning logician, puts it:

148

'If it hadn't been for Klamm Hans wouldn't have been unhappy and wouldn't have been sitting doing nothing in the garden, if it hadn't been for Klamm Hans wouldn't have seen you sitting there, if it hadn't been that you were unhappy a shy man like Hans would never have ventured to speak, if it hadn't been for Klamm Hans would never have found you in tears . . . if it hadn't been for Klamm you wouldn't have been indifferent to what life still offered you, and therefore would never have married Hans. Now in all this there's enough of Klamm already, it seems to me. But that's not all. If you hadn't been trying to forget, you certainly wouldn't have overtaxed your strength so much and done so splendidly with the inn. So Klamm was there too' (C, 84).

And if now Gardena can only become aware of Klamm by a calculated act of memory then she has failed to incorporate Klamm, and the experience of him, into her normal life.

What precisely is Klamm's power? The answer we get from Olga again :

'Klamm's a kind of tyrant over women, he orders first one and then another to come to him, puts up with none of them for long, and orders them to go just as he ordered them to come. . . . But we do know that women can't help loving the officials once they give them any encouragement, yes, they even love them beforehand, let them deny it as much as they like' (C, 185f.).

The women's love for Klamm and the officials is then, in the words of W. Emrich, 'eine unmittelbare Bestimmtheit durch Gefühle, die sowohl vor wie nach der Begegnung mit den Beamten dauernd wirksam sind' ('a direct conditioning through feelings which are perpetually operative both before and after contact with the officials').[7] Klamm is a personification of impersonal love, of love itself, of the powerful spirit which, according to the idealist tradition in European literature and philosophy, permeates the whole universe. Particularly at a very early stage in the lives of men, in what Hofmannsthal called 'prae-existence' (when potential is everything, and concretion of human emotions and spiritual matters at a minimum), this power can be experienced in its unattached purity. It is felt as a feeling of supreme happiness, like first love, long after it has ceased to be operative in its pure form, in Gardena's case as a happy memory which she is loath to contaminate with the more impure feelings of a real life-situation, her marriage. The encounter with Klamm is experienced as an encounter with the impersonal power of love, an encounter which can neither be anticipated nor avoided. The impression made by the encounter on the human beings selected (in Kafka exclusively women) is one of overwhelming but indefinable significance. 'The response of the imagination to such a presence or significance is a passion of awe',[8] as W. H. Auden put it, commenting on the nature of our experience of the sacred. Auden's account of the matter perfectly describes Gardena's and Frieda's relationship to Klamm : 'A sacred being may . . . be an object of desire but the imagination does not desire it. A desire can be a sacred being but the imagination is without desire. In the presence of the sacred, it is self-forgetful. . . . A sacred being may also demand to be loved or obeyed, it may reward or punish, but the imagination is unconcerned. . . . To the imagination a sacred being is self-sufficient, and like Aristotle's God can have no need of friends.'[9] It is again Olga who provides the evidence for this :

'The relation existing between the women and the officials, believe me, is very difficult, or rather very easy to determine. Love always enters into it. There's no such thing as an official's unhappy love affair. So in that respect it's no praise to say of a girl—I'm referring to many others besides Frieda—that she gave herself to an official out of love. She loved him and gave herself to him, that was all, there's nothing praiseworthy in that' (C, 186f.).

There may be good reasons for the fact that 'Klamm's notorious for his rudeness, he can apparently sit dumb for hours and then suddenly brings out something so brutal that it makes one shiver' (C, 184). The point is that behavioural factors of this kind do not and cannot influence the experience of pure love, a 'sacred' state of mind in Auden's terminology, once it has been entered into. Klamm's actions are of no importance. His significance lies not in what he *does*, but in what he *is*. His influence cannot be measured in terms of anything obviously useful but more generally in terms of 'a distinction that cannot be lost'. This of course raises the problem of Klamm's relation to the world of social experience, which cannot be measured in terms of potential or states of consciousness but only in terms of action. As we shall see later, Frieda is the only woman who recognises the need of both retaining an awareness of Klamm and disengaging herself from him completely. The happiness Klamm promises, and the 'truth' he stands for, can only be experienced at rare moments of insight ('for a second or two'), in the form of hopes, despairs, and longings rather than in the form of anything more concrete. But human beings must above all learn to accept the more limited happiness and truth of what they have to live by day in day out : individual love. All they can hope to do is to find a way of assimilating the 'higher' love to their own kind of loving. The question of course arises whether this is possible or not. Unfortunately, the gap between the seen and unseen order is a serious one, as the realistic Olga is quick to see : 'Of course we're all supposed to belong to the Castle, and there's supposed to be no gulf between us, and nothing to be bridged over, and that may be true enough on ordinary occasions, but we've had grim evidence that it's not true when anything really important crops up' (C, 185). It is K.'s passionate desire, however, to remove all gulfs between the world of the Castle and his own. He severely criticises Gardena for having unsuccessfully combined her experience of Klamm with her experience as a married woman. Gardena had a promising starting-point, in that she was selected by Klamm, but once left on her own (in the world of human reality) everything went wrong. Her husband Hans would have been better off with a simple girl who gave him her first love. He would not now have to stand in the inn, as if completely lost. And Gardena too would not be the unhappy woman she is. Her health-destroying involvement in her work is merely a substitute for her secret yearning for Klamm. When she asks K. what she and Hans failed to do, K. answers : 'To ask Klamm'. In other words, to make sure whether the anonymous power of love found its appropriate object in real life. 'The blessing was over you', K. says, 'but they [those responsible for her marriage] didn't know how to bring it down' (C, 85).

During the same conversation K. reveals the secret of his own interest in Klamm :

'Firstly, I want to see him at close quarters; then I want to hear his voice; then I want to get from him what his attitude is to our [Frieda's and K.'s] marriage. What I shall ask from him after that depends on the outcome of our interview. Lots of things may come up in the course of talking, but still the most important thing for me is to be confronted with him. You see I haven't yet spoken with a real official. That seems to be more difficult to manage than I had thought. But now I'm put under the obligation of speaking to him as a private person, and that, in my opinion, is much easier to bring about. As an official I can only speak to him in his bureau in the Castle, which may be inaccessible, or—and that's questionable, too—in the Herrenhof. But as a private person I can speak to him anywhere, in a house, in the street, wherever I happen to meet him. If I should find the official in front of me, then I would be glad to accost him as well, but that's not my primary object' (C, 86).

K. draws a significant distinction between Klamm the 'official' and Klamm as a 'private person', a distinction which contradicts the general attitude to Klamm. In the words of the landlady:

'Klamm as a private person . . . who can imagine him as a private person? . . . Just because Frieda was Klamm's mistress, d'you think she saw him as a private person, just because we love him, d'you think we love him as a private person? One can't say of a real official that he is sometimes more, sometimes less of an official—he is always an official through and through.'

That is to say, the women's love for Klamm has nothing to do with human love. It is rather a rare state of consciousness, a feeling of total trust in the power of life (or love) itself, something that cannot be explained or experienced in terms of individual emotions. As we shall see later, it is Kafka's assumption that women are securely embedded in the undercurrent of impersonal forces. They are committed, to a much higher degree than men, to a mode of existence which might almost be called mystical. 'Love for Klamm' is Kafka's metaphor for this commitment, the 'official' in Klamm his metaphor for the realm of the impersonal. Whilst women have an instinctual relationship to this realm, men are doomed to seek for it by analytical methods. In doing so they demonstrate the typical behaviour-pattern of the non-mystic, of questers whose quest turns into a 'fight' motivated by the desire to force a personal confrontation with the impersonal. Thus K.'s wishful dream to speak to Klamm as 'a private person' rather than in his capacity as an 'official'. This dream is no other than a dream for Faustian goals, which K., having no Mephisto to help him, pursues by Socratic means.

The hermetic nature of the non-human sphere is metaphorically suggested towards the end of chapter nine:

Klamm was far away. Once the landlady had compared Klamm to an eagle, and that had seemed absurd in K.'s eyes, but it did not seem absurd now; he thought of Klamm's remoteness, of his impregnable dwelling, of his silence, broken perhaps only by cries such as K. had never yet heard, of his downward-pressing gaze, which could never be proved or disproved, of his wheelings which could never be disturbed by anything that K. did down below, which far above he followed at the behest of incomprehensible laws and which only for instants were visible (C, 113f.).

What is striking in this passage is not so much the emphasis on the inaccessibility of Klamm but the hint at Klamm's painfully endured loneliness. Though Klamm is irredeemably trapped by his own laws his far-away gaze is 'downward-pressing' and sometimes he interrupts the silence of his existence by unimaginable cries, as if he too is crying out for K. as K. is crying out for him. And indeed, Klamm *is* writing 'personal' letters to K. rather than 'official' ones. The powerful theme of *The Trial* is introduced once more. Existence 'up there' is meaningless if no link can be established with 'down here'. 'They' are reaching out for 'us' as we are reaching out for them. On the other hand 'they' are trapped by laws of their own as we are trapped by the conditions of human existence. As Kafka put it somewhere else : 'The crows claim that a single crow could destroy heaven. That is undoubtedly so but proves nothing against heaven, since heavens mean precisely : impossibility of crows.' This is the paradox, in *The Trial* as well as in *The Castle*. Is there a way out? Two ways of breaking the 'lock' (Schloss) are explored at length in *The Castle*, as it happens both with negative results. One way occurs to K. himself—marriage with Frieda. The other is suggested by an official of the Castle (Bürgel)—mystical experience. Let us examine these two possibilities in turn.

K. and Frieda

The Frieda chapters in the novel parade once more the intricate problems of love and marriage with which Kafka had wrestled, shrewdly but unsuccessfully, in the diaries and, above all, in his letters to Felice Bauer. Years after his final separation from Felice he is no less preoccupied with the implications and consequences of the choice he made at the time. But he is at least able to stand back now and, instead of erecting yet another monument to his personal guilt, to firmly integrate his experience into the cool scheme of his last novel. Kafka's main interest centres on the question of whether both the 'realist' and 'idealist' in the loving person can be satisfied by marriage as a social institution.

Frieda is 'an unobtrusive little girl with fair hair, sad eyes, and hollow cheeks'—features which in Kafka's work are always distinguishing attributes of characters striving for the 'unknown'. She began as a milk-maid at the inn by the bridge but then attained, without much effort of her own, her distinguished position in the bar of the Herrenhof, where K. meets her for the first time. He is impressed by 'her look' which seems to decide 'something concerning himself, something which he had not known to exist, but which her look assured him did exist' (C, 40). K. discovers that he is not dealing with an ordinary woman but with somebody of ambitions similar to his own. Her eyes speak to him 'far more of conquests still to come than of conquests past' (C, 42). He is quick to offer his help, 'the help of a man who's fighting his way up too, even though he's a small and uninfluential man'. Above all, Frieda is Klamm's mistress, and therefore a valuable link with him.

To his surprise K. has no difficulty in persuading Frieda to leave Klamm and become his sweetheart instead. In a matter of seconds they find themselves rolling among the puddles of beer and other refuse collected on the floor.

There, hours went past, hours in which they breathed as one, in which their hearts beat as one, hours in which K. was haunted by the feeling that he was losing himself or wandering into a strange country, farther than ever man had wandered before, a country so strange that not even the air had anything in common with his native air, one might die of strangeness, and yet whose enchantment was such that one could only go on and lose oneself further (C, 45f.).

When Klamm's 'authoritative, impersonal voice' calls for Frieda, she answers rebelliously : 'I'm with the Land Surveyor !', thereby confirming her desire to leave Klamm for ever. This is not what the horrified K. expected. What can he hope to get from Frieda, now that she has betrayed everything? But Frieda sees things differently. She may have lost Klamm, but then she has won K. Frieda has made an important choice, to extricate herself from a situation in which love (and existence) remain a mere potentiality, in favour of a situation in which love (and existence) are a human reality. Her position behind the bar—the German

'Ausschank' (a counter where drinks are dispensed) conveys the symbolic content better than the English 'bar' or 'taproom'—was a characteristically intermediate position. Neither did she have any real contact with Klamm—only through a hole in the door —nor with ordinary human beings. To the customers of the Herrenhof Frieda is something of an untouchable. They either respect her or whisper behind her back, but they do not communicate with her. In coming to K. Frieda has come down on one side of the 'fence'. But in doing so she has exchanged one extreme for another, the condition of pure love for the condition of pure sexuality. The puddles of beer on the floor, in which the two 'fallen' lovers roll, are reminiscent of Klamm's brandy 'which seemed hardly more than a sweet perfume' until K. spills it, transforming the rare spirit into 'a drink fit for a coachman'. Frieda and K., rolling to and fro and 'landing with a thud on Klamm's door', have become partners in a self-annihilating ritual.

Kafka's meaning is clearer when, a little later on, he describes a similar scene. Back in K.'s room at the Brückenhof, the two repeat their earlier performance, but this time matters are no longer as simple as the first time round :

There they lay, but not in the forgetfulness of the previous night. She was seeking and he was seeking, they raged and contorted their faces and bored their heads into each other's bosoms in the urgency of seeking something, and their embraces and their tossing limbs did not avail to make them forget, but only reminded them of what they sought; like dogs desperately tearing up the ground they tore at each other's bodies, and often, helplessly baffled, in a final effort to attain happiness they nuzzled and tongued each other's face. Sheer weariness stilled them at last and brought them gratitude to each other. Then the maids came in. 'Look how they're lying there,' said one, and sympathetically cast a coverlet over them (C, 49).

What earlier on was a new and transporting experience—at least for Frieda who sought to liberate herself from Klamm (K., in search of Klamm, tried in fact to 'master' his 'state of unconsciousness')—has now become a desperate quest for what they both lost in their all too human love-making : Klamm. But, in the condition they are in, their quest is in vain, the two lovers merely 'die' in each other's arms and have to be covered up like corpses.

In chapter thirteen the dilemma of their love is explored further through the image of the grave. It is Frieda who gives expression to the secret terror of their situation :

'I feel that here in this world there's no undisturbed place for our love, neither in the village nor anywhere else; and I dream of a grave, deep and narrow, where we could clasp each other in our arms as with iron bars, and I would hide my face in you and you would hide your face in me, and nobody would ever see us any more' (C, 134).

Nor would they themselves, with their faces hidden in each other's breasts, be able to see each other any more. What is left of their love is, in the words of Erich Heller, 'the desperate desire for spiritual certainty'.[10] At this point the real nature of their situation uncannily reveals itself, as a classic case of Romantic love. K. and Frieda have become partners in their pursuit of a purer world rather than lovers in the ordinary sense. Their love is not 'the fulfilling of the law'[11] but, as music to Gregor Samsa, a guide to the unknown and therefore an irredeemably distancing factor in their life. It merely confirms the separation between the ideal and the real rather than fusing the two. Frieda is acutely aware of this when in her desperation she suggests to K. to take her away, as far as possible, from Klamm, to the South of France or to Spain. Her desire is for a purely terrestrial love, for a straightforward situation in which the lovers are spared the perpetual agony of confusing the planes of being. In the village there is

'too much of Klamm! it's to escape from him that I want to go away. It's not Klamm that I miss, it's you. I want to go away for your sake, because I can't get enough of you, here where everything distracts me. I would gladly lose my pretty looks, I would gladly be sick and ailing, if I could be left in peace with you' (C, 133).

Frieda is now prepared to renounce the advantages of knowing Klamm, fine looks and a cocoon-like protection from the laws of becoming, and to direct all her feelings toward the welfare of K. She envisages a love-relationship which would be based on mutual trust, on the tacit understanding that both would actualise their potentialities for the sake of the happiness of the other. Frieda does not in fact mean to exclude Klamm entirely from the life she desires. What she longs for is a balance between Klamm, infinite love, and themselves, finite love. Klamm ought to be present in their relationship just as he is present in the assistants: 'Their eyes—those ingenuous and yet flashing eyes—remind me somehow of Klamm's', Frieda says, 'yes, that's it, it's Klamm's glance that sometimes runs through me from their eyes' (C, 135). Klamm will manifest himself in the form of tender looks, sweet words and caresses exchanged between the lovers. Frieda is not merely oversensitive when she criticises K. for failing to utter her name with the same affection with which he utters the name of Barnabas. She is acutely aware of the lack of tenderness in K.'s dealings with her, of his opportunism and calculating mind. K. sadly fails to live up to Frieda's almost Hegelian vision of love. The feeling of love makes its appearance 'through the bodily members themselves', Hegel wrote, 'through a look, the facial expression, or in a still more spiritual way through the voice tones or a word'.[12] Bürgel similarly refers to opportunities in which more can be achieved 'by means of a word, a glance, a sign of trust . . . than by means of lifelong exhausting efforts' (C, 245). K. has never demonstrated anything of this sort to Frieda. His love for her develops from physical infatuation to a conscious strategy for purposes of transcending his own situation and of reaching Klamm—and absolutes lying beyond Klamm. As Frieda puts it:

'It's only since you have known me that you've become aware of your goal. That's because you believe you have secured in me a sweetheart of Klamm's, and so possess a hostage which can only be ransomed at a great price. Your one endeavour is to treat with Klamm about this hostage. As in your eyes I am nothing and the price everything, so you are ready for any concession so far as I'm concerned, but as for the price you're adamant. So it's a matter of indifference to you that I've lost my post at the Herrenhof and that I've had to leave the Bridge Inn as well, a matter of indifference that I have to endure the heavy work here in the school. You have no tenderness to spare for me, you have hardly even time for me, you leave me to the assistants, the idea of being jealous never comes into your mind, my only value for you is that I was once Klamm's sweetheart' (C, 148f.).

Marriage to Frieda has merely intensified K.'s quest for Klamm instead of bestowing peace on him. Moreover, he searches for Klamm outside his marriage rather than inside it. Life with Frieda is thus no more than a rational and respectable means for the pursuit of higher ends. Frieda's own quest for a spiritual union with K. is frustrated by K.'s inability to surrender his self-consciousness and to forget himself in another self rather than in the search for abstract love. In his dealings with real things and people, K. suffers from an acute sense of unreality. Thus he is not a Romantic hero, as is frequently asserted, because he has no inclination to find out about the absolute through an intensive examination of his own mental and emotional life or that of others. Instead he feels compelled to avoid all emotional involvement and to consider all human realities as a mere stepping-stone to matters beyond them. Frieda is a victim of K.'s 'Realism' (in the medieval sense of the word) or, to put it in more modern terms, of his neurasthenic temper. When she leaves K. for Jeremiah, one of the assistants, she liberates herself from a humiliating position, but merely reverses her role without achieving her desired goal: physical *and* spiritual union with her new partner in love.

As one of Klamm's servants Jeremiah is an 'attractive' person. Imbued with the spirit of his master he is youthful and full of innocent playfulness. Frieda watches his 'stupid tricks with respect and admiration' and is moved by the way he and Arthur 'would hop round like children and stretch out their arms to me like men' (C, 135). Moreover, Jeremiah used to be a playmate of Frieda's in her childhood—'we played together on the slope of the Castle Hill, a lovely time, you've never asked me anything about my past' (C, 233), she tells K. As he does in the *Metamorphosis* Kafka establishes a link here between spiritual and adolescent love. After leaving Klamm Jeremiah quickly turns into 'a rather unhealthy elderly creature' (C, 232), but his fearless and passionate nature still commands Frieda's respect, as she explains to K.:

'When he's in service he fears the slightest look of his master, but when he's not in service there's nothing he's afraid of. He came and took me; forsaken by you, commanded by him, my old friend, I couldn't resist. I didn't unlock the school door. He smashed the window and lifted me out. We flew here, the landlord looks up to him, nothing could be more welcome to the guests, either, than to have such a waiter, so we were taken on, he isn't living with me, but we are staying in the same room' (C, 233f.).

This arrangement, with its flavour of an apparently genuine involvement in a human situation, also reflects Frieda's tragic predicament. K. cannot resist giving his view of the matter:

'Since you're no longer his master's fiancée, you're by no means such a temptation for him as you used to be. You may be the friend of his childhood, but . . . in my opinion he doesn't lay much weight on such sentimental considerations. I don't know why he should seem a passionate person in your eyes. His mind seems to me on the contrary to be particularly cold. He received from Galater [a harbinger of death] certain instructions relating to me . . . one of them was to wreck our relationship. . . . Of love for you he hasn't a trace, he frankly admitted it to me . . . you don't love him, you only think you do, and you'll be thankful to me for ridding you of your illusion. For think, if anybody wanted to take you away from me, without violence, but with the most careful calculation, he could only do it through the two assistants. In appearance, good, childish, merry, irresponsible youths, fallen from the sky, from the Castle, a dash of childhood's memories with them too; all that of course must have seemed very nice, especially when I was the antithesis of it all. . . . The whole thing was simply a wicked but very clever exploitation of the failings in our relationship . . . you were torn away from Klamm, I can't calculate how much that must have meant, but a vague idea of it I've managed to arrive at gradually, you stumbled, you couldn't find yourself, and even if I was always ready to help you, still I wasn't always there, and when I was there you were held captive by your dreams or by something more palpable . . . in short there were times when you turned away from me, longed, poor child, for vague inexpressible things, and at those periods any passable man had only to come within your range of vision and you lost yourself to him, succumbing to the illusion that mere fancies of the moment, ghosts, old memories, things of the past and things receding ever more into the past, life that had once been lived—that all this was your actual present-day life . . . even if you thought that the assistants were sent by Klamm —it's quite untrue, they come from Galater—and even if they manage by the help of this illusion to charm you so completely that even in their disreputable tricks and their lewdness you thought you found traces of Klamm, just as one fancies one catches a glimpse of some precious stone that one has lost in a dung heap, while in reality one wouldn't be able to find it even if it were there—all the same they're only hobbledehoys like the servants in the stall, except that they're not healthy like them, and a little fresh air makes them ill and compels them to take to their beds, which I must say that they know how to snuffle out with a servant's true cunning' (C, 234ff.).

This anti-Hegelian analysis of Frieda's situation is directed against what, in K.'s view, is her illusion that innocent flirtatious behaviour is a signal of higher love. Where Frieda sees Klamm, K. sees Galater, the devil's machinations, a corrupt ritual of temptation and seduction. Jeremiah represents the flesh contaminating the spirit. Once he has achieved his aim his former sprightliness and 'those ingenuous and yet flashing eyes' will no longer be in evidence. He will not even possess the powerful sexual instincts of the servants in the stable. Together with his rapidly decaying body—'he was like a patient who had escaped from hospital' (C, 237)—his mind too turns cold and unresponsive. Frieda's devotion to the task of nursing Jeremiah back to life is just as hopeless an attempt to retain Klamm as were her earlier attempts to obtain Klamm out of K.'s body. But her present situation at least leaves her free from despair and unfulfilled longing. In renouncing 'the only dream' (C, 237) she had, to be with K., Frieda demonstrates the kind of courageous realism Kafka admired in women. The only thing she can do now is to return to her former position behind the bar, to some kind of spiritual no-man's-land. However, her decision to stay with Jeremiah, though not live with him, is an outward sign of her attempts to combine the physical and the spiritual in love.

The promise of mystical experience

Frieda sets an example, which K. cannot follow. The problem about his quest is that, unlike Frieda, he has never experienced anything purer than his immediate self. What he is seeking he knows only in the form of an obsession, not in the form of an intuition. In this sense he is worse off than Joseph K. in *The Trial*. As Dr Gray has pointed out, 'in making K. come to the village and so to the Castle organisation, rather than letting it come to him, Kafka was deliberately reversing the situation of *The Trial*'.[13] Whereas potential knowledge of the Law had been bestowed on Joseph K. the new K. is without such knowledge. His conquering spirit is a measure of both his ignorance and his obsession. He is indeed a man 'who would have at least attempted to pass the guard at the gate of the Law in the Court-chaplain's parable'.[13] This makes K. somebody not only dangerous to himself but also to others. He has no ability to absorb what he conquers, merely to destroy it. He could not destroy Frieda herself, only her 'dream', but he has successfully destroyed their marriage.

By turning it into a public institution, a grotesque affair in the School house for everybody to see, he achieves the opposite of what Frieda intended—an intimate and self-contained relationship. In his contacts with the concrete world, whether human, animal or physical, K. manages to make it more absurd than it already is. Where he desires to redeem reality he merely exhibits its rawness and absurdity. Where he revolts against it he unwittingly blocks all paths to a purer reality.

If to K. reality is not the kind of mediating agency nineteenth-century literature and theology frequently made it out to be, is there another possibility of reaching those unknown powers which we cannot ban from our consciousness? At least one Castle official, Bürgel (diminutive of 'Bürge', guarantor), thinks that such a possibility exists. The Bürgel episode has had as many interpretations as there are critics, most of them concentrating on what they regard as a 'missed opportunity' on the part of K. Since the last paragraph of the relevant chapter appears to contradict this reading I would argue that on the contrary K. does not miss anything but consciously refuses what Bürgel holds out to him.

On his way to Erlanger's office at the Herrenhof K. enters, by mistake, another official's room. There he encounters, lying in a huge bed, Bürgel, Friedrich's (the name suggests, like Frieda's, peace) secretary. As the Castle's 'Verbindungssekretär' Bürgel is responsible for the 'liaison between Friedrich and the village', or, metaphorically speaking, between the human world and the metaphysical world. His position as mediator between the two finds expression in his very appearance :

He was a small, well-looking gentleman whose face had a certain contradictoriness in that the cheeks were chubby as a child's and the eyes merry as a child's, but that the high forehead, the pointed nose, the narrow mouth, the lips of which would scarcely remain closed, the almost vanishing chin, were not like a child's at all, but revealed superior intellect. It was doubtless his satisfaction with this, his satisfaction with himself, that had preserved in him a marked residue of something healthily child-like (C, 241).

The combination of gay innocence and stark intellectualism (qualities which are rarely possessed together) makes him feel at peace with himself. His first question to K.—'Do you know Friedrich?'—has therefore a highly ironic ring about it. Peace with himself is the very thing K. has never known. Bürgel offers K. a place 'on the edge of the bed' (C, 242), i.e. on the border which divides the human and the non-human worlds. Indeed, Bürgel's formula for salvation, which he now offers K., is about none other than the possibility of removing this boundary. The place K. is asked to occupy is 'not an official place' but one 'only intended for nocturnal conversations'. That is to say it is a vantage-point from which private contact between an official and a human being, between worlds which are normally separated from each other by both our blind striving and 'their' perpetual display of 'official' bureaucracy, becomes possible. How is this contact to be realised? The problem is so simple that K.'s reaction is one of disbelief. The fact is, however, as Bürgel explains, that the officials are not only 'resilient' (i.e. tough in their resistance against the human world) but also 'vulnerable' (i.e. weak in their dangerous longing for human contact). If an applicant takes a secretary of the Castle by surprise, if, in the middle of the night and almost unconscious of what happens to him, he slips like a grain of sand through the fine sieve of the Castle's nigh-perfect screening mechanism, then this secretary cannot help but yield to the intruder. Moreover, the Castle, in the person of this one secretary, must grant the unsuspecting applicant what he unintentionally came to ask for. Bürgel himself is at great pains to point out that the chances of this paradoxical situation ever arising are practically nil. And it is probably quite easy to prove 'that there is no room for it in this world' (C, 252). But who knows, one night,

'the never-beheld, always-expected applicant, truly thirstingly expected and always reasonably regarded as out of reach—there this applicant sits. By his mute presence, if by nothing else, he constitutes an invitation to penetrate into his poor life, to look around there as in one's own property and there to suffer with him under the weight of his futile demands. This invitation in the silent night is beguiling. One gives way to it, and now one has actually ceased to function in one's official capacity. It is a situation in which it very soon becomes impossible to refuse to do a favour. To put it precisely, one is desperate; to put it still more precisely, one is very happy. Desperate, for the defenceless position in which one sits here waiting for the applicant to utter his plea and knowing that once it is uttered one must grant it, even if, at least in so far as one has oneself a general view of the situation, it positively tears the official organisation to shreds: this is, I suppose, the worst thing that can happen to one in the fulfilment of one's duties. . . . For it is inherent in our position that we are not empowered to grant pleas such as that with which we are here concerned, yet through the proximity of this nocturnal applicant our official powers do in a manner of speaking grow, we pledge ourselves to do things that are outside our scope; indeed, we shall even fulfil our pledges. The applicant wrings from us in the night, as the robber does in the forest, sacrifices of which we should otherwise never be capable' (C, 252f.).

This passage has that 'eternal unanimity'[14] about it which we find in mystical utterances. The mystical union cannot be willed; it most likely occurs during the hours of the night; it induces both despair and happiness; it tears down the barrier between the seen and the unseen order; it raises our normal powers to unimaginable limits, making nonsense of the function and demands of our ordinary waking consciousness; and we feel as if we had been soaked up and absorbed by the opposite power. It speaks for the extraordinary artistic sophistication of Kafka that he gives us an account of mystical experience from 'the other side', as it were, not from K.'s point of view but from the Castle's. This device enables him to bring an effect of alienation to a predictable and potentially embarrassing subject-matter. At the same time K. can be shown to be the sceptical character he is in the face of alien experience. K.'s response can now be presented as a convenient test-case of the human ability or inability to transcend normal states of consciousness.

Ironically enough K. is in exactly the situation required for the kind of mutual façade-dropping envisaged by Bürgel. He has come at night, stumbled into a room without meaning to do so or without being expected, and has found a most 'vulnerable' official. Not only is he sitting in the right spot but tired to the point of exhaustion, so that he is hardly bothered by his normally over-active consciousness. He has only one wish, that his loquacious host should stop talking and make room for him to lie down on the bed. When K. finally falls asleep he has the following interesting dream :

A secretary, naked, very like the statue of a Greek god, was hard pressed by K. in the fight. It was very funny and K. in his sleep smiled gently about how the secretary was time and again startled out of his proud attitude by K.'s assaults and would hastily have to use his raised arm and clenched fist to cover unguarded parts of his body and yet was always too slow in doing so. The fight did not last long; step for step, and they were very big steps, K. advanced. Was it a fight at all? There was no serious obstacle, only now and then a squeak from the secretary. This Greek god squeaked like a girl being tickled. And finally he was gone, K. was alone in the large room; ready for battle he turned round, looking for his opponent; but there was no longer anyone there (C, 248).

This dream, a pale echo of the Nietzschean dichotomy between Apollonian and Dionysian tendencies, is presented as mystical experience in progress. K.'s 'tiresome consciousness had gone' (C, 248). The simplest rudiment of mystical states, the sense of the timeless, is also characteristic of K.'s dream. It throws up events which 'were repeated once again or perhaps not repeated at all, but only took place now and had already been celebrated earlier and there was no leaving off celebrating it' (C, 248). Above all, the whole thing is, up to a certain point, a dream-version of what Bürgel is spelling out in words. K.'s dream and Bürgel's chatter are in fact carefully synchronised by Kafka. But it is precisely here that the problem lies. The actual miracle, the mystical union, never happens. The dream is no more than a dream about the metaphysical duality of things. The mystery and the enlargement of K.'s perception which seem imminent are never accomplished. What we get is hardly more than a caricature of K.'s predicament, of his waking dream to reach unknown powers which, however, retreat before his attack. Moreover, the possibility of eliminating consciousness altogether must remain an illusion. What K. desires, a state of mind free from all consciousness and 'without dreaming or being disturbed' (C, 250), could only be achieved by by-passing the problem altogether: 'Between the competent secretaries on the one hand and the non-competent on the other, and confronted with the crowd of fully occupied applicants, he would sink into deep sleep and in this way escape everything' (C, 250). But this would be tantamount to giving in to death, which K. has come to conquer. 'It's high time for him to come over' (C, 254), as the Mephisto-like Erlanger (suggestive of 'erlangen', to get, to gain) now shouts from next door, knocking vigorously 'on the partition wall'. The chance in a million does not happen after all. Bürgel's possibility remains no more than a 'rumour'. K.'s consciousness has been pushed to its limits but the partition wall between him and 'them' remains intact. Even Bürgel has to concede this and face the facts :

'Who can help the fact that precisely this limit is significant in other ways too? No, nobody can help it. That is how the world itself corrects the deviations in its course and maintains the balance. This is indeed an excellent, time and again unimaginably excellent arrangement, even if in other respects dismal and cheerless' (C, 254).

But in particular K. suffers from the cheerlessness of it all. Bürgel's lesson has only taught him that the barriers exist. Realising the futility of staying any longer in the room K. decides to leave, thus repudiating the possibility offered by mysticism. The final sentences of the Bürgel chapter are both a raison d'être of K.'s decision and an account of the dreariness of post-mystical experience :

How indescribably dreary this room seemed to him. Whether it had become so or had been so all the time, he did not know. Here he would not even succeed in going to sleep again. This conviction was indeed the decisive factor; smiling a little at this, he rose supporting himself wherever he found any support, on the bed, on the wall, on the door, and, as though he had long ago taken leave of Bürgel, left without saying good-bye.

A divine comedy

Having left Bürgel for good K. becomes the involuntary observer of a curious spectacle in the corridors of the Herrenhof : the distribution of files at the crack of dawn. The scene is one of the most original metaphysical fantasies in literature, a comic allegory of timeless existence. Life for the officials is an integrated and joyous affair, 'like the jubilation of children getting ready for a picnic, another time like day-break in a hen-roost, like the joy of being in complete accord with the awakening day. Somewhere indeed a gentleman imitated the crowing of a cock' (C, 257). There is no distinction between ordinary time and working time. If the officials appear to be tired they are not, like K., exhausted but tired 'amid happy work', as one is tired at noon, as part of the happy natural course of day. ' "For the gentlemen here it is always noon," K. said to himself.' What may look like fatigue is actually indestructible repose, indestructible peace.

When the files are being distributed to the officials events take on a cartoon-like quality. The whole passage begins to buzz with the opening and shutting of doors, with early-morning heads appearing and instantly disappearing again. Confusion arises when the servants deliver the wrong files to the wrong doors, or when an official does not get enough files or does not get his files quickly enough. On such occasions the servants have a hard time in appeasing the officials who, deprived of their allocation, make a great din inside their room, clapping their hands, stamping their feet, and continuously shouting a particular file-number out into the passage through the chink of the door. An impatient official 'was often made still more impatient by the attempts to appease him . . . he did not want consolation, he wanted files' (C, 259). This unquenchable thirst for files reveals the officials' desire to involve themselves in human affairs. The files are of course none other than the complex dossiers on the Castle's petitioners. But the officials have their own way of dealing with human matters. They cannot face such matters directly but only indirectly. They enthusiastically browse in the applicants' records but they shy away from direct contact like little girls. As the landlady explains to K. later, they cannot endure the natural order and those who are part of it. Since the sight of the applicants would be unendurable to them by day, they examine them quickly and at night, 'by artificial light, with the possibility of, immediately after the interrogation, forgetting all the ugliness of it in sleep' (C, 266). The sight of an applicant, 'in all its truth to nature', is the greatest shock to an official. Herein lies the paradox. The Castle organisation exists only with regard to the human world, but it has turned its dealings with this world into a self-contained and self-perpetuating business. Parkinson's law is also a law within the Law. K. watches the Chaplinesque comedy of the officials fighting for their files with great sympathy and understanding, because it dawns on him that the Castle is a mirror not only of our mysterious hopes and desires but also of our comic and unsuccessful ways of realising them. What K. watches is a caricature of man's striving for harmony with the supernatural world. What he has yet to learn is to accept the necessity of looking for harmony within our self rather than outside it. 'The merry bustle among the gentlemen' (C, 268) may demonstrate the absurdity of their ineffective ritual, but it also demonstrates their satisfaction with, and acceptance of it. Whilst K. is unhappy and frustrated in his grim pursuit of the impossible, the officials are happy and flamboyant in their child-like acceptance of an apparently futile situation. Where he gets tragically entangled, they are merely comically involved. By making striving itself an integral part of the metaphysical scheme of things Kafka demonstrates the possibility of striving without an aim. *The Castle* presents thus a complete parody of the human situation. According to Kafka life must not become a human tragedy but some kind of divine comedy.

The parody of self-importance

Above all K. is an unnatural person. His mind is full of lofty abstractions, but otherwise he lacks all natural instincts, which would secure his happiness amongst his own kind. Since he does not know jealousy, for example, he has no sense of whether he really loves Frieda or not. Worse than that, he has no sense of shame, and so lacks the most natural of our instincts, to hide our nakedness. Even the Greek god K. encounters in his dream is concerned with covering 'unguarded parts of his body'. One of the officials' most pronounced qualities is their bashfulness. They are unable to expose themselves to the gaze of strangers. However completely dressed they might be, they always feel 'too naked to show themselves' (C, 267). Their sense of shame has the important function of safeguarding their identity. The point, or truth, of their existence lies in their grace and cheerfulness. With them 'Truth is a bashful thing'. With K. 'Truth is a whore', something that prostitutes existence and destroys its innermost core. Kafka's model here is no doubt borrowed from German Romanticism—one must not give away one's 'secret' to strangers —but the message is clear enough. Truth lies in the enjoyment and exercise of our limited powers, in the firm embrace of the place we occupy. If we have any sense we do not reach beyond what is given us. 'Does not even the nocturnal moth, the poor creature, when day comes seek out a quiet cranny, flatten itself out there, only wishing it could vanish and being unhappy because it cannot?' (C, 266). K. lacks all those instincts which make the lowest of creatures seek out its most suitable habitat. Instead he plants himself precisely 'where he is most visible'. His place is at best in the 'taproom', far away from the sensitive officials themselves. In order to rid themselves of K.'s embarrassing presence the officials have to ring the bell and call for help. Though it is not quite clear what the meaning of the piece of paper is which one of the servants tears up—K. thinks it might refer to his own case (the most insignificant of all)—it is possible that the gesture signifies the Castle's revenge for K.'s unwarranted intrusion. If so the occurrence is at least a faint echo of the ending of *The Trial*, where not only Joseph K.'s file but he himself is destroyed. As Joseph K. agrees to his own death, the new K. does not protest against this administrative 'irregularity' but excuses it by attributing it to the servants' 'accumulated annoyance'. This indeed is the beginning of K.'s metamorphosis, which we shall explore later.

The positive quality of 'bashfulness' is replaced in K. by an inflated sense of self-importance. This effectively prevents him from understanding the general laws of existence. All he is concerned with is the pursuit of self-interest. The Castle, in its wisdom, has taken steps to put K. on the right path by assigning 'assistants' to him. Their function is to correct K.'s attitude to his quest, to cheer him up and quite generally to make him forget himself a little.

For a full understanding of the function of the assistants in *The Castle*, a curious paradox must first be resolved. Arthur and Jeremiah are referred to, at various times, as both K.'s 'old' and 'new' assistants. Who are they really? Let us take a close look at the relevant passage. Having been saluted by the two, 'in Erinnerung an seine Militärzeit, an diese glücklichen Zeiten' ('in memory of his military service, of those happy days'), K. asks them :

'Who are you?' . . . 'Your assistants,' they answered. . . . 'What?' said K., 'are you my old assistants whom I told to follow me and whom I am expecting?' They answered in the affirmative. 'That's good,' observed K. after a short pause. 'I'm glad you've come.' 'Well,' he said, after another pause, 'you've come very late, you're slack.' 'It was a long way to come,' said one of them. 'A long way?' repeated K., 'but I met you just now coming from the Castle.' 'Yes,' said they without further explanation. 'Where is the apparatus?' asked K. 'We haven't any,' said they. 'The apparatus I gave you?' said K. 'We haven't any,' they reiterated. 'Oh, you are fine fellows!'

said K., 'do you know anything about surveying?' 'No,' said they. 'But if you are my old assistants you must know something about it,' said K. They made no reply (C, 24).

The crucial points made about the assistants are that (1) they remind K. of his military service (i.e. of a real-life situation which they have presumably once shared with K.), (2) they have taken a long time to come (i.e. they have enjoyed a long life, whilst K. has been busy trying to settle down in the land of death), (3) they are coming straight from the Castle (i.e. they, or their death, has been accepted by the Castle without further ado whilst K. is not yet considered to be ready) and (4) they have no equipment or any knowledge of land surveying (i.e. they could not bring their former possessions and skills with them). Death, the great leveller, has also made them indistinguishable from each other. K., in accepting this new, paradoxical situation, decides to treat them like identical twins and to call both of them Arthur.

Kafka has found an astonishingly simple way of establishing the metaphorical significance of the assistants. So unobtrusive is his method that, as far as the novel's plot is concerned, the origin and assignment of Arthur and Jeremiah remain a puzzle to most readers. The paradox of the two being both K.'s old and new assistants can only be resolved if we grasp the allegorical basis of *The Castle*. (It certainly does not help to explain the matter away by taking the Castle to have made a mistake, as traditional Kafka criticism would have it.) If it is correct to conclude that the novel's episodes and images are decisively orientated towards the theme of death then this should also manifest itself on the level of plot. This is indeed so. In having come to the Castle K. has put himself in his own coffin, as it were. Unlike his assistants, he has come uninvited and with impossible designs on what must remain the supreme mystery not only to him but to any man. (Cf. the quotation on page 179.) K.'s 'old' assistants followed him, but only after their time had come. And it is only after their arrival in the kingdom of death that they can be employed by the Castle authorities as their master's 'new' assistants. But it must be said that Kafka left this point obscure on purpose. A rigid allegorical structure would not have allowed him to explore his grand theme in all its complexity. The plot had to be left as ambiguous and open-ended as the thematic implications of the novel.

In due course K. receives the following letter from Klamm:

To the Land Surveyor at the Bridge Inn. The surveying work which you have carried out thus far has been appreciated by me. The work of the assistants, too, deserves praise. You know how to keep them at their jobs. Do not slacken in your efforts! Carry your work on to a fortunate conclusion. Any interruption would displease me (C, 115).

K., naturally, is puzzled. Not only has he done nothing that could remotely be called 'land surveying' but, much worse, the assistants have in the meantime fully lived up to their original confession that they do not know a thing about their supposed job. K. of course does not realise that the Castle has all along taken his activity figuratively rather than literally. What else could it have done? Representing an order different from the human order it cannot begin to accept, or even understand, purely human activities. But it can at least try, however reluctantly, to monitor those objectives of K.'s consciousness that are aggressively orientated towards itself. The inn, with its traditional overtones of a last resting-place in the *paysage mort*, is K.'s personal purification chamber within the larger purgatory of the village. Whatever he does, or omits to do, at this stage will be noted by the Castle. Like his counterpart in *The Trial* K. has plenty of helpers at his disposal, to advise him and warn him of the mistakes he is likely to make. Though he does not know it K.'s most watchful guardians are the two clownish assistants. They cannot protect K. from blundering but they can at least provide a kind of running theatrical commentary on their master's activity. Wherever K. goes the assistants go. Not only are they present in K.'s very bedroom but sometimes even manage to sleep between Frieda and him. K. conducts his quest on the same functional and rationalised, rather impersonal lines typified by the organised way in which he intends to survey the land, or in which Joseph K. runs his business in the bank. Everything has first to be considered, then carried out in an orderly, efficient manner and with a minimum personal involvement and display of emotion. The clownish behaviour of the assistants is the comic mirror-image of all this. It is the silhouette of K.'s activity distorted into a farce, a radical parody of human solemnity. This is how things look from 'beyond'. When K. later questions Jeremiah on the complaints the assistants intend to put in about K.'s rough treatment of them, he answers :

'That you can't understand a joke. What have we done? Jested a little, laughed a little, teased your fiancée a little. And all according to our instructions, too. When Galater sent us to you . . . he said . . . : You are to go down there as assistants to the Land Surveyor. We replied : But we don't know anything about the work. Thereupon he replied : That's not the main point : if it's necessary, he'll teach you it. The main thing is to cheer him up a little. According to the reports I've received he takes everything too seriously. He has just got to the village, and starts off thinking that a great experience, whereas in reality it's nothing at all. You must make him see that' (C, 219).

K., however, gives the assistants little chance to fulfil their mission. He drives them from his presence whenever possible, maltreating them physically if they provoke him too much. On one occasion he sends Jeremiah out into the snow and lets him freeze at the railings. ' "His obstinacy is really wonderful," K. told himself, but had to add, "he'll freeze to the railings if he keeps it up". Outwardly, however, K. had nothing for the assistant but a threatening gesture with his fist' (C, 154). Railings, or lattice-work, are one of Kafka's symbols of the human predicament. 'I am like a living lattice-work, a lattice that is solidly planted and would like to tumble down' (D2, 31), he writes in the Diaries. Jeremiah's determination to freeze at the railings rather than give up his attempt to get into the house is an example of the absurd endurance-test which our life represents. The 'inner' K. realises this. But the 'outer' K. acts against the insight of his better self. The scene also reveals that the fate of the assistants and that of K.'s better self are synchronised. Like the warder Franz in *The Trial* they are K.'s doubles, or Counter-K.s. In terms of the allegorical schemes of *The Castle* Arthur and Jeremiah are K.'s 'new' assistants assigned to him in order to make him understand the limits of man's striving. In terms of the novel's psychology they are his 'old' assistants, metaphors of genuinely human qualities—this is why Frieda feels so attached to them—and of our realistic instincts and sense of perspective. Because of K.'s obstinacy they can do hardly more than demonstrate 'how every person is lost in himself beyond hope of rescue'. But beneath their apparently destructive clowning, and undetected by K., lies a more positive message, that salvation is not to be sought in the promotion of self-interest but in our ability 'to observe other people and the law governing them and everything' (D2, 10).

Amalia and Olga

In the chapter on *The Trial* it was briefly shown how Kafka establishes a significant relationship between sexual and spiritual feelings. In *The Castle* the opposition of female sexuality and male spirituality acquires the dimensions of a major theme. A short excursion into the psychological thinking of the period, as far as the problem of the erotic is concerned, will reveal that this theme is in no way peculiar to Kafka. On the contrary, in his attempt to associate female existence with elementary forces he could rely on what was already spelt out fully in the prolific literature around him. Here is a typical example from the Austrian writer Richard Beer-Hofmann :

> The male alone was weaned, while woman yet
> May ever dream upon the bosom of the earth,
> Close to the springs of life. Not yet expelled
> From ancient mystic covenants,
> Submitting to the movement of the stars
> That likewise govern seas and tides, she
> With every moon that wanes, mid blood and pain,
> Is bidden—like an erring priestess—to reflect
> Upon her earthly mission. What to men
> Appears as riddle, conflict, charm perhaps
> Is this : that she, akin to nature's elements—
> Perhaps herself the last-born of their line—
> Is for him the only tie which conjoins
> His fate with cosmic destinies.[15]

These are the kind of clichés the turn of the century repeated *ad nauseam* in the course of its renewed interest in a favourite nineteenth-century topic, the daemonic female. The subject was not only confined to the arts but was frequently discussed within the prestige disciplines of the time, psychology, physiology, and even sociology. One of the most notorious books was Otto Weininger's *Geschlecht und Charakter* (1903), in which the author explores, with the high-flown rhetoric of a pseudo-scientific pathos, the kind of sentiments Beer-Hofmann expressed in free verse. Here is Weininger's version of the harmony assumed to exist between women and universal forces:

Coitus is the only thing which acquires an exclusively positive value in the eyes of woman, at all times and in all places: woman is the bearer of the communal principle in general. The supreme value which woman places on coitus is not confined to one individual, not even to the individual who evaluates, it refers to Being *as such*, it is not personal but *inter*-personal, *supra*-personal, it is as it were . . . the transcendental *function of woman. For if womanliness is coupling, womanliness is universal sexuality. Coitus is the supreme value for woman, she seeks to achieve it always and in all places.* Her individual sexuality represents only a limited portion of this unlimited desire.[16]

The corresponding ideas which we find in Kafka's *The Trial* and *The Castle* merely demonstrate the degree to which Kafka's language is emancipated from turn-of-the-century jargon. Otherwise there is a very close analogy. Though Kafka pursues his own complex aims with ideas of this kind, his view of women, like D. H. Lawrence's, is quite clearly based on a well-established literary and anthropological topos, that of an assumed transcendental function of female sexuality. We may now appreciate why women like Frieda and Gardena are, almost in an *a priori* sense, in the grip of Klamm's power; or why the court official's wife in *The Trial* so easily succumbs to sexual advances, no matter from whom they come; or why, quite generally, the women in Kafka's work are an integral part of the order the K.s try to penetrate.

One of the most obvious examples of the daemonic female in Kafka is Leni, the Advocate's nurse, in *The Trial*. When Joseph K. encounters her for the first time she appears like a figure of virtue and light, wearing a long white apron and holding a candle in her hand. She is described as having a doll-like rounded face and great dark, somewhat protuberant, eyes. Though she looks like a delicate Pre-Raphaelite painting K. is soon to experience the irresistible power of her seductive art. Her beauty is marred by a sinister deformity of her hand. The web-like growth between her fingers designates her as a figure whose real roots are in the mud and slime of the primeval swamp. Leni is quite generally described in animal-like terms. K. calls her a 'cherishing little creature'; she gives out an animal-like 'odour as of pepper'

173

and when she kisses K. she bites him on the neck. Physical disfigurement, like Fräulein Montag's limp or the spinal deformity of the girl in Titorelli's house (*The Trial*), is a sign of the daemonic element in women. But the term 'daemonic' must not be applied to Kafka in too narrow a sense. It mirrors the whole range of ambiguities with which Kafka habitually viewed the transcendental. Leni's sexual aggressiveness is sinister because the powers that have challenged Joseph K. and his tidy rational world are, to his bourgeois imagination, irrational and debased. Pepi in *The Castle*, Frieda's temporary successor in the bar and another chthonic creature (she lives in a damp cellar), has none of Leni's evilness about her. Her bonds with the elemental reflect a positive situation, and the reconciled K. advises her to stay in her dark maid's room rather than aspire to higher positions. Frieda and Gardena can no longer be called daemonic females at all. They represent the kind of transcendental function Weininger attributes to women in general, and therefore the kind of puzzle Beer-Hofmann is referring to. They raise the hope in K. of being able to participate one day in the mysterious order from which he feels so hopelessly cut off.

We are now in a position to understand the complex fate of the most enigmatic of Kafka's females, Amalia of the Barnabas family. It is often assumed by readers of Kafka that the attempts of his protagonists, in their most arrogant mood, to force the authorities to yield, is the worst human crime Kafka could imagine. A crime much worse than that, if indeed it can be called a crime, is committed by Amalia. Her tragic story is revealed to K. by her sister Olga, who reports the following incident. One day in July the Fire Brigade gave a celebration. The Castle too had made its contribution in the form of a new fire-engine, which was handed over by the official Sortini. The attraction of the day was Amalia who had been decked out like a bride for the occasion. She was not exactly beautiful, but her 'sombre glance' and authoritative appearance commanded everybody's respect. By far the proudest man was Amalia's father, who urged the crowd to take a good look at the new apparatus:

'he laughed with delight when he saw it, the new fire-engine made him happy, he began to examine it and explain it to us, he wouldn't hear of any opposition or holding back, but made everyone of us stoop and almost crawl under the engine if there was something there he had to show us, and he smacked Barnabas for refusing. Only Amalia paid no attention to the engine, she stood upright beside it in her fine clothes and nobody dared to say a word to her' (C, 179).

Sortini, who for a long time did nothing but wearily scan one guest after another, 'as if sighing to find that there was still another and another to look at', suddenly leapt over the shaft ('sprang über die Deichsel') at the sight of Amalia, to get nearer to her. The gesture is interpreted by everybody as a declaration of love to Amalia. Sortini did not do much else after that except sit on the wagon pole with his arms folded until the Castle carriage came to fetch him. The next day Amalia received a letter from Sortini, which was 'couched in the vilest language' and ordered the girl to come and see the sender at once. Amalia was so offended by the obscene document that she tore it up immediately. Soon after that the results of Amalia's hasty action began to show. Her father was asked to resign from the Fire Brigade, friends and neighbours withdrew from the family until its life was reduced, both socially and economically, to a mere vegetable existence. They had become outsiders in every sense of the word. Within months the parents' former health and energy changed to a crippling disease, which rendered them completely helpless. Amalia made it her exclusive business to nurse the parents; she also developed a habit of attending to her mother first whenever the two required her services. What are we to make of this tale?

Ever since Erich Heller briskly dismissed Max Brod's notorious interpretation—that Sortini's designs on Amalia should be seen as a parallel to the sacrifice of Isaac—as one of 'the comic escapades of literary criticism', critics have been less frequently tempted to attach religious significance to the Sortini episode. But even the more recent 'existential' interpretations, accusing Amalia of 'bad faith', seem to miss the main point. And it is certainly misleading to draw too close a parallel between Amalia's and K.'s predicaments.

The meaning of Amalia's action is best understood by an analysis of the sustained sexual metaphor through which the whole episode is presented. The Fire Brigade's celebrations are more than a *sacre du printemps* (Politzer), they are an explicit invitation to everybody present at the festival to familiarise themselves with the primary mechanism of sexual love and procreation. The father's enthusiasm about the new fire-engine is a measure of his sexual potency, his demonstration of it like a demonstration of the male organ itself. But it is again the transcendental function of the sexual activity that is emphasised. The Castle too has its own fire brigade, but it is outmoded and needs restructuring. A deputation from the Castle has seen the performance of the village's fire brigade, has expressed great approval and compared the Castle brigade unfavourably with the village brigade. That is to say, it has praised an activity that is a great unifying factor in the relationship between the village and the Castle. The village brigade's celebrations are in fact so successful that the Castle cannot resist establishing, through the person of one of its secretaries, Sortini, a significant link between itself and the human community. The occasion generates one of those moments when, in Bürgel's words, an official is surprised in his own weakness. Against his will the stiff and normally withdrawn Sortini leaps over the shaft in order to make an approach to Amalia. The German 'sprang über die Deichsel' makes clearer what is meant here. In Kafka's days, and until quite recently, cows were used by Czech and Austrian peasants to pull carts. When sexually excited the cows would frequently leap over the shaft of the cart rather than move forward. The phrase 'über die Deichsel springen' is then also used figuratively, to denote uncontrolled sexual behaviour amongst humans. Since Kafka reproduces the phrase exactly (which is odd in the case of a fire-engine) we must assume that he quite consciously brings its standard figurative meaning into play. When after the leap Sortini goes and sits on the shaft then he confirms the Castle's intention to give the object, and the celebrations evolving around it, its fullest blessing. It is now up to the villagers to make the best use of their chance. As is normal on such occasions only one person receives the crucial invitation, and whatever that person does to meet the challenge is done in the name of the whole community. The same happened, as Olga points out, when Frieda and Gardena were selected and sent for under comparable circumstances.

In refusing to even look at the fire-engine and in tearing up Sortini's letter the next day Amalia offends, in the eyes of the villagers, against an absolute law. The point is made repeatedly in the novel that women cannot help loving the officials, however crude or obscene their approaches may be. Being selected by one of them is the greatest possible honour that can be bestowed on a woman. Frieda and Gardena followed Klamm willingly, Olga thinks nothing of spending every night for two years in the stable with the Castle's servants, and all those women who have not yet been selected patiently wait for their great chance. Only Amalia is the odd woman out. To understand her reaction we must take into account what is said about her character. Despite her many positive qualities she is lacking in good-nature and generosity. She is above all of the domineering type. 'Amalia was so masterful that she not only took to herself whatever was said in her presence, but induced other people of their own free will to include her in everything' (C, 162). Her 'cold hard eye' has repelled K. from the beginning. Unlike everybody else she is not interested in what she calls 'Castle gossip'. 'I heard once of a young man,' she tells K., 'who thought of nothing but the Castle day and night, he neglected everything else and people feared for his reason, his mind was so wholly absorbed by the Castle' (C, 193). She has no patience with Olga's and Barnabas's despairing struggle to gain access to the Castle. Their tragic failure to arrive at any certainty in matters of their unrequited endeavour is proof enough for Amalia that the Castle is not worth bothering about. She therefore remains indifferent to any attempts to bridge the gulf between the world she knows and the world she cannot and does not want to know. In her rebellion against the transcendental Amalia is Kafka's only truly absurdist character. She is a living testimony against the influence of outside powers, and against the perversions created by these powers in the human world. Her action is thus not so much a crime but a heroic protest against an alien order. We are told that Amalia probably loved Sortini, and there are signs that she loves K. But she protests against the perverted conditions which result from all attempts to reconcile the seen and unseen order. She loved the 'small, frail, reflective-looking gentleman' in Sortini, his aloof intelligence, but she is frustrated by the way the official's purity communicated itself to a human being. She cannot accept Olga's apologetic interpretation of the ghastly incident: when the officials rise from their desk 'they feel out of place in the ordinary world and in their distraction they say the most beastly things. . . . Now when a man so unused to society as Sortini suddenly felt himself in love with a village girl, he'll naturally take it quite differently from, say, the joiner's apprentice next door. And one must remember, too, that between an official and a village cobbler's daughter there's a great gulf fixed which has to be somehow bridged over, and Sortini tried to do it in that way, where someone else might have acted differently' (C, 184f.).

Olga's mind is practical and conciliatory, she accepts the absurd, the fact that the spiritual gets perverted into the sordid when it is translated into the human sphere. Though the Amalia chapters are incomplete it is clear enough that Kafka was groping for what Camus expressed in *The Rebel*, in the chapter on 'Metaphysical Rebellion' :

Metaphysical rebellion is the means by which a man protests against his condition and against the whole of creation. It is metaphysical because it disputes the ends of man and creation. The slave protests against the condition of his state of slavery; the metaphysical rebel protests against the human condition in general. The rebel slave affirms that there is something in him which will not tolerate the manner in which his master treats him; the metaphysical rebel declares that he is frustrated by the universe. For both of them it is not only a problem of pure and simple negation. In fact in both cases we find an assessment of values in the name of which the rebel refuses to accept the condition in which he finds himself.[17]

These values Amalia finds in herself, in her job—she makes expensive dresses for the more distinguished women in the village—and, last but not least, in looking after her parents rather than after Castle matters. Her rebellion is therefore an aspiration to a human order, a demand for clarity and unity as only human intelligence can achieve it. But Kafka is not thinking of male intelligence, a kind of rational constructivism, but of female intelligence, a combination of reason and moral authority. The fact that Amalia gives preferential treatment to her mother also appears to indicate that the human order envisaged is of a matriarchal type.

Amalia's metaphysical revolt is an expression of her non-conciliatory form of intelligence. She is not against the Castle as such, as one might think, but against its confusing interference with the village world. Where others tortuously try to make sense of the Castle, she simply blasphemes, primarily in the name of human dignity, by denouncing it, and everything it stands for, as the supreme disillusionment. Of necessity, Amalia lives her life according to a philosophy of domination, as described by Olga. Her whole existence is like a 'silent restraint' on others, an unspoken demand to follow her example. As her exclusive devotion to the dying parents proves, her ultimate goal is no less than to conquer death itself. This much she shares with K. The difference however is that Amalia tries to achieve her aims by strengthening the human position to the utmost, whilst K. pursues his aims by undermining this position and by trying to operate within the Castle itself.

In the end Amalia's way will be rejected by the others. As Olga puts it : 'We couldn't go on living like that, without hope of any kind we could not live, and we began each in his or her own fashion with prayers or blustering to beg the Castle's forgiveness' (C, 199). But this does not mean that Amalia's exceptional courage is not acknowledged. It is her perceptive sister again who puts the matter most eloquently :

'Amalia not only suffered, she had the understanding to see her suffering clearly, we saw only the effects, but she knew the cause, we hoped for some small relief or other, she knew that everything was decided, we had to whisper, she had only to be silent. She stood face to face with the truth and went on living and endured her life then as now' (C, 197).

Conclusion

In Kafka's *Wedding Preparations* we find the following astute comment on the relationship between life and death :

Anyone who has once been in a state of suspended animation can tell terrible stories about it, but he cannot say what it is like after death, he has actually been no nearer to death than anyone else, fundamentally he has only 'lived' through an extraordinary experience, and not-extraordinary, everyday life has become more valuable to him as a result. It is similar with everyone who has experienced something extraordinary. For instance, Moses certainly experienced something 'extraordinary' on Mount Sinai, but instead of submitting to this extraordinary experience, like someone in a state of suspended animation, not answering and remaining quiet in his coffin, he fled down the mountain and, of course, had valuable things to tell and loved, even more than before, the people to whom he had fled and then sacrificed his life for them, one might say : in gratitude.[18]

Herein lies the ultimate meaning of *The Castle*, in the hero's return to life from a state of apparent death. The urge to transcend life led Moses to Mount Sinai, K. in the opposite direction, to some kind of underworld. In their own ways they have been witnesses of extraordinary conditions, but the value of their respective experience lies in the same thing, in its re-application to normal conditions. What one gains through a temporary absence from the ordinary world is not the acquisition of 'higher' truths but a sharpened apprehension of life. At almost the same time as Kafka was writing the above lines, the Swiss painter Paul Klee made a similar point in his diaries : 'Imagine that you had died : after long years of absence you are enabled to cast a single glance towards earth. You see a street lamp and an old dog, lifting its leg. You would then sob with sheer emotion.'[19] In this sense *The Castle* can be understood as an immense 'Vexierbild', as a given account of an estranged experience through which the contours of normal experience come into focus once more. K.'s excursions into the unknown lead to the rediscovery of life as it is, when uncontaminated by our aspirations. By surprising the officials in the Herrenhof at their most private business K. has pushed his quest to its limits and, faced with those limits, is forced to conclude that his spiritual escapades were an aberration of the mind rather than a valid search for truth. K.'s conversation with Pepi at the end of the novel is a subdued homage to the intrinsic value of our appointed station in life. Pepi is to stay in her dark room, and not to aspire after Frieda's position in the taproom. 'You chambermaids are used to spying through keyholes', K. warns her, 'and from that you get this way of thinking, of drawing conclusions, as grand as they are false, about the whole situation from some little thing you really see' (C, 290). Frieda's job is really a job like any other, but in her dreaminess Pepi would turn it into some kind of heaven, would consequently set about everything with exaggerated eagerness, and 'trick yourself out as in your opinion the angels are tricked out—but in reality they are different' (C, 291). Pepi's designs on higher things are not a true reflection of her natural self, they were sparked off by K.'s own striving, i.e. by following a bad example. At first she had no serious intentions of getting on in the world. Being herself in love with K. she particularly disliked Frieda's ambition and her 'artfulness'. All she desired was to lower herself and to teach K.

what true love was, which he would never be able to learn from Frieda and which was independent of all positions of honour in the world. But then everything turned out differently. And what was to blame for this? . . . Above all, K. For what was he after, what sort of strange person was he? What was he trying to get, what were these important things that kept him busy and made him forget what was nearest of all, best of all, most beautiful of all? . . . anyone who had the strength to set fire to the whole Herrenhof and burn it down, burn it to the ground, so that not a trace of it was left, burn it up like a piece of paper in the stove, *he* would today be Pepi's chosen love (C, 274).

The passage is reminiscent of what Kafka wrote as early as 1902 to his friend Oskar Pollak :

Prague does not let go—either of you or of me. This little mother has claws. There is nothing for it but to give in or—. We should have to set it on fire from two sides, at the Vysehrad and at the Hradschin, only thus could we free ourselves.[20]

The city with its great variety of cultural traditions (both Western and Eastern) and its rich intellectual past is experienced as a burden rather than a liberating force by the young generation. Like the Castle to Pepi, it is a unique spiritual phenomenon which inspires both love and hate in those who still have to make their choices in life. Pepi's wish to see the Herrenhof burning is a reflection of her instinctive knowledge that anything K. is after is a distraction from true, that is to say terrestrial happiness. When K. does not reciprocate her love she herself begins to think of a career connecting her with the Castle. Kafka has made the point once before, in *The Trial*. The unknown powers will take possession of us as soon as we either disengage ourselves from life or are frustrated in our spontaneous commitment to it.

The K. who emerges from the corridors of the Herrenhof is a changed person. He has learnt the essential lesson, that the officials, the 'gentlemen' are hardly better off than normal human beings. Real life may be sombre, disagreeable, and like a millstone round our neck, but it is at least authentic, not the kind of meaningless spiritual arcadia the officials inhabit. Their serenity may be a fine thing to contemplate, but it is also acquiescence in the futility of it all. Their concern for files may be impressive to the applicants, but to the objective observer it is hardly more than a substitute for actual contact. And is their 'bashfulness' and 'shame' such a positive thing, as the landlady at the Herrenhof suggests? It is after all not a natural instinct but a consequence of the Fall (mythologically speaking) or a product of alienated human consciousness and culture (sociologically speaking). This reminds us again that the whole Castle-world is ultimately none other than a Fata Morgana created by the demiurge for the purpose of confusing the innocent. And yet when all is said and done this world will never cease to present an intriguing, even necessary, challenge to the human imagination. The novel's ambiguity is sustained until the very end. Pepi's sudden interest in Klamm implies both the risk of alienation and the possibility of escaping a lower level of existence. Whether the former is an evil and the latter a good thing we shall never know. In each case there are gains and losses. Moreover, one seems to imply the other at any time. To strive *and* not to strive appears to be the paradoxical message of *The Castle*. This postulate of practical reason at least allows life to become a self-correcting process within its own limits. It is not a doctrine of salvation. Ironically enough, K. is reminded of Death, more forcefully than ever, as soon as he has renounced all his former ambitions. The novel's last words are spoken by the Herrenhof landlady, the Madame la Mort of the book, and addressed to K. whilst 'Gerstäcker was clutching at his sleeve again' : 'I am getting a new dress tomorrow, perhaps I shall send for you.' But now this will not be a 'Scheintod', a state of suspended animation, but real death, the decisive moment which puts man in the coffin, or on Mount Sinai, without any chance of return. It would be futile for the novelist, or any man, to reflect further on the matter—though he may amuse himself by either asking, or attempting to answer, the question of which land the enigmatic and unseen Count Westwest inhabits. Towards the end of his life, and stricken by an incurable disease (tuberculosis), Kafka may have wanted to write a novel about Death. All he could attempt was an exploration of human experience on the margins of existence.

Notes

Full bibliographical details, where not found in the Notes, are given in the Select Bibliography

1. Kafka's World

1 *Der Habsburgische Mythos in der österreichischen Literatur*, Otto Müller, Salzburg, 1966.

2 Martin Swales, *Arthur Schnitzler. A Critical Study*, Oxford, at the Clarendon Press, 1971, p.5 (Dr Swales' book contains an excellent summary of the writer's position in *fin de siècle* Austria.)

3 *Da geht Kafka*, Artemis Verlag, Zurich and Stuttgart, 1965, p.6.

4 *The Diaries of Franz Kafka 1914–1924*, tr. M. Greenberg, p.145.

5 Cf., for example, his *Streitbares Leben* (Kindler, Munich, 1960) and *Der Prager Kreis* (Kohlhammer, Stuttgart, 1966). In the context of this chapter I have also found useful E. Goldstücker's (ed.) *Weltfreunde: Konferenz über die Prager deutsche Literatur* (Luchterhand, Berlin, 1967).

6 Quoted from Franz Baumer, op. cit., p.62.

7 Janouch, *Conversations with Kafka*, p.103.

8 Ibid., p.86.

9 Quoted from Franz Baumer, op. cit., p.64.

10 Janouch, op. cit., p.85.

11 Leo Tolstoy, *A Confession, The Gospel in Brief, What I Believe*, tr. A. Maude, Oxford University Press, London, 1967 (1940), p.52. (The World's Classics, p.229.)

12 Max Stirner, *The Ego and His Own*, tr. S. T. Byington, introd. J. L. Walker, London, 1915, p.199. (The German text was originally published in 1846.)

13 Ibid., pp.199f.

14 Robert Musil, *The Man Without Qualities*, Vol. 1, tr. Eithne Wilkins and Ernst Kaiser, Secker & Warburg, London, 1953, p.54.

15 All we know is that Stirner was much talked about at the turn of the century and that the anarchist Vohryzek lectured on Stirner in 1902 to the Young People's Club in Prague. 'Stirnerism' was introduced to the late Nineties through J. H. Mackay's biography of Stirner (1898) and his edition of the philosopher's *Kleinere Schriften und Entgegnungen* (1898). When Kafka was asked one day by Gustav Janouch whether he had studied Ravachol's life he answered: 'Yes. And not only Ravachol's but the lives of various other anarchists. I went deeply into the lives and ideas of Godwin, Proudhon, Stirner, Bakunin, Kropotkin, Tucker and Tolstoy . . .' (*Conversations with Kafka*, p.90).

16 W. H. Sokel, *The Writer in Extremis*, McGraw-Hill, New York, Toronto and London, 1964, p.35.

17 Hugo von Hofmannsthal, 'The

Letter of Lord Chandos', in *Selected Prose*, tr. M. Hottinger and T. and J. Stern, Routledge & Kegan Paul, London, 1952, pp.129–41.

18 S. T. Coleridge, 'To William Sotheby', in Coleridge, *Select Poetry and Prose*, ed. Stephen Potter, The Nonesuch Press, London, 1950, p.599.

19 Ibid.

20 Quoted from William James, *The Varieties of Religious Experience*, ed. A. D. Nock, Fontana, London and Glasgow, 1960, p.161. I have quoted from James because the translation he uses is particularly close to turn-of-the-century terminology. But cf. also Leo Tolstoy, *A Confession* (see note 11), pp.20f. For close analogies between Tolstoy's *Confession* and Hofmannsthal's *Letter* see pp.17ff., 23f., 44f., 52f. and 58.

21 Hugo von Hofmannsthal, *Prosa I*, ed. H. Steiner, Fischer, Frankfurt am Main, 1950, p.191.

22 'Hofmannsthal's Essays, 1900–1908', in *Hofmannsthal. Studies in Commemoration*, ed. F. Norman, London, 1963, p.51.

23 'Hofmannsthal's Bibliothek', in *Euphorion*, LV (1961), p. 22.

24 Frank Kermode, 'A Babylonish Dialect', in *T. S. Eliot. The Man and His Work*, ed. Allen Tate, London, 1967, p.234.

25 *'Description of a Struggle'* and *'The Great Wall of China'*, tr. W. and E. Muir and T. and J. Stern, Secker & Warburg, London, 1960, p.51.

26 Ibid., p. 48.

27 Ibid., p.49f.

28 Ibid., p.52.

29 Albert Einstein was professor of theoretical physics at the German University in Prague (1911–12), where the philosophical implications of his new work on the generalisation of the special theory of relativity aroused great interest in intellectual circles. He met Kafka, and became particularly friendly with Hugo Bergmann and Max Brod. The latter portrayed Einstein's personality in his novel *The Redemption of Tycho Brahe*. (Cf. Philipp Frank, *Einstein. His Life and Times*, Cape, London, 1948, pp.106ff.)

30 Cf. Georg Lukacs, *The Meaning of Contemporary Realism*, tr. J. and N. Mander, Merlin Press, London, 1962, p.27.

2. Literature as Corrective Punishment

1 Op. cit., pp.248, 290.

2 Sokel, *Tragik und Ironie*, p.94.

3 Ibid., p.192. (My translation.)

4 The verbal allusion in the two passages is unfortunately lost in the Muirs' translation: 'And it was like a confirmation of their new dreams and excellent intentions that at the end of their journey their daughter sprang to her feet first and stretched her young body' (M, 63).

'It showed a lady . . . sitting upright and holding out to the spectator a huge fur muff into which the whole of her forearm vanished' (M, 9).

5 Leopold von Sacher-Masoch, *Venus in Furs*, Sphere Books, London, 1969, p.9.

6 Ibid., p.13.

7 Ibid.

8 Ibid.

9 Ibid., p.26.

10 Kafka's idea of 'Verhaftung', which is hinted at here but more fully developed in *The Trial*, seems a curious mixture of Rousseau's idea of a 'contrat social' and of Kafka's notion of metaphysical guilt.

11 *Venus in Furs*, p.82.

12 James Cleugh, *The First Masochist*, Anthony Blond, London, 1967, p.60.

13 D1, pp.297f.

14 In his exhaustive *Studien zu einer historisch-kritischen Ausgabe von Robert Musil's Roman 'Der Mann ohne Eigenschaften'*, Rowohlt Verlag, 1964.

15 *James Joyce*, Oxford University Press, New York, 1959, p.662.

16 R. M. Adams, *Surface and Symbol. The Consistency of James Joyce's 'Ulysses'*, Oxford University Press, New York, 1962, p.246.

17 Cf. also Ernst Kaiser and Eithne Wilkins, 'Musil und die Quadratwurzel aus minus eins', in *Robert Musil, Leben, Werk, Wirkung*, Reinbeck, Vienna, 1960, pp.157–74; W. Bausinger, op. cit., pp.93ff.; Ulrich Karthaus, *Der andere Zustand. Zeitstrukturen im Werke Robert Musils*, Erich Schmidt Verlag, Berlin, 1965, pp.53ff.; H. W. Schaffnit, *Mimesis als Problem*, Walter de Gruyter, Berlin, 1971, pp.1–7, 35–47.

18 Op. cit., p.252.

19 Ibid., p.248.

20 D1, p.276.

21 Harry Levin, *James Joyce. A Critical Introduction*, Faber & Faber, London, 1944 (1960), p.20.

22 I have borrowed this phrase from Harry Levin.

23 Charles Robert Maturin, *Melmoth the Wanderer*, ed. with an introduction by Douglas Grant, Oxford University Press, London, 1968, p.135.

24 Fyodor Dostoyevsky, *Notes from Underground*, tr. R. E. Matlaw, E. P. Dutton, New York, 1960, p.114.

25 Frank Kermode, *Modern Essays*, Fontana Books, London, 1971, p.118.

26 Maturin, op. cit., p.157.

27 Max Born (ed.), *The Born-Einstein Letters*, tr. Irene Born, Macmillan, London, 1971, p.4.

28 W. M. Johnston, *The Austrian Mind. An Intellectual and Social History, 1848–1938*, University of California Press, Berkeley, Los Angeles and London, 1972, p.273.

29 Immanuel Kant, *Critique of Pure Reason*, tr. N. K. Smith, Macmillan, London, 1963 (1933), p.22. (I have slightly amended the English text.)

30 Emile Durkheim, *The Elementary Forms of the Religious Life*, tr. J. W. Swain, Allen & Unwin, London, 1964 (1915), p.2.

31 Ibid., p.16.

3. *Metamorphosis*

1 In *Stories of Three Decades*, tr. H. T. Lowe-Porter, Secker & Warburg, London, 1936, p.385.

2 Fyodor Dostoyevsky, *Notes from Underground*, tr. R. E. Matlaw, E. P. Dutton, New York, 1960, p.6.

3 Ibid., p.7.

4 Ibid., p.5.

5 In this context the following passage by Karl Marx on alienation is of interest: as a result of alien-

ation 'man (the worker) no longer feels himself to be freely active in any but his animal functions . . . and in his human functions he no longer feels himself to be anything but animal. What is animal becomes human and what is human becomes animal'. (Quoted from Istvan Mészáros, *Marx's Theory of Alienation*, Merlin Press, London, 1970, p.177.)

6 Kurt Weinberg, op. cit., p.264. (My translation.)
7 R. A. Nisbet, *The Sociological Tradition*, Heinemann, London, 1970, p.306.
8 Ibid., p.270.
9 Cf. also H. Stuart Hughes, *Consciousness and Society. The Reorientation of European Social Thought 1890–1930*, MacGibbon & Kee, London, 1967, pp.336–78.

4. *America*

1 J. M. S. Pasley, 'Introduction' to his edition of *Franz Kafka: Der Heizer, In der Strafkolonie, Der Bau*, Cambridge University Press, 1966, p.13.
2 Graham Hough, *A Preface to 'The Faerie Queene'*, Duckworth, London, 1962, p.102f.
3 Cf. W. S. Sokel, *Franz Kafka. Tragik und Ironie*, pp.312ff.
4 Mark Spilka, *Dickens and Kafka. A Mutual Interpretation*.
5 F. D. Luke, 'The Metamorphosis', in *Franz Kafka Today*, ed. A. Flores and H. Swander, p.41.
6 Pasley, op. cit., p.11.
7 M. Greenberg, op. cit., p.96.
8 Cf. Gerhard Loose, *Franz Kafka und Amerika*, Klostermann, Frankfurt am Main, 1968.
9 *A Friend of Kafka and Other Stories*, Jonathan Cape, London, 1972, p.12.
10 *Language, Thought and Reality*, ed. John B. Carroll, M.I.T. Press, Cambridge, Mass., 1970 (1956), p.73.
11 Karl Mannheim, *Ideology and Utopia*, Routledge & Kegan Paul, London, 1960, pp.206ff.
12 Weinberg, op. cit., p.5
13 Quoted from J. Bauer, *Kafka and Prague*, p.101.
14 Emrich, op. cit., p.244.
15 Politzer, *Franz Kafka. Parable and Paradox*, p.151.
16 David Riesman, *The Lonely Crowd*, Yale University Press, New Haven and London, 1961 (1950), p.15.
17 Cf. Gerhard Loose, *Franz Kafka und Amerika*.

5. *The Trial*

1 Kafka and Felice had their crucial talks when walking through the Berlin Zoo, and the subsequent letters refer to the 'Reden im Tiergarten' ('conversations in the zoo'), a short-hand for Felice's suspicious attitude and the humiliation Kafka had to suffer.
2 Cf. also *Diaries*, February 14, 1914 where Kafka repeats the sentence amongst thoughts of suicide ('I can't find any other way of resolving it'), adding that 'F. is fortuitously the person through whom my destiny reveals itself'.
3 Joseph Conrad, *Three Short*

Novels, ed. Edward Weeks, Bantam Books, New York, 1960, p.40.
4 Robert Musil, *Young Törless*, tr. Eithne Wilkins and Ernst Kaiser, Panther Books, London, 1971, p.24.
5 Friedrich Nietzsche, *The Birth of Tragedy*, tr. Francis Golffing, Doubleday Anchor Books, New York, 1956, p.30.
6 Anthony Thorlby, op. cit., pp.53–68.
7 Ibid., pp.67f.

6. *The Castle*

1 W. G. Sebald, 'The Undiscover'd Country: The Death Motif in Kafka's Castle', in *Journal of European Studies*, II, 1 (1972), p.23.
2 Ibid., p.25.
3 Politzer, *Franz Kafka. Parable and Paradox*, p.235.
4 Gray, *Kafka's Castle*, p.19.
5 Ibid., p.18.
6 Sebald, op. cit., p.33.
7 Emrich, op. cit., p.316.
8 W. H. Auden, 'Making, Knowing and Judging' (An Inaugural Lecture delivered before the University of Oxford on June 11, 1956), at the Clarendon Press, Oxford, 1956, p.28.
9 Ibid., p.28f.
10 *The Disinherited Mind*, p.223.
11 The Epistle of Paul to the Romans, xiii, 10.
12 Quoted from Jack Kaminsky, *Hegel on Art*, State University of New York Press, Albany, 1962 (1970), p.90f.
13 *Franz Kafka*, p.142.
14 William James, *The Varieties of Religious Experience*, Collins (Fontana Library), 1960, p.404.
15 'Entwöhnt ward nur der Mann;
      das Weib, es darf
    noch immer träumen an der
      Erde Brüsten,
    dem Werden nah. Noch nicht
      entlassen aus
    geheimnisvollen alten Urver-
      trägen,
    dem selben Nachtgestirne
      unterworfen,
    das auch dem Meer befiehlt,
      wird sie von jedem
    erfüllten Mondeslauf, mit Blut
      und Schmerzen,
    —wie eine säum'ge Priesterin
      —gemahnt,
    was hier ihr Amt! Und was
      dem Mann an ihr
    als Zwiespalt, Rätsel—Reiz
      vielleicht—erscheint—
    ist: dass sie noch so nah den
      Elementen
    —das letzte jüngste selbst viel-
      leicht—für ihn
    das einz'ge Band noch ist, das
      sein Geschick
    an aller Welten ew'ges Schick-
      sal bindet!—'
(From Richard Beer-Hofmann, *Der Graf von Charolais*, S. Fischer, Berlin, 1913 (6th ed.), pp.111f.)
16. '*Der Koitus ist das einzige, allerwärts und immer, von der Frau ausschliesslich positiv Bewertete; die Frau ist die Trägerin des Gemeinschaftsgedankens überhaupt.* Die weibliche Höchstwertung des Koitus ist nicht auf ein Individuum, auch nicht auf das wertende Individuum, beschränkt, sie bezieht sich auf Wesen *überhaupt,* sie ist nicht individuell, sondern *inter*individuell, *über*individuell, sie ist sozusagen . . . die *transcendentale Funktion des Weibes. Denn wenn Weiblichkeit Kuppelei ist, so ist Weiblichkeit*

universale Sexualität. Der Koitus ist der höchste Wert der Frau, ihn sucht sie immer und überall zu verwirklichen. Ihre eigene Sexualität bildet von diesem unbegrenzten Wollen nur einen begrenzten Teil.'
(From Otto Weininger, *Geschlecht und Charakter*, 15th ed., Vienna and Leipzig, 1916, p.354.)

17 Albert Camus, *The Rebel*, tr. A. Bower, Hamish Hamilton, London, 1953 (1960), p.29.
18 Op. cit., p.429.
19 Paul Klee, *Tagebücher 1898–1918*, DuMont, Cologne, 1957, p.187. (My translation.)
20 Kafka, *Briefe 1902–1924*, p.14.

Chronology of Kafka's Works

(Date of first publication is shown in brackets)

1. Works published in Kafka's lifetime:

Betrachtung, 1904–12 (1913).
Das Urteil (*The Judgment*), 1912 (1913).
Der Heizer (*The Stoker*), 1912 (1913).
Die Verwandlung (*Metamorphosis*), 1912 (1915).

In der Strafkolonie (*In the Penal Settlement*), 1914 (1919).
Ein Landarzt. Kleine Erzählungen (*A Country-Doctor* and other pieces), 1914–17 (1919).
Ein Hungerkünstler. Vier Geschichten (*A Hunger-Artist*. Four stories), 1921–24 (1924).

2. Works published after Kafka's death

Beschreibung eines Kampfes (*Description of a Struggle*), 1904–05 (1936).
Hochzeitsvorbereitungen auf dem Lande (*Wedding Preparations in the Country*), 1907 (1953).
Der Verschollene (= *America*), 1912 (1927).

Der Prozess (*The Trial*), 1914 (1925).
Beim Bau der chinesischen Mauer (*The Great Wall of China*), 1917 (1931).
Das Schloss (*The Castle*), 1922 (1926).

Select Bibliography

Editions

German editions

The latest German edition is the second edition of the *Gesammelte Werke*, edited by Max Brod and published by Fischer Verlag, Frankfurt am Main:

Der Prozess, 1950.
Das Schloss, 1951.
Tagebücher 1910–1923, 1951.
Briefe an Milena, ed. W. Haas, 1952.
Erzählungen, 1952.
Amerika, 1953.
Hochzeitsvorbereitungen auf dem Lande und andere Prosa aus dem Nachlass, 1953.
Beschreibung eines Kampfes.

Novellen, Skizzen, Aphorismen aus dem Nachlass, 1954.
Briefe 1902–1924, 1958.

Sämtliche Erzählungen, ed. P. Raabe, Fischer, Frankfurt am Main, 1970.
Briefe an Felice und andere Korrespondenz, ed. and introd. E. Heller, Fischer, Frankfurt am Main, 1967.

English editions

Definitive editions in English (paperback editions indicated undated in brackets)

America, tr. Willa and Edwin Muir, Secker & Warburg, London, 1961 (and Penguin); entitled *Amerika,* Schocken Books, New York, 1962 (also paperback).

The Trial, tr. W. and E. Muir, with additional material tr. E. M. Butler, Secker & Warburg, 1956 (and Penguin); Alfred A. Knopf, New York, 1957 (and Modern Library); Schocken paperback, 1968.

The Castle, tr. W. and E. Muir, with additional material tr. Eithne Wilkins and Ernst Kaiser, Secker & Warburg, 1953 (and Penguin); Alfred A. Knopf, 1954 (and Modern Library); Schocken paperback, 1974.

The Penal Colony: Stories and Short Pieces (includes *The Metamorphosis*), tr. W. and E. Muir, Schocken Books, 1948 (also paperback); entitled *In the Penal Settlement*, Secker & Warburg, 1949 (*Metamorphosis* included in *Metamorphosis and Other Stories*, Penguin).

The Great Wall of China and Other Pieces, tr. W. and E. Muir, Secker & Warburg, 1933; entitled *The Great Wall of China. Stories and Reflections*, Schocken Books, new edition, 1970 (also paperback).

Letters to Milena, ed. Willy Haas, tr. Tania and James Stern, Secker & Warburg, 1953; Schocken Books, 1953 (also paperback).

Wedding Preparations in the Country, and Other Posthumous Prose Writings, tr. E. Kaiser and E. Wilkins, Secker & Warburg, 1954.

Description of a Struggle, tr. T. and J. Stern, Schocken Books, 1958; included in *Description of a Struggle and The Great Wall of China,* tr. T. and J. Stern and W. and E. Muir, Secker & Warburg, 1960.

Letters to Felice, ed. Erich Heller and Jürgen Born, tr. James Stern and Elisabeth Duckworth, Schocken Books, 1973; Secker & Warburg, 1974.

Shorter Works, tr. and ed. Malcolm Pasley, Vols 1 and 2, Secker & Warburg, 1973 and 1974.

The Complete Stories, ed. Nahum N. Glatzer, Schocken Books, 1972.

The Diaries of Franz Kafka 1910–1913, ed. Max Brod, tr. Joseph Kresh, Secker & Warburg, 1948; Schocken Books, 1948 (also paperback).

The Diaries of Franz Kafka 1914–1923, ed. Max Brod, tr. Martin Greenberg with the co-operation of Hannah Arendt, Secker & Warburg, 1949; Schocken Books, 1949 (also paperback).

The Diaries of Franz Kafka 1910–1923, Penguin, 1972 (selects from the two-volume edition).

Anthologies of Criticism and Symposia

J. Born *et al.* (eds), *Kafka-Symposium,* Verlag Klaus Wagenbach, Berlin, 1965.

A. Flores and H. Swander (eds), *The Kafka Problem,* New Directions, New York, 1946.

— *Franz Kafka Today,* University of Wisconsin Press, Madison, 1958.

E. Goldstücker and F. Kautmann (eds), *Franz Kafka aus Prager Sicht,* Academia, Prague, 1966.

R. Gray (ed.), *Kafka. A Collection of Critical Essays,* Prentice-Hall, Englewood Cliffs, N.J., 1962 (Twentieth Century Views).

P. F. Neumeyer, *Twentieth Century Interpretations of The Castle,* Prentice-Hall, Englewood Cliffs, N.J., 1969.

W. T. Zyla (ed.), *Franz Kafka: His Place in World Literature* (Proceedings of the Comparative Literature Symposium), Texas Tech. University, Lubbock, 1971.

Bibliographies

R. Hemmerle, *Franz Kafka. Eine Bibliographie,* Lerche, Munich, 1958.

H. Järv, *Die Kafka-Literatur. Eine Bibliographie,* Bo Cavefors, Malmö and Lund, 1961.

Biographies

M. Brod, *Franz Kafka. Eine Biographie*, Fischer, Frankfurt, 1954. — *Franz Kafka. A Biography*, tr. G. H. Roberts and R. Winston, Schocken Books, New York, 1960 (2nd enlarged ed.).

K. Wagenbach, *Franz Kafka. Eine Biographie seiner Jugend (1883–1912)*, Francke, Berne, 1958. — *Franz Kafka in Selbstzeugnissen und Bilddokumenten*, Rowohlt, Hamburg, 1964.

Writings on Kafka

In German

J. Bauer, *Kafka und Prag*, Belser, Stuttgart, 1971.

H. Binder, *Motiv und Gestaltung bei Franz Kafka*, H. Bouvier, Bonn, 1966.

E. Canetti, *Der andere Prozess. Kafkas Briefe am Felice*, Carl Hanser, Munich, 1969.

W. Emrich, *Franz Kafka*, Athenäum, Frankfurt am Main and Bonn, 1957.

H. Hillmann, *Franz Kafka. Dichtungstheorie und Dichtungsgestalt*, H. Bouvier, Bonn, 1964.

D. Jakob, *Das Kafka-Bild in England*, Oxford and Erlangen, 1971.

G. Janouch, *Gespräche mit Kafka*, Fischer, Frankfurt am Main, 1968 (2nd rev. and enlarged ed.).

H. Politzer, *Franz Kafka, der Künstler*, Fischer, Frankfurt am Main, 1965.

W. S. Sokel, *Franz Kafka, Tragik und Ironie*, Albert Langen and Georg Müller, Munich and Vienna, 1964.

K. Weinberg, *Kafkas Dichtungen. Die Travestien des Mythos*, Francke, Berne and Munich, 1963.

M. Walser, *Beschreibung einer Form. Versuch über Franz Kafka*, Carl Hanser, Munich, 1961.

In English

G. Anders, *Franz Kafka*, tr. A. Steer and A. K. Thorlby, Bowes & Bowes; Hillary House, New York, 1960.

J. Bauer, *Kafka and Prague*, tr. P. S. Falla, Pall Mall Press, London; Praeger, New York, 1971.

F. Baumer, *Franz Kafka*, tr. A. Farbstein, Frederick Ungar, New York, 1971 (Modern Literature Monographs).

E. T. Beck, *Kafka and the Yiddish Theatre*, University of Wisconsin Press, Madison, 1971.

A. P. Foulkes, *The Reluctant Pessimist. A Study of Franz Kafka*, Mouton, The Hague; Humanities Press, New York, 1967.

M. Friedmann, *Problematic Rebel. An Image of Modern Man (Kafka, Melville, Dostoyevski, Camus)*, Random House, New York, 1963; 2nd rev. ed., University of Chicago Press, Chicago and London, 1970.

R. Gray, *Kafka's Castle*, Cambridge University Press, Cambridge, 1956.

— *Franz Kafka*, Cambridge University Press, Cambridge, 1973.

M. Greenberg, *The Terror of Art. Kafka and Modern Literature*, Basic Books, New York, 1968. (*The Terror of Art: Analysis of the Works of Kafka*, Deutsch, London, 1971.)

E. Heller, 'The World of Franz Kafka', in *The Disinherited Mind*, Bowes & Bowes, London; Barnes and Noble, New York, 3rd rev. ed. 1971.

P. Heller, 'Kafka: The Futility of Striving', in *Dialectics and Nihilism*, University of Massachusetts Press, 1966.

G. Janouch, *Conversations with Kafka,* tr. G. Rees, André Deutsch, London (2nd rev. and enlarged ed.); New Directions, New York, 1971.

G. Lukacs, 'Franz Kafka or Thomas Mann?', in *The Meaning of Contemporary Realism*, tr. J. and N. Mander, Merlin Press, London, 1963.

C. Osborne, *Franz Kafka*, Oliver and Boyd, Edinburgh; Barnes and Noble, New York, 1967 (Writers and Critics).

H. Politzer, *Franz Kafka. Parable and Paradox*, Cornell University Press, Ithaca, New York, 1962.

W. S. Sokel, *Franz Kafka*, Columbia University Press, New York, 1966 (Columbia Essays on Modern Writers).

M. Spilka, *Dickens and Kafka. A Mutual Interpretation*, Indiana University Press, Bloomington, 1963.

A. Thorlby, *Kafka: A Study*, Heinemann, London; Rowman and Littlefield, Totowa, N.J., 1972.

H. Weinberg, *The New Novel in America. The Kafkan Mode in Contemporary Fiction*, Cornell University Press, Ithaca and London, 1970.

Index

Adams, Robert Martin, 40, 41
Adler, Friedrich, 15
Die Aktion, 18
apocalypse, 21, 70, 94, 120
Auden, W. H., 150
Austrian literature, 13ff, 20

Bacon, Francis, 26
Bakunin, Mikhail, 183n
Balzac, Honoré de, 34
Barrès, Maurice, 22, 23
Bauer, Erna, 104
Bauer, Felice, 33, 44, 99–107, 111, 153, 186n
Bauer, Johann, 90
Baum, Oskar, 17
Bausinger, Wilhelm, 39
Beckett, Samuel, 40
Beer-Hofmann, Richard, 172, 174, 187n
Benjamin, Walter, 44
Bergmann, Hugo, 184n
Bergmann, Ingmar, 142
The Bible, 18, 115
Biese, Alfred, 29
Bildungsroman, 66, 88
Bloch, Grete, 101, 103, 104–107, 108
Born, Hedwig, 45
Brecht, Bertolt, 62
Brentano, Franz, 67
Broch, Hermann, 20
Brod, Max, 9, 17ff, 30, 43, 69, 99, 102, 103, 175, 183n, 184n

Camus, Albert, 21, 109; *The Rebel*, 178
Carroll, Lewis, 68; *Alice in Wonderland*, 143
Chaplin, Charlie, 114
Cleugh, James, 37
Coleridge, S. T., 28, 64
Conrad, Joseph, *Heart of Darkness*, 57, 119
Corneille, Pierre, 13

Dickens, Charles, 65, 66, 95
Donne, John, 138
Dostoyevsky, Fyodor, 9, 20, 22, 49, 124; *The Brothers Karamazov*, 19f; *Notes from Underground*, 50, 52
Durkheim, Emile, 48, 62, 63

Edschmid, Kasimir, 29
egoism, 24, 25, 32
Ehrenfels, Christian, *Kosmogonie*, 45f
Einstein, Albert, 32, 45, 184n
Eliot, T. S., 27, 89, 112, 116; 'Little Gidding', 30
Ellmann, Richard, 40
Emrich, Wilhelm, 92, 149
existentialism, 25, 116, 175

Flaubert, Gustave, 18, 42
Flores, A. and H. Swander, 11
Franklin, Benjamin, 67
Freud, Sigmund, 22, 42, 64
Frühling, 17
Fürnberg, Louis, 18

German novel, 94
Gilbert, Mary, 29
Godwin, William, 183n
Goethe, Johann Wolfgang von, 16, 18, 20, 36, 107, 136
Gogol, Nikolay Vasilievich, 25
Goldstücker, Eduard, 183n
Gray, Ronald, 139, 160
Greenberg, Martin, 66
Grillparzer, Franz, 20

Haas, Willy, 17
'Habsburg myth', 14, 19
Hadwiger, Victor, 17
Hamburger, Michael, 30
Handke, Peter, 20
Hartmann von Aue, *Gregorius*, 58f
Hasek, Jaroslav, 90
Hegel, Georg Wilhelm Friedrich, 32, 46, 157, 159
Heller, Erich, 10, 99, 101, 156, 175
Herder, Johann Gottfried, 18
Herder-Blätter, 17, 18
Hesse, Hermann, 63, 69
Hiller, Kurt, 18
Hoffmann, Camill, 15
Hoffmann, E. T. A., 123
Hofmannsthal, Hugo von, 14, 23, 67, 69, 149, 184n; 'Chandos Letter', 26–30
Höllerer, Walter, 29

Homer, 18
Hugo, Victor, 39
Hough, Graham, 64
Husserl, Edmund, 67

Ibsen, Henrik, 22, 39

James, William, 183n
Janouch, Gustav, 10, 19, 183n
Jens, Walter, 29
Johnston, W. M., 185n
Joyce, James, 12, 27, 40ff, 128, 129; *Ulysses*, 40, 41, 92; *Finnegans Wake*, 40

Kácha, Michal, 90
Kafka, Franz (for German titles of works *see* chronological list, p. 189) *America*, 11, 21, 64–98; 'The Burrow', 68; *The Castle*, 9, 11, 20, 21, 32, 45, 62, 67, 68, 79, 136–82; *Description of a Struggle*, 30; *The Great Wall of China*, 19, 20; 'A Hunger-Artist', 21, 62; 'The Judgement', 33, 42f, 53, 64, 136, 143, 144; 'Letter to His Father', 11; 'Metamorphosis', 11, 19, 33ff, 39, 41, 43, 49–63, 64, 66, 136, 146, 158; 'In the Penal Settlement', 33, 64, 65, 88, 92; 'The Stoker', 64, 65, 68–76; *The Trial*, 11, 20, 25, 32, 33, 44, 45, 63, 64, 67, 68, 79, 89, 99–135, 136, 143, 145, 146, 153, 170, 171, 172, 173, 181, 185n; *Wedding Preparations in the Country*, 179

alienation, 37, 62f; *avant-garde*, 43; Chaplinesque, 89, 166; consistent dualism, 45f, 79f, 103, 109, 116–120, 135; Copernican revolution, 47; crisis of consciousness, 26–32, 57, 116–120; critique of a harmonious order, 32, 47; gnosticism, 46; the grotesque, 66; idealism, 59, 62, 149, 154; identity, 22, 28, 31, 73, 96, 127; inwardness, 13, 65, 69f, 74, 77ff, 94f, 98; language and experience, 28f, 71f, 132, 134; literature, Kafka and, 20f, 33–48, 99–107; logical positivism, 47; masochism, 33ff; mysticism, mystical experience, 26, 32, 160–165; narrative method, 65ff, 67ff; perspectivism, 67f, pessimism, 15, 21, 26; the picaresque, 66, 87; realism, 65f, 158; reductionism, 67f; sex and the transcendental, 120f, 126, 152, 172ff; Socialism,

16, 18, 19f; social criticism, 47f, 49ff, 81, 86, 89f, 124; 'sociological tradition', 63; spiritual quest, 22, 56, 58f, 103f, 109; symbolism, 60f, 64f
Kafka, Ottla (sister), 105, 111
Kant, Immanuel, *Critique of Pure Reason*, 47, 185n
Kermode, Frank, 44, 94
Kierkegaard, Søren, 20, 25, 32, 46
Kisch, Erwin Egon, 17
Klee, Paul, 180
Kleist, Heinrich von, 20; *Prince of Homburg*, 101
Kornfeld, Paul, 17
Kraus, Karl, 14
Kropotkin, Peter, 90, 183n
Kubin, Alfred, *The Other Side*, 46, 144
Kuznetsov, Boris, 9

Lawrence, D. H., 120, 173
Leibniz, Gottfried Wilhelm von, 32, 46
Leppin, Paul, 15, 17
Levin, Harry, 185n
Loose, Gerhard, 186n
Ludwig II of Bavaria, 39
Lukács, Georg, 10, 13
Luke, F. D., 66

Mach, Ernst, 22
Maeterlinck, Maurice, 22
Magris, Claudio, 14
Mann, Thomas, 13, 23, 39, 63; *The Magic Mountain*, 40, 59; *Death in Venice*, 49f, 66, 139
Mannheim, Karl, 78
Marcionism, 45ff, 144
Mareš, Michael, 19
Martini, Fritz, 29
Marx, Karl, 185n
Maturin, Charles Robert, *Melmoth*, 43, 45
Mazzeo, J. A., 11
Metternich, Klemens, 14
Meyrink, Gustav *Golem*, 46
Moderne Flugblätter, 17
Modernism, Moderns, 15f, 17, 22f, 26, 29f, 32; language and experience, 28f, 41, 44; mode of existence of allusions, 39ff
Mörike, Eduard, 18
Moses, 180
Musil, Robert, 20, 39f, 67, 69, 128; *The Man Without Qualities*, 24f, 41; *Young Törless*, 26, 91, 120

Naipaul, V. S., 60
narcissism, 25f

Nietzsche, Friedrich, 23, 24, 26, 33, 59, 68, 73, 109, 124, 126; *The Birth of Tragedy*, 21, 131
Nisbet, R. A., 63

Pasley, Malcolm, 64
Pirandello, Luigi, 63
Plato, 18
politics and intellectuals, 93
Politzer, Heinz, 11, 33, 92, 138, 175
Pollak, Oskar, 181
Prague, 16ff, 181; anarchism, 90f; German literature of, 13ff, 15ff; 'Young Prague', 17; 'Young People's Club', 90, 91, 183n
Proudhon, Pierre, 183n
Proust, Marcel, 27, 63

Racine, Jean, 13
Ravachol, Francois-Claudius, 183n
Riesmann, David, 74, 94
Rilke, Rainer Maria, 17, 67, 69, 110, 142; 'Der Panther', 42
Romanticism, Romantic, 27f, 56, 127, 156, 167
Rousseau, Jean-Jacques, 185n

Sacher-Masoch, Leopold von, 43; *Venus in Furs*, 33ff
Sade, Marquis de, 34
Salus, Hugo, 15
Sartre, Jean-Paul, 115, 116
Schiller, Friedrich von, 13, 18
Schnitzler, Arthur, 20
Schopenhauer, Arthur, 20, 21, 24, 59
Sebald, W. G., 137
Simmel, Georg, 62
Singer, Isaac Bashevis, 68

Spilka, Mark, 65
Sokel, Walter H., 34, 35, 69
Stifter, Adalbert, 18
Stirner, Max, 23ff, 32, 90, 183n
Strindberg, August, 20
Der Sturm, 18
Swales, Martin, 183n

Thorlby, Anthony, 132, 134
Tieck, Ludwig, 97
Tolstoy, Count Lev Nikolayevich, 124, 183n, 184n; *A Confession*, 22f, 28
Trakl, Georg, 29, 30
Tucker, Abraham, 183n

Urzidil, Johannes, 16
utopia, utopian, 21, 67, 78, 94f, 146

Wagner, Richard, 24
Wassermann, Jakob, 42
Weber, Max, 62
Weinberg, Helen, 87
Weinberg, Kurt, 34, 35, 58, 60
Weininger, Otto, 172f, 174, 187n
Weiskopf, F. C., 18
Weiss, Ernst, 104
Weltsch, Felix, 17, 103
Werfel, Franz, 17, 30, 42
Whorf, Benjamin Lee, 68
Wiener, Oskar, 17
Wilkinson, E. M., 11
Wir, 17
Witiko, 18
Wolff, Kurt, 68

Zola, Emile, 39

196